Manner

by Mrs. Joh.

PREFACE.

There is no country where there are so many people asking what is "proper to do," or, indeed, where there are so many genuinely anxious to do the proper thing, as in the vast conglomerate which we call the United States of America. The newness of our country is perpetually renewed by the sudden making of fortunes, and by the absence of a hereditary, reigning set. There is no aristocracy here which has the right and title to set the fashions.

But a "reigning set," whether it depend upon hereditary right or adventitious wealth, if it be possessed of a desire to lead and a disposition to hospitality, becomes for a period the dictator of fashion to a large number of lookers-on. The travelling world, living far from great centres, goes to Newport, Saratoga, New York, Washington, Philadelphia, Boston, and gazes on what is called the latest American fashion. This, though exploited by what we may call for the sake of distinction the "newer set," is influenced and shaped in some degree by people of native refinement and taste, and that wide experience which is gained by travel and association with broad and cultivated minds. They counteract the tendency to vulgarity, which is the great danger of a newly launched society, so that our social condition improves, rather than retrogrades, with every decade.

There may be many social purists who will disagree with us in this statement. Men and women educated in the creeds of the Old World, with the good blood of a long ancestry of quiet ladies and gentlemen, find modern American society, particularly in New York and at Newport, fast, furious, and vulgar. There are, of course, excesses committed everywhere in the name of fashion; but we cannot see that they are peculiar to America. We can only answer that the creed of fashion is one of perpetual change. There is a Council of Trent, we may say, every five years, perhaps even every two years, in our new and changeful country, and we learn that, follow as we may either the grand old etiquette of England or the more gay and shifting social code of France, we still must make an original etiquette of our own. Our political system alone, where the lowest may rise to the highest preferment, upsets in a measure all that the Old World insists upon in matters of precedence and formality. Certain immutable principles remain common to all elegant people who assume to gather society about them, and who wish to enter its portals; the absent-minded scholar from his library should not ignore them, the fresh young farmer from the countryside feels and recognizes their importance. If we are to live together in unity we must make society a pleasant thing, we must obey certain formal rules, and these rules must conform to the fashion of the period.

And it is in no way derogatory to a new country like our own if on some minor points of etiquette we presume to differ from the older world. We must fit our garments to the climate, our manners to our fortunes and to our daily lives. There are, however, faults and inelegancies of which foreigners accuse us which we may do well to consider. One of these is the greater freedom allowed in the manners of our young women a freedom which, as our New World fills up with people of foreign birth, cannot but lead to social disturbances. Other national faults, which English writers and critics kindly point out, are our bumptiousness, our spread- eagleism, and our too great familiarity and lack of dignity, etc.

Instead of growing angry over these criticisms, perhaps we might as well look into the matter dispassionately, and see if we cannot turn the advice in some degree to our advantage. We can, however, decide for ourselves on certain points of etiquette which we borrow from nobody; they are a part of our great nation, of our republican institutions, and of that continental hospitality which gives a home to the Russian, the German, the Frenchman, the Irishman, man, and the "heathen Chinee." A somewhat wide and elastic code, as boundless as the prairies, can alone meet the needs of these different citizens. The old traditions of stately manners, so common to the Washington and Jefferson days, have almost died out here, as similar manners have died out all over the world. The war of 1861 swept away what little was left of that once important American fact--a grandfather. We began all over again; and now there comes up from this newer world a flood of questions: How shall we manage all this? How shall we use a fork? When wear a dress-coat? How and when and on whom shall we leave our cards? How long and for whom shall we wear mourning? What is the etiquette of a wedding? How shall we give a dinner-party? The young housekeeper of Kansas writes as to the manners she shall teach to her children; the miner's wife, having become rich, asks how she shall arrange her house, call on her neighbors, write her letters? Many an anxious girl writes as to the propriety of "driving out with a gentleman," etc. In fact, there is one great universal question, What is the etiquette of good society?

Not a few people have tried to answer these questions, and have broken down in the attempt. Many have made valuable manuals, as far as they went; but writers on etiquette commonly fail, for one or two different reasons. Many attempt to write who know nothing of good society by experience, and their books are full of ludicrous errors. Others have had the disadvantage of knowing too much, of ignoring the beginning of things, of supposing that the person who reads will take much for granted. For a person who has an intuitive knowledge of etiquette, who has been brought up from his mother's knee in the best society, has always known what to do, how to dress, to whom to bow, to write in the simplest way about etiquette would be impossible; he would never know how little the reader, to whose edification he was addressing himself, knew of the matter.

If, however, an anxious inquirer should write and ask if "mashed potato must be eaten with a knife or a fork," or if "napkins and finger bowls can be used at breakfast," those questions he can answer.

It is with an effort to answer thousands of these questions, written in good faith to Harper's Bazar, that this book is undertaken. The simplicity, the directness, and the evident desire "to improve," which characterize these anonymous letters, are all much to be commended. Many people have found themselves suddenly conquerors of material wealth, the most successful colonists in the world, the heirs of a great inheritance, the builders of a new empire. There is a true refinement manifested in their questions. Not only do men and women like to behave properly themselves, but all desire to know what is the best school of manners, that they may educate their children therein. Such minds are the best conservators of law and order. It is not a communistic spirit that asks, "How can I do this thing in a better way?" It is that wise and liberal conservatism which includes reverence for law, respect for age, belief in religion, and a desire for a refined society. A book on etiquette, however patiently considered and honestly written, must have many shortcomings, and contain disputed testimony. All we can do is endeavor to mention those fashions and customs which we believe to be the best, remembering always, as we have said, that the great law of change goes on forever, that our stately grandfathers had fashions which we should now consider gross and unbecoming, while we have customs, particularly of speech, which would have shocked them. This law of change is not only one which time modifies, but with us the South, the North, the East, and the West differ as to certain points of etiquette. All, however, agree in saying that there is a good society in America whose mandates are supreme. All feel that the well-bred man or woman is a "recognized institution." Everybody laughed at the mistakes of Daisy Miller, and saw wherein she and her mother were wrong. Independent American girls may still choose to travel without a chaperon, but they must be prepared to fight a well-founded prejudice if they do. There is a recognition of the necessity of good manners, and a profound conviction, let us hope, that a graceful manner is the outcropping of a well-regulated mind and of a good heart.

MANNERS AND SOCIAL USAGES.

CHAPTER I

WOMEN AS LEADERS.

Nothing strikes the foreigner so much (since the days of De Tocqueville, the first to mention it) as the prominent position of woman in the best society of America. She has almost no position in the political world. She is not a leader, an intrigante in politics, as she is in France. We have no Madame de Stael, no Princess Belgioso, here to make and unmake our Presidents; but women do all the social work, which in Europe is done not only by women, but by young bachelors and old ones, statesmen, princes, ambassadors, and attaches. Officials are connected with every court whose business it is to visit, write and answer invitations, leave cards, call, and perform all the multifarious duties of the social world.

In America, the lady of the house does all this. Her men are all in business or in pleasure, her sons are at work or off yachting. They cannot spend time to make their dinner calls--"Mamma, please leave my cards" is the legend written on their banners.

Thus to women, as the conductors of social politics, is committed the card--that pasteboard protocol, whose laws are well defined in every land but our own.

Now, in ten different books on etiquette which we have consulted we find ten different opinions upon the subject of first calls, as between two women. We cannot, therefore, presume to decide where so many doctors disagree, but give the commonly received opinions as expressed by the customs of New York society.

When should a lady call first upon a new and a desirable acquaintance? Not hastily. She should have met the new and desirable acquaintance, should have been properly introduced, should feel sure that her acquaintance is desired. The oldest resident, the one most prominent in fashion, should call first; but, if there is no such distinction, two women need not forever stand at bay each waiting for the other to call. A very admirable and polite expedient has been: substituted for a first call in the sending out of cards, for several days in the month, by a lady who wishes to begin her social life, we will say, in a new city. These may or may not be accompanied by the card of some well-known friend. If these cards bring the desired visits or the cards of the desired guests, the beginner may feel that she has started on her society career with no loss of self respect. Those who do not respond are generally in a minority. Too much haste in making new acquaintances, however--"pushing," as it is called-cannot be too much deprecated.

First calls should be returned within a week. If a lady is invited to any entertainment by a new acquaintance, whether the invitation come through a friend or not, she should immediately leave cards, and send either a regret or an acceptance. To lose time in this matter is a great rudeness. Whether she attend the entertainment or not, she should call after it within a week. Then, having done all that is polite, and having shown herself a woman of good-breeding, she can keep up the acquaintance or not as she pleases. Sometimes there are reasons why a lady does not wish to keep up the acquaintance, but she must not, for her own sake, be oblivious to the politeness extended. Some very rude people in New York have sent back invitations, or failed to recognize the first attempt at civility, saying, "We don't know the people." This is not the way to discourage unpleasant familiarity. In New York, Boston, and Philadelphia, and in the large cities of the West, and generally in the country: towns, residents call first upon new-comers; but in Washington this custom is reversed, and the new-comer calls first upon the resident. Every one--officials of the highest down to the lowest grade returns these cards. The visitor generally finds himself invited to the receptions of the President and his Cabinet, etc. This arrangement is so convenient that it is a thousand pities it does not go into operation all over the country, particularly in those large cities where the resident cannot know if her dearest friend be in town unless informed in some such way of the fact.

This does not, as might be supposed, expose society to the intrusion of unwelcome visitors. Tact, which is the only guide through the mazes of society, will enable a woman to avoid anything like an unwelcome intimacy or a doubtful acquaintance, even if such a person should "call first."

Now the question comes up, and here doctors disagree: When may a lady call by proxy, or when may she send her card, or when must she call in person?

After a dinner-party a guest must call in person and inquire if the hostess is at home. For other entertainments it is allowed, in New York, that the lady call by proxy, or that she simply send her card. In sending to inquire for a person's health, cards may be sent by a servant, with a kindly message.

No first visit should, however, be returned by card only; this would be considered a slight, unless followed by an invitation. The size of New York, the great distances, the busy life of a woman of charities, large family, and immense circle of acquaintances may render a personal visit almost impossible. She may be considered to have done her duty if she in her turn asks her new acquaintance to call on her on a specified day, if she is not herself able to call.

Bachelors should leave cards (if they ever leave any) on the master and mistress of the house, and, in America, upon the young ladies. A gentleman does not turn down the corners of his card--indeed, that fashion has become almost obsolete, except, perhaps, where a lady wishes it distinctly understood that she has called in person. The plainer the card the better. A small, thin card for a gentleman, not glazed, with his name in small script and his address well engraved in the corner, is in good taste. A lady's card should be larger, but not glazed or ornamented in any way. It is a rule with sticklers for good-breeding that after any entertainment a gentleman should leave his card in person, although, as we have said, he often commits it to some feminine agency.

No gentleman should call on a lady unless she asks him to do so, or unless he brings a letter of introduction, or unless he is taken by a lady who is sufficiently intimate to invite him to call. A lady should say to a gentleman, if she wishes him to call, "I hope that we shall see you," or, "I am at home on Monday," or something of that sort. If he receives an invitation to dinner or to a ball from a stranger, he is bound to send an immediate answer, call the very next day, leave his card, and then to call after the entertainment.

This, at least, is foreign etiquette, and we cannot do better than import it. This rule holds good for the entertainments of bachelors, who should leave their cards on each other after an entertainment, unless the intimacy is so great that no card- leaving is expected.

When a lady returns to town, after an absence in Europe or in the country, it is strict etiquette that she should leave cards on all her acquaintances and friends if she expects to entertain or to lead a gay, social winter; but as distances in our great cities are formidable, as all ladies do not keep a carriage, as most ladies have a great deal else to do besides making visits, this long and troublesome process is sometimes simplified by giving a tea or a series of teas, which enables the lady, by staying at home on one evening of a week, or two or three afternoons of a month, to send out her cards to that effect, and to thus show her friends that she at least remembers them. As society and card-leaving thus become rapidly complicated, a lady should have a visiting-book, into which her list is carefully copied, with spaces for days and future engagements.

A servant must be taught to receive the cards at the door, remember messages, and recollect for whom they are left, as it is not proper in calling upon Mrs. Brown at a private house to write her name on your card. At a crowded hotel this may be allowed, but it is not etiquette in visiting at private houses. In returning visits, observe the exact etiquette of the person who has left the first card. A call must not be returned with a card only, or a card by a call. If a person send you a card by post, return a card by post; if a personal visit is made, return it by a personal visit; if your acquaintance leave cards only, without inquiring if you are at home, return the same courtesy. If she has left the cards of the gentlemen of her family, return those of the gentlemen of your family.

A young lady's card should almost always be accompanied by that of her mother or her chaperon. It is well, on her entrance into society, that the name of the young lady be engraved on her mother's card. After she has been out a year, she may leave her own card only. Here American etiquette begins to differ from English etiquette. In London, on the other hand, no young lady leaves her card: if she is motherless, her name is engraved beneath the name of her father, and the card of her chaperon is left with both until she becomes a maiden lady of somewhat mature if uncertain age.

It is rare now to see the names of both husband and wife engraved on one card, as "Mr. and Mrs. Brown." The lady has her own card, "Mrs. Octavius Brown," or with the addition, "The Misses Brown." Her husband has his separate card; each of the sons has his own card. No titles are used on visiting-cards in America, save military, naval, or judicial ones; and, indeed, many of our most distinguished judges have had cards printed simply with the name, without prefix or affix. "Mr. Webster," "Mr. Winthrop," "Henry Clay" are well-known instances of simplicity. But a woman must always use the prefix "Mrs." or "Miss." A gentleman may or may not use the prefix "Mr.," as he pleases, but women must treat themselves with more respect. No card is less proper than one which is boldly engraved "Gertrude F. Brown;" it should be "Miss Gertrude F. Brown."

A married lady always bears her husband's name, during his life, on her card. Some discussion is now going on as to whether she should continue to call herself "Mrs. Octavius Brown" or "Mrs. Mary Brown" after his death. The burden of opinion is in favor of the latter--particularly as a son may bear his father's name, so there will be two Mrs. Octavius Browns. No lady wishes to be known as "old Mrs. Octavius Brown," and as we do not use the convenient title of Dowager, we may as well take the alternative of the Christian name. We cannot say "Mrs. Octavius Brown, Jr.," if the husband has ceased to be a junior. Many married ladies hesitate to discard the name by which they have always been known. Perhaps the simple "Mrs. Brown" is the best, after all. No lady should leave cards upon an unmarried gentleman, except in the case of his having given entertainments at which ladies were present. Then the lady of the house should drive to his door with the cards of herself and family, allowing the footman to leave them.

The young ladies' names, in such a case as this, should be engraven on their mother's card.

"We have no leisure class," as Henry James says in his brilliant "International Episode;" but still young men should try to make time to call on those who entertain them, showing by some sort of personal attention their gratitude for the politeness shown them. American young men are, as a rule, very remiss about this matter of calling on the hostess whose hospitality they accept.

A gentleman should not call on a young lady without asking for her mother or her chaperon. Nor should he leave cards for her alone, but always leave one for her mother.

Ladies can, and often do, write informal invitations on the visiting-card. To teas, readings, and small parties, may be added the day of reception. It is convenient and proper to send these cards by post. Everything can be sent by post now, except an invitation to dinner, and that must always be sent by private hand, and an answer must be immediately returned in the same formal manner.

After balls, amateur concerts, theatrical parties, garden-parties, or "at homes," cards should be left by all invited guests within a week after the invitation, particularly if the invited guest has been obliged to decline. These cards may be left without inquiring for the hostess, if time presses; but it is more polite to inquire for the hostess, even if it is not her day. If it is her reception day, it would be rude not to inquire, enter, and pay a personal visit. After a dinner, one must inquire for the hostess and pay a personal visit. It is necessary to mention this fact, because so many ladies have got into the habit (having large acquaintances) of leaving or sending cards in by a footman, without inquiring for the hostess (who is generally not at home), that there has grown up a confusion, which leads to offence being taken where none is meant.

It is not considered necessary to leave cards after a tea. A lady leaves her cards as she enters the hall, pays her visit, and the etiquette of a visiting acquaintance is thus established for a year. She should, however, give a tea herself, asking all her entertainers.

If a lady has been invited to a tea or other entertainment through a friend without having known her hostess, she is bound to call soon; but if the invitation is not followed up by a return card or another invitation, she must understand that the acquaintance is at an end. She may, however, invite her new friend, within a reasonable time, to some entertainment at her own house, and if that is accepted, the acquaintance goes on. It is soon ascertained by a young woman who begins life in a new city whether her new friends intend to be friendly or the reverse. A resident of a town or village can call, with propriety, on any new-comer. The newcomer must return this call; but, if she does not desire a further acquaintance, this can be the end of it. The time of calling must in every town be settled by the habits of the place; after two o'clock and before six is, however, generally safe.

In England they have a pleasant fashion of calling to inquire for invalids or afflicted friends, and of pencilling the words "kind inquiries." It has not obtained that popularity in America which it deserves, and it would be well to introduce it. If a lady call on a person who is a stranger to her, and if she has difficulty in impressing her name on the servant, she sends up her card, while she waits to see if the lady will receive her. But she must never on any occasion hand her own card to her hostess. If she enters the parlor and finds her hostess there, she must introduce herself by pronouncing her own name distinctly. If she is acquainted with the lady, she simply gives her name to the servant, and does not send up her card.

Wedding-cards have great prominence in America, but we ignore those elaborate funeral-cards and christening-cards, and printed cards with announcements of engagements, and many other cards fashionable abroad. With us the cards of the bride and her parents, and sometimes of the _fianc‚_, are sent to all friends before the wedding, and those of the invitation to the wedding to a few only, it may be, or to all, as the family desire. After the marriage, the cards of the married pair, with their address, are sent to all whose acquaintance is desired.

Husbands and wives rarely call together in America, although there is no law against their doing so. It is unusual because, as we have said, we have no "leisure class." Gentlemen are privileged to call on Sunday, after church, and on Sunday evenings. A mother and daughter should call together, or, if the mother is an invalid, the daughter can call, leaving her mother's card.

"Not at home" is a proper formula, if ladies are not receiving; nor does it involve a falsehood. It merely means that the lady is not at home to company. The servant should also add, "Mrs. Brown receives on Tuesdays," if the lady has a day. Were not ladies able to deny themselves to callers there would be no time in crowded cities for any sort of work, or repose, or leisure for self-improvement. For, with the many idle people who seek to rid themselves of the pain and penalty of their own vapid society by calling and making somebody else entertain them, with the wandering book-agents and beggars, or with even the overflow of society, a lady would find her existence muddled away by the poorest and most abject of occupations--that of receiving a number of inconsiderate, and perhaps impertinent, wasters of time.

It is well for all house-keepers to devote one day in the week to the reception of visitors--the morning to tradespeople and those who may wish to see her on business, and the afternoon to those who call socially. It saves her time and simplifies matters.

Nothing is more vulgar than that a caller should ask the servant where his mistress is, when she went out, when she will be in, how soon she will be down, etc. All that a well-bred servant should say to such questions is, "I do not know, madam." A mistress should inform her servant after breakfast what he is to say to all comers. It is very offensive to a visitor to be let in, and then be told that she cannot see the lady of the house. She feels personally insulted, and as if, had she been some other person, the lady of the house would perhaps have seen her.

If a servant, evidently ignorant and uncertain of his mistress and her wishes, says, "I will see if Mrs. Brown will see you," and ushers you into the parlor, it is only proper to go in and wait. But it is always well to say, "If Mrs. Brown is going out, is dressing, or is otherwise engaged, ask her not to trouble herself to come down." Mrs. Brown will be very much obliged to you. In calling on a friend who is staying with people with whom you are not acquainted, always leave a card for the lady of the house. The lack of this attention is severely felt by new people who may entertain a fashionable woman as their guest--one who receives many calls from those who do not know her hostess. It is never proper to call on a guest without asking for the hostess.

Again, if the hostess be a very fashionable woman, and the visitor decidedly not so, it is equally vulgar to make one's friend who may be a guest in the house a sort of entering wedge for an acquaintance; a card should be left, but unaccompanied by any request to see the lady of the house. This every lady will at once understand. A lady who has a guest staying with her who receives really calls should always try to place a parlor at her disposal where she can see her friends alone, unless she be a very young person, to whom the chaperonage of the hostess is indispensable.

If the lady of the house is in the drawing-room when the visitor arrives to call on her guest, she is, of course, introduced and says a few words; and if she is not in the room, the guest should inquire of the visitor if the lady of the house will see him or her, thus giving her a chance to accept or decline.

In calling on the sons or the daughters of the house, every visitor should leave a card for the father and mother. If ladies are at home, cards should be left for the gentlemen of the family.

In Europe a young man is not allowed to ask for the young ladies of the house in formal parlance, nor is he allowed to leave a card on them--socially in Europe the "_jeune fille_" has no existence. He calls on the mother or chaperon; the young lady may be sent for, but he must not inquire for her first. Even if she is a young lady at the head of a house, he is not allowed to call upon her without some preliminaries; some amiable female friend must manage to bring them together.

In America the other extreme has led to a very vicious system of etiquette, by which young ladies are recognized as altogether leaders of society, receiving the guests and pushing their mothers into the background. It would amaze a large number of ambitious young ladies to be told that it was not proper that young men should call on them and be received by them alone. But the solution would seem to be that the mother or chaperon should advance to her proper place in this country, and while taking care of her daughter, appearing with her in public, and receiving visits with her, still permit that good-natured and well-intended social intercourse between young men and women which is so seldom abused, and which has led to so many happy marriages. It is one of the points yet debatable how much liberty should be allowed young ladies. Certainly, however, we do not wish to hold our young girls up to the scorn and ridicule of the novelist or the foreign critic by ignoring what has been a recognized tenet of good manners since society was formed. The fact that the chaperon is a necessary institution, and that to married ladies and to elderly ladies should be paid all due respect, is a subject of which we shall treat later. No young lady who is visiting in a strange city or country town should ever receive the visits of gentlemen without asking her hostess and her daughters to come down and be introduced to them; nor should she ever invite such persons to call without asking her hostess if it would be agreeable. To receive an ordinary acquaintance at any hour, even that of the afternoon reception, without her hostess would be very bad manners. We fear the practice is too common, however. How much worse to receive a lover, or a gentleman who may aspire to the honor of becoming one, at unusual hours, without saying anything to the lady of the house! Too many young American girls are in the habit of doing so: making of their friend's house a convenience by which an acquaintance with a young man may be carried on--a young man too, perhaps, who has been forbidden her own home.

A bride receives her callers after she has settled down in her married home just as any lady does. There is no particular etiquette observed. She sends out cards for two or three reception days, and her friends and new acquaintances call or send cards on these days. She must not, however, call on her friends until they have called upon her.

As many of these callers--friends, perhaps, of the bridegroom--are unknown to the bride, it is well to have a servant announce the names; and they should also leave their cards in the hall that she may be able to know where to return the visits.

What has so far been said will serve to give a general idea of the card and its uses, and of the duties which it imposes upon different members of society. Farther on in this volume we will take up, in much more particular fashion, the matters only alluded to in this opening chapter.

We may say that cards have changed less in the history of etiquette and fashion than anything else. They, the shifting pasteboards, are in style about what they were fifty--nay, a hundred--years ago.

The plain, unglazed card with fine engraved script cannot be improved upon. The passing fashion for engraved autographs, for old English, for German text, all these fashions have had but a brief hour. Nothing is in worse taste than for an American to put a coat-of-arms on his card. It only serves to make him ridiculous.

A lady should send up her card by a servant, but not deliver it to the lady of the house; a card is yourself, therefore if you meet a lady, she does not want two of you. If you wish to leave your address, leave a card on the hall table. One does right in leaving a card on the hall table at a reception, and one need not call again. An invitation to one's house cancels all indebtedness. If a card is left on a lady's reception, she should make the next call, although many busy society women now never make calls, except when they receive invitations to afternoon teas or receptions.

When a gentleman calls on ladies who are at home, if he knows them well he does not send up a card; the servant announces his name. If he does not know them well, he does send up a card. One card is sufficient, but he can inquire for them all. In leaving cards it is not necessary to leave seven or eight, but it is customary to leave two--one for the lady of the house, the other for the rest of the family or the stranger who is within their gates. If a gentleman wishes particularly to call on any one member, he says so to the servant, as "Take my card up to Miss Jones," and he adds, "I should like to see all the ladies if they are at home." The trouble in answering this question is that authorities differ. We give the latest London and New York fashion, so far as we know, and also what we believe to be the common-sense view. A gentleman can ask first for the lady of the house, then for any other member of the family, but he need never leave more than two cards. He must in this, as in all etiquette, exercise common-sense. No one can define all the ten thousand little points.

CHAPTER II

OPTIONAL CIVILITIES.

There are many optional civilities in life which add very much to its charm if observed, but which cannot be called indispensable. To those which are harmless and graceful we shall give a cursory glance, and to those which are doubtful and perhaps harmful we shall also briefly allude, leaving it to the common-sense of the reader as to whether he will hereafter observe in his own manners these so-called optional civilities.

In France, when a gentleman takes off his hat in a windy street or in an exposed passage-way, and holds it in his hand while talking to a lady, she always says, "_Couvrez vous_" (I beg of you not to stand uncovered). A kind-hearted woman says this to a boatman, a coachman, a man of low degree, who always takes off his hat when a lady speaks to him. Now in our country, unfortunately, the cabmen have such bad manners that a lady seldom has the opportunity of this optional civility, for, unlike a similar class in Europe, those who serve you for your money in America often throw in a good deal of incivility with the service, and no book of etiquette is more needed than one which should teach shop-girls and shop-men the beauty and advantages of a respectful manner. If men who drive carriages and street cabs would learn the most advantageous way of making money, they would learn to touch their hats to a lady when she speaks to them or gives an order. It is always done in the Old World, and this respectful air adds infinitely to the pleasures of foreign travel.

In all foreign hotels the landlords enforce such respect on the part of the waiters to the guests of the hotel that if two complaints are made of incivility, the man or woman complained of is immediately dismissed. In a livery-stable, if the hired coachman is complained of for an uncivil answer, or even a silence which is construed as incivility, he is immediately discharged. On the lake of Como, if a lady steps down to a wharf to hire a boat, every boatman takes off his cap until she has finished speaking, and remains uncovered until she asks him to put on his hat.

Now optional civilities, such as saying to one's inferior, "Do not stand without your hat," to one's equal, "Do not rise, I beg of you," "Do not come out in the rain to put me in my carriage," naturally occur to the kind-hearted, but they may be cultivated. It used to be enumerated among the uses of foreign travel that a man went away a bear and came home a gentleman. It is not natural to the Anglo-Saxon race to be overpolite. They have no petits soins. A husband in France moves out an easy-chair for his wife, and sets a footstool for every lady. He hands her the morning paper, he brings a shawl if there is danger of a draught, he kisses her hand when he comes in, and he tries to make himself agreeable to her in the matter of these little optional civilities. It has the most charming effect upon all domestic life, and we find a curious allusion to the politeness observed by French sons towards their mothers and fathers in one of Moliere's comedies, where a prodigal son observes to his father, who comes to denounce him, "Pray, sir, take a chair," says Prodigal; "you could scold me so much more at your ease if you were seated."

If this was a piece of optional civility which had in it a bit of sarcasm, we can readily see that civility lends great strength to satire, and take a hint from it in our treatment of rude people. A lady once entering a crowded shop, where the women behind the counter were singularly inattentive and rude even for America, remarked to one young woman who was lounging on the counter, and who did not show any particular desire to serve her,

"My dear, you make me a convert to the Saturday-afternoon early-closing rule, and to the plan for providing seats for saleswomen, for I see that fatigue has impaired your usefulness to your employer."

The lounger started to her feet with flashing eyes. "I am as strong as you are," said she, very indignantly.

"Then save yourself a report at the desk by showing me some lace," said the lady, in a soft voice, with a smile.

She was served after this with alacrity. In America we are all workers; we have no privileged class; we are earning money in various servitudes, called variously law, medicine, divinity, literature, art, mercantile business, or as clerks, servants, seamstresses, and nurses, and we owe it to our work to do it not only honestly but pleasantly. It is absolutely necessary to success in the last-mentioned profession that a woman have a pleasant manner, and it is a part of the instruction of the training-school of nurses, that of civility. It is not every one who has a fascinating manner. What a great gift of fortune it is! But it is in every one's power to try and cultivate a civil manner.

In the matter of "keeping a hotel"--a slang expression which has become a proverb--how well the women in Europe understand their business, and how poorly the women in America understand theirs! In England and all over the

Continent the newly arrived stranger is received by a woman neatly dressed, with pleasant, respectful manners, who is overflowing with optional civilities. She conducts the lady to her room, asks if she will have the blinds drawn or open, if she will have hot water or cold, if she would like a cup of tea, etc.; sends a neat chambermaid to her to take her orders, gets her pen and paper for her notes--in fact, treats her as a lady should treat a guest. Even in very rural districts the landlady comes out to her own door to meet the stranger, holds her neat hand to assist her to alight, and performs for her all the service she can while she is under her roof.

In America a lady may alight in what is called a tavern, weary, travel-stained, and with a headache. She is shown into a waiting-room where sits, perhaps, an overdressed female in a rocking-chair violently fanning herself. She learns that this is the landlady. She asks if she can have a room, some hot water, etc. The answer may be, "I don't know; I don't have to work; perhaps Jim will tell you." And it is to the man of the house that the traveller must apply. It is a favorable sign that American men are never ashamed to labor, although they may not overflow with civility. It is a very unfavorable sign for the women of America when they are afraid or ashamed of work, and when they hesitate to do that which is nearest them with civility and interest.

Another test of self-respect, and one which is sometimes lacking in those whom the world calls fashionable, those who have the possessions which the majority of us desire, fine houses, fine clothes, wealth, good position, etc., is the lack or the presence of "fine courtesy," which shall treat every one so that he or she is entirely at ease.

"Society is the intercourse of persons on a footing of apparent equality," and if so, any one in it who treats other people so as to make them uncomfortable is manifestly unfit for society. Now an optional courtesy should be the unfailing custom of such a woman, we will say, one who has the power of giving pain by a slight, who can wound amour propre in the shy, can make a _d‚butante_ stammer and blush, can annoy a shy youth by a sneer. How many a girl has had her society life ruined by the cruelty of a society leader! how many a young man has had his blood frozen by a contemptuous smile at his awkwardness! How much of the native good-will of an impulsive person has been frozen into a caustic and sardonic temper by the lack of a little optional civility? The servant who comes for a place, and seats herself while the lady who speaks to her is standing, is wanting in optional civility. She sins from ignorance, and should be kindly told of her offence, and taught better manners. The rich woman who treats a guest impolitely, the landlady who sits in her rocking-chair while the traveller waits for those comforts which her house of call invites, all are guilty of the same offence. It hurts the landlady and the servant more nearly than it does the rich woman, because it renders their self-imposed task of getting a living the more difficult, but it is equally reprehensible in all three.

Good manners are said to be the result of a kind heart and careful home training; bad manners, the result of a coarse nature and unwise training. We are prone to believe that bad manners in Americans are almost purely from want of thought. There is no more generous, kindly, or better people in the world than the standard American, but he is often an untrained creature. The thousands of emigrants who land on our shores, with privileges which they never thought to have thrust upon them, how can they immediately learn good manners? In the Old World tradition of power is still so fresh that they have to learn respect for their employers there. Here there are no such traditions.

The first duty, then, it would seem, both for those to whom fortune has been kind and for those who are still courting her favors, would be to study optional civility; not only the decencies of life, but a little more. Not only be virtuous, but have the shadows of virtue. Be polite, be engaging; give a cordial bow, a gracious smile; make sunshine in a shady place. Begin at home with your optional civility. Not only avoid those serious breaches of manners which should cause a man to kick another man down-stairs, but go further than good manners--have better manners. Let men raise their hats to women, give up seats in cars, kiss the hand of an elderly lady if she confers the honor of her acquaintance upon them, protect the weak, assist the fallen, and cultivate civility; in every class of life this would oil the wheels; and especially let American women seek to mend their manners.

Optional civility does not in any way include familiarity. We doubt whether it is not the best of all armor against it. Familiarity is "bad style." It is not civility which causes one lady to say to another, "Your bonnet is very unbecoming; let me beg of you to go to another milliner." That is familiarity, which however much it may be supposed to be excess of friendship, is generally either caused by spite or by a deficiency of respect The latter is never pardonable. It is in doubtful taste to warn people of their faults, to comment upon their lack of taste, to carry them disagreeable tidings, under the name of friendship. On the Continent, where diffidence is unknown, where a man, whoever he may be, has a right to speak to his fellow-man (if he does it civilly), where a woman finds other women much more polite to her than women are to each other in this country, there is no familiarity. It is almost an insult to touch the person; for instance, no one places his hand on the arm or shoulder of another person unless there is the closest intimacy; but everywhere there is an optional civility freely given between poor and poor, rich and poor, rich and rich, superiors and inferiors, between equals. It would be pleasant to follow this out in detail, the results are so agreeable and so honorable.

CHAPTER III

GOOD AND BAD SOCIETY.

Many of our correspondents ask us to define what is meant by the terms "good society" and "bad society." They say that they read in the newspapers of the "good society" in New York and Washington and Newport, and that it is a record of drunkenness, flirtation, bad manners and gossip, backbiting, divorce, and slander. They read that the fashionable people at popular resorts commit all sorts of vulgarities, such as talking aloud at the opera, and disturbing their neighbors; that young men go to a dinner, get drunk, and break glasses; and one ingenuous young girl remarks, "We do not call that good society in Atlanta."

Such a letter might have been written to that careful chronicler of "good society" in the days of Charles II., old Pepys of courtly fame. The young maiden of Hertfordshire, far from the Court, might well have thought of Rochester and such "gay sparks," and the ladies who threw glasses of wine at them, as not altogether well-bred, nor entitled to admission into "good society." We cannot blame her.

It is the old story. Where, too, as in our land, pleasure and luxury rule a certain set who enjoy no tradition of good manners, the contradiction in terms is the more apparent. Even the external forms of respect to good manners are wanting. No such overt vulgarity, for instance, as talking aloud at the opera will ever be endured in London, because a powerful class of really well-born and well-bred people will hiss it down, and insist on the quiet which music, of all other things, demands. That is what we mean by a tradition of good manners.

In humbler society, we may say as in the household of a Scotch peasant, such as was the father of Carlyle, the breaches of manners which are often seen in fashionable society would never occur. They would appear perfectly impossible to a person who had a really good heart and a gentle nature. The manners of a young man of fashion who keeps his hat on when speaking to a lady, who would smoke in her face, and would appear indifferent to her comfort at a supper-table, who would be contradictory and neglectful--such manners would have been impossible to Thomas or John Carlyle, reared as they were in the humblest poverty. It was the "London swell" who dared to be rude in their day as now.

But this impertinence and arrogance of fashion should not prevent the son of a Scotch peasant from acquiring, or attempting to acquire, the conventional habits and manners of a gentleman. If he have already the grace of high culture, he should seek to add to it the knowledge of social laws, which will render him an agreeable person to be met in society. He must learn how to write a graceful note, and to answer his invitations promptly; he must learn the etiquette of dress and of leaving cards; he must learn how to eat his dinner gracefully, and, even if he sees in good society men of external polish guilty of a rudeness which would have shocked the man who in the Scotch Highlands fed and milked the cows, he still must not forget that society demands something which was not found in the farm-yard. Carlyle, himself the greatest radical and democrat in the world, found that life at Craigenputtock would not do all for him, that he must go to London and Edinburgh to rub off his solitary neglect of manners, and strive to be like other people. On the other band, the Queen of England has just refused to receive the Duke of Marlborough because he notoriously ill-treated the best of wives, and had been, in all his relations of life, what they call in England a "cad." She has even asked him to give back the Star and Garter, the insignia once worn by the great duke, which has never fallen on shoulders so unworthy as those of the late Marquis of Blandford, now Duke of Marlborough. For all this the world has great reason to thank the Queen, for the present duke has been always in "good society," and such is the reverence felt for rank and for hereditary name in England that he might have continued in the most fashionable circles for all his bad behaviour, still being courted for name and title, had not the highest lady in the land rebuked him.

She has refused to receive the friends of the Prince of Wales, particularly some of his American favorites, this good Queen, because she esteems good manners and a virtuous life as a part of good society.

Now, those who are not "in society" are apt to mistake all that is excessive, all that is boorish, all that is snobbish, all that is aggressive, as being a part of that society. In this they are wrong. No one estimates the grandeur of the ocean by the rubbish thrown up on the shore. Fashionable society, good society, the best society, is composed of the very best people, the most polished and accomplished, religious, moral, and charitable.

The higher the civilization, therefore, the better the society, it being always borne in mind that there will be found, here and there, the objectionable outgrowths of a false luxury and of an insincere culture. No doubt, among the circles of the highest nobility, while the king and queen may be people of simple and unpretending manners, there may be some arrogant and self-sufficient master of ceremonies, some Malvolio whose pomposity is in strange contrast to the good-breeding of Olivia. It is the lesser star which twinkles most. The "School for Scandal" is a lasting picture of the folly and frivolity of a certain phase of London society in the past, and it repeats itself in every decade. There is always a Mrs. Candour, a Sir Benjamin Backbite, and a scandalous college at Newport, in New York, Milwaukee, Philadelphia, Boston, Baltimore, Chicago, Saratoga, Long Branch, wherever society congregates. It is the necessary imperfection, the seamy side. Such is the reverse of the pattern. Unfortunately, the right side is not so easily described. The colors of a beautiful bit of brocade are, when seen as a whole, so judiciously blended that they can hardly be pronounced upon individually: one only admires the _tout ensemble_, and that uncritically, perhaps.

That society is bad whose members, however tenacious they be of forms of etiquette and elaborate ceremonials, have one code of manners for those whom they deem their equals, and another for those whom they esteem to be of less importance to them by reason of age, pecuniary condition, or relative social influence. Bad manners are apt to prove the concomitant of a mind and disposition that are none too good, and the fashionable woman who slights and wounds people because they cannot minister to her ambition, challenges a merciless criticism of her own moral shortcomings. A young girl who is impertinent or careless in her demeanor to her mother or her mother's friends; who goes about without a chaperon and talks slang; who is careless in her bearing towards young men, permitting them to treat her as if she were one of themselves; who accepts the attention of a young man of bad character or dissipated habits because he happens to be rich; who is loud in dress and rough in manner--such a young girl is "bad society," be she the daughter of an earl or a butcher. There are many such instances of audacity in the so-called "good society" of America, but such people do not spoil it; they simply isolate themselves.

A young man is "bad society" who is indifferent to those older than himself, who neglects to acknowledge invitations, who sits while a lady stands, who goes to a ball and does not speak to his host, who is selfish, who is notoriously immoral and careless of his good name, and who throws discredit on his father and mother by showing his ill-breeding. No matter how rich, how externally agreeable to those whom he may wish to court, no matter how much varnish of outward manner such a man may possess, he is "bad society."

A parvenue who assumes to keep other people out of the society which she has just conquered, whose thoughts are wholly upon social success (which means, with her, knowing somebody who has heretofore refused to know her), who is climbing, and throwing backward looks of disdain upon those who also climb--such a woman, unfortunately too common in America, is, when she happens to have achieved a fashionable position, one of the worst instances of bad society. She may be very prominent, powerful, and influential. She may have money and "entertain," and people desirous of being amused may court her, and her bad manners will be accepted by the careless observer as one of the concomitants of fashion. The reverse is true. She is an interloper in the circles of good society, and the old fable of the ass in the lion's skin fits her precisely. Many a duchess in England is such an interloper; her supercilious airs betray the falsity of her politeness, but she is obliged by the rules of the Court at which she has been educated to "behave like a lady;" she has to counterfeit good-breeding; she cannot, she dare not, behave as a woman who has suddenly become rich may sometimes, nay does, behave in American society, and still be received.

It will thus be seen, as has been happily expressed, that "fashion has many classes, and many rules of probation and admission." A young person ignorant of its laws should not be deluded, however, by false appearances. If a young girl comes from the most secluded circles to Saratoga, and sees some handsome, well-dressed, conspicuous woman much courted, lionized, as it were, and observes in her what seems to be insolent pretence, unkindness, frivolity, and superciliousness, let her inquire and wait before she accepts this bit of brass for pure gold. Emerson defines "sterling fashion as funded talent." Its objects may be frivolous or objectless; but, in the long-run, its purposes are neither frivolous nor accidental. It is an effort for good society; it is the bringing together of admirable men and women in a pleasant way. Good-breeding, personal superiority, beauty, genius, culture, are all very good things. Every one delights in a person of charming manners. Some people will forgive very great derelictions in a person who has charming manners, but the truly good society is the society of those who have virtue and good manners both.

Some Englishman asked an American, "What sort of a country is America?" "It is a country where everybody can tread on everybody's toes," was the answer.

It is very bad society where any one wishes to tread on his neighbor's toes, and worse yet where there is a disposition to feel aggrieved, or to show that one feels aggrieved. There are certain people new in society who are always having their toes trodden upon. They say: "Mrs. Brown snubbed me; Mrs. Smith does not wish to know me; Mrs. Thompson ought to have invited me. I am as good as any of them." This is very bad society. No woman with self-respect will ever say such things. If one meets with rudeness, take no revenge, cast no aspersions. Wit and tact, accomplishments and social talents, may have elevated some woman to a higher popularity than another, but no woman will gain that height by complaining. Command of temper, delicacy of feeling, and elegance of manner--all these are demanded of the persons who become leaders of society, and would remain so. They alone are "good society." Their imitators may masquerade for a time, and tread on toes, and fling scorn and insult about them while in a false and insecure supremacy; but such pretenders to the throne are soon unseated. There is a dreadful Sedan and Strasburg awaiting them. They distrust their own flatterers; their "appanage" is not a solid one.

People who are looking on at society from a distance must remember that women of the world are not always worldly women. They forget that brilliancy in society may be accompanied by the best heart and the sternest principle. The best people of the world are those who know the world best. They recognize the fact that this world should be known and served and treated with as much respect and sincerity as that other world, which is to be our reward for having conquered the one in which we live now.

CHAPTER IV

ON INTRODUCING PEOPLE.

A lady in her own house can in these United States do pretty much as she pleases, but there is one thing in which our cultivated and exclusive city fashionable society seems agreed, and that is, that she must not introduce two ladies who reside in the same town. It is an awkward and an embarrassing restriction, particularly as the other rule, which renders it easy enough--the English rule--that the "roof is an introduction," and that visitors can converse without further notice, is not understood. So awkward, however, are Americans about this, that even in very good houses one lady has spoken to another, perhaps to a young girl, and has received no answer, "because she had not been introduced;" but this state of ignorance is, fortunately, not very common. It should be met by the surprised rejoinder of the Hoosier school-mistress: "Don't yer know enough to speak when yer spoken to?" Let every woman remember, whether she is from the backwoods, or from the most fashionable city house, that no such casual conversation can hurt her. It does not involve the further acquaintance of these two persons. They may cease to know each other when they go down the front steps; and it would be kinder if they would both relieve the lady of the house of their joint entertainment by joining in the conversation, or even speaking to each other.

A hostess in this land is sometimes young, embarrassed, and not fluent. The presence of two ladies with whom she is not very well acquainted herself, and both of whom she must entertain, presents a fearful dilemma. It is a kindness to her, which should outweigh the dangers of making an acquaintance in "another set," if those ladies converse a little with each other.

If one lady desires to be introduced to another, the hostess should ask if she may do so, of course unobtrusively. Sometimes this places one lady in an unlucky position towards another. She does not know exactly what to do. Mrs. So-and-so may have the gift of exclusiveness, and may desire that Mrs. That-and-that shall not have the privilege of bowing to her. Gurowski says, in his very clever book on America, that snobbishness is a peculiarity of the fashionable set in America, because they do not know where they stand. It is the peculiarity of vulgar people everywhere, whether they sit on thrones or keep liquor-shops; snobs are born--not made. If, ever, a lady has this gift or this drawback of exclusiveness, it is wrong to invade her privacy by introducing people to her.

Introducing should not be indiscriminately done either at home or in society by any lady, however kind-hearted. Her own position must be maintained, and that may demand a certain loyalty to her own set. She must be careful how she lets loose on society an undesirable or aggressive man, for instance, or a great bore, or a vulgar, irritating woman. These will all be social obstacles to the young ladies of her family, whom she must first consider. She must not add to the embarrassments of a lady who has already too large a visiting list. Unsolicited introductions are bad for both parties. Some large-hearted women of society are too generous by half in this way. A lady should by adroit questions find out how a new acquaintance would be received, whether or not it is the desire of both parties to know each other; for, if there is the slightest doubt existing on this point, she will be blamed by both. It is often the good-natured desire of a sympathetic person that the people whom she knows well should know each other. She therefore strives to bring them together at lunch or dinner, but perhaps finds out afterwards that one of the ladies has particular objections to knowing the other, and she is not thanked. The disaffected lady shows her displeasure by being impolite to the pushing lady, as she may consider her. Had no introduction taken place, she argues, she might have Still enjoyed a reputation for politeness. Wary women of the world are therefore very shy of introducing two women to each other.

This is the awkward side. The more agreeable and, we may say, humane side has its thousands and thousands of supporters, who believe that a friendly introduction hurts no one; but we are now not talking of kindness, but of etiquette, which is decidedly opposed to indiscriminate introductions.

Society is such a complicated organization, and its laws are so lamentably unwritten, yet so deeply engraved on certain minds, that these things become important to those who are always winding and unwinding the chains of fashion.

It is therefore well to state it as a received rule that no gentleman should ever be introduced to a lady unless her permission has been asked, and she be given an opportunity to refuse; and that no woman should be introduced formally to another woman unless the introducer has consulted the wishes of both women. No delicate-minded person would ever intrude herself upon the notice of a person to whom she had been casually introduced in a friend's drawing-room; but all the world, unfortunately, is not made up of delicate-minded persons.

In making an introduction, the gentleman is presented to the lady with some such informal speech as this: "Mrs. A, allow me to present Mr. B;" or, "Mrs. A, Mr. B desires the honor of knowing you." In introducing two women, present the younger to the older woman, the question of rank not holding good in our society where the position of the husband, be he judge, general, senator, or president even, does not give his wife fashionable position. She may be of far less importance in the great world of society than some Mrs. Smith, who, having nothing else, is set down as of the highest rank in that unpublished but well-known book of heraldry which is so thoroughly understood in America as a tradition. It is the proper thing for a gentleman to ask a mutual friend or an acquaintance to introduce him to a lady, and there are few occasions when this request is refused. In our crowded ballrooms, chaperons often ask young men if they will be introduced to their charges. It is better before asking the young men of this present luxurious age, if they will not only be introduced, but if they propose to dance, with the young lady, else that young person may be mortified by a snub. It is painful to record, as we must, that the age of chivalry is past, and that at a gay ball young men appear as supremely selfish, and desire generally only introductions to the reigning belle, or to an heiress, not deigning to look at the humble wall-flower, who is neither, but whose womanhood should command respect. Ballroom introductions are supposed to mean, on the part of the gentleman, either an intention to dance with the young lady, to walk with her, or to talk to her through one dance, or to show her some attention.

Men scarcely ever ask to be introduced to each other, but if a lady, through some desire of her own, wishes to present them, she should never be met by indifference on their part. Men have a right to be exclusive as to their acquaintances, of course; but at a lady's table, or in her parlor, they should never openly show distaste for each other's society before her.

In America it is the fashion to shake hands, and most women, if desirous of being cordial, extend their hands even on a first introduction; but it is, perhaps, more elegant to make a bow only, at a first introduction.

In her own house a hostess should always extend her hand to a person brought to her by a mutual friend, and introduced for the first time. At a dinner-party, a few minutes before dinner, the hostess introduces to a lady the gentleman who is to take her down to the dining-room, but makes no further introductions, except in the case of a distinguished stranger, to whom all the company are introduced. Here people, as we have said, are shy of speaking, but they should not be, for the room where they meet is a sufficient guarantee that they can converse without any loss of dignity.

At large gatherings in the country it is proper for the lady to introduce her guests to each other, and it is perfectly proper to do this without asking permission of either party. A mother always introduces her son or daughter, a husband his wife, or a wife her husband, without asking permission.

A gentleman, after being introduced to a lady, must wait for her to bow first before he ventures to claim her as an acquaintance.

This is Anglo-Saxon etiquette. On the Continent, however, the gentleman bows first. There the matter of the raising the hat is also important. An American gentleman takes his hat quite off to a lady; a foreigner raises it but slightly, and bows with a deferential air. Between ladies but slightly acquainted, and just introduced, a very formal bow is all that is proper; acquaintances and friends bow and smile; intimate male friends simply nod, but all gentlemen with ladies raise the hat and bow if the lady recognizes a friend.

Introductions which take place out-of-doors, as on the lawn-tennis ground, in the hunting field, in the street, or in any casual way, are not to be taken as necessarily formal, unless the lady chooses so to consider them. The same may be said of introductions at a watering-place, where a group of ladies walking together may meet other ladies or gentlemen, and join forces for a walk or drive. Introductions are needful, and should be made by the oldest lady of the party, but are not to be considered as making an acquaintance necessary between the parties if neither should afterwards wish it. It is universally conceded now that this sort of casual introduction does not involve either lady in the net-work of a future acquaintance; nor need a lady recognize a gentleman, if she does not choose to do so, after a watering-place introduction. It is always, however, more polite to bow; that civility hurts no one.

There are in our new country many women who consider themselves fashionable leaders--members of an exclusive set--and who fear if they should know some other women out of that set that they would imperil their social standing. These people have no titles by which they can be known, so they preserve their exclusiveness by disagreeable manners, as one would hedge a garden by a border of prickly-pear. The result is that much ill-feeling is engendered in society, and people whom these old aristocrats call the "_nouveaux riches_," "parvenus," etc., are always having their feelings hurt. The fact remains that the best-bred and most truly aristocratic people do not find it necessary to hurt any one's feelings. An introduction never harms anybody, and a woman with the slightest tact can keep off a vulgar and a pushing person without being rude. It is to be feared that there are vulgar natures among those who aspire to be considered exclusive, and that they are gratified if they can presumably increase their own importance by seeming exclusive; but it is not necessary to dwell on such people.

The place given here to the ill-bred is only conceded to them that one may realize the great demands made upon the tact and the good feeling of a hostess. She must have a quick apprehension; she may and will remember, however, that it is very easily forgiven, this kind-heartedness--that it is better to sin against etiquette than to do an unkind thing.

Great pains should be taken by a hostess to introduce shy people. Young people are those whose pleasure must depend on introductions.

It is well for a lady in presenting two strangers to say something which may break the ice, and make the conversation easy and agreeable; as, for instance, "Mrs. Smith, allow me to present Mr. Brown, who has just arrived from New Zealand;" or, "Mrs. Jones, allow me to present Mrs. Walsingham, of Washington--or San Francisco," so that the two may naturally have a question and answer ready with which to step over the threshold of conversation without tripping.

At a five-o'clock tea or a large reception there are reasons why a lady cannot introduce any one but the daughter or sister whom she has in charge. A lady who comes and knows no one sometimes goes away feeling that her hostess has been inattentive, because no one has spoken to her. She remembers Europe, where the roof-tree has been an introduction, and where people spoke kindly to her and did not pass her by. Dinner-parties in stiff and formal London have this great attraction: a gentleman steps up and speaks to a lady, although they have never met before, and often takes her down to dinner without an introduction. The women chat after dinner like old friends; every one knows that the roof is a sufficient guarantee. This is as it should be; but great awkwardness results in the United States if one lady speaks to another and receives no answer. "Pray, can you tell me who the pianist is?" said a leader of society to a young girl near her at a private concert. The young lady looked distressed and blushed, and did not answer. Having seen a deaf-mute in the room whom she knew, the speaker concluded that this young lady belonged to that class of persons, and was very much surprised when later the hostess brought up this silent personage and introduced her.

"I could not speak to you before because I had not been introduced--but the pianist is Mr. Mills," remarked this punctilious person. "I, however, could speak to you, although we had not been formally presented. The roof was a sufficient guarantee of your respectability, and I thought from your not answering that you were deaf and dumb," said the lady.

The rebuke was deserved. Common-sense must interpret etiquette; "nice customs courtesy to great kings." Society depends upon its social soothsayers for all that is good in it. A disagreeable woman can always find precedents for being formal and chilling; a fine-tempered woman can always find reasons enough for being agreeable. A woman would rather be a benediction than a curse, one would think. We hold it proper, all things considered, that at dinner-parties and receptions a hostess may introduce her friends to each other. So long as there is embarrassment, or the mistake made by the young lady above mentioned who would not answer a civil question; so long as these mistakes and others are made, and the result be stupidity and gloom, and a party silent and thumb-twisting, instead of gayly conversing, as it should be; so long as people do not come together easily--it is manifestly proper that the hostess should put her finger on the social pendulum, and give it a swing to start the conversational clock. All well-bred people recognize the propriety of speaking to even an enemy at a dinner-party, although they would suffer no recognition an hour later. The same principle holds good, of course, if, in the true exercise of her hospitality, the hostess should introduce some person whom she would like to commend. These are the exceptions which form the rule.

Care should be taken in presenting foreigners to young ladies; sometimes titles are dubious. Here, a hostess is to be forgiven if she positively declines. She may say, politely, "I hardly think I know you well enough to dare to present you to that young lady. You must wait until her parents (or guardians, or chaperon) will present you."

But the numbers of agreeable people who are ready and waiting to be introduced are many. The woman of literary distinction and the possessor of an honored name may be invincibly shy and afraid to speak; while her next neighbor, knowing her fame perhaps, and anxious to make her acquaintance, misconstrues shyness for pride--a masquerade which bashfulness sometimes plays; so two people, with volumes to say to each other, remain silent as fishes, until the kindly magician comes along, and, by the open sesame of an introduction, unlocks the treasure which has been so deftly hidden. A woman of fashion may enter an assembly of thinkers and find herself dreaded and shunned, until some kind word creates the entente cordiale. In the social entertainments of New York, the majority prefer those where the hostess introduces her guests--under, of course, these wise and proper limitations.

As for forms of introduction, the simplest are best. A lady should introduce her husband as "Mr. Brown," "General Brown," "Judge Brown." If he has a title she is always to give it to him. Our simple forms of titular respect have been condemned abroad, and we are accused of being all "colonels" and "generals;" but a wife should still give her husband his title. In addressing the President we say "Mr. President," but his wife should say, "Allow me to introduce the President to you." The modesty of Mrs. Grant, however, never allowed her to call her many-titled husband anything but "Mr. Grant," which had, in her case, a sweetness above all etiquette.

Introductions in the homely German fatherland are universal, everybody pronouncing to everybody else the name of the lady to whom he is talking; and among our German fellow-citizens we often see a gentleman convoying a lady through a crowded assemblage, introducing her to everybody. It is a simple, cordial, and pleasant thing enough, as with them the acquaintance stops there; and a bow and smile hurt nobody.

No one of heart or mind need feel afraid to talk and be agreeable, whether introduced or not, at a friend's house; even if she meets with the rebuff of a deaf-and-dumb neighbor, she need not feel heart-broken: she is right, and her stiff acquaintance is wrong.

If a gentleman asks to be presented to a lady, she should signify her assent in a pleasant way, and pay her hostess, through whom the request comes, the compliment of at least seeming to be gratified at the introduction. Our American ladies are sometimes a little lacking in cordiality of manner, often receiving a new acquaintance with that part of their conformation which is known as the "cold shoulder." A brusque discourtesy is bad, a very effusive courtesy and a too low bow are worse, and an overwhelming and patronizing manner is atrocious. The proper salutation lies just between the two extremes: the_ juste milieu_ is the proper thing always. In seeking introductions for ourselves, while we need not be shy of making a first visit or asking for an introduction, we must still beware of "push." There are instincts in the humblest understanding which will tell us where to draw the line. If a person is socially more prominent than ourselves, or more distinguished in any way, we should not be violently anxious to take the first step; we should wait until some happy chance brought us together, for we must be as firm in our self-respect as our neighbor is secure in her exalted position. Wealth has heretofore had very little power to give a person an exclusively fashionable position. Character, breeding, culture, good connections--all must help. An aristocrat who is such by virtue of an old and honored name which has never been tarnished is a power in the newest society as in the oldest; but it is a shadowy power, felt rather than described. Education is always a power.

To be sure, there is a tyranny in large cities of what is known as the "fashionable set," formed of people willing to spend money; who make a sort of alliance, offensive and defensive; who can give balls and parties and keep certain people out; who have the place which many covet; who are too much feared and dreaded. If those who desire an introduction to this set strive for it too much, they will be sure to be snubbed; for this circle lives by snubbing. If such an aspirant will wait patiently, either the whole autocratic set of ladies will disband--for such sets disentangle easily--or else they in their turn will come knocking at the door and ask to be received. _L'art de tenir salon_ is not acquired in an hour. It takes many years for a new and an uninstructed set to surmount all the little awkwardnesses, the dubious points of etiquette, that come up in every new shuffle of the social cards; but a modest and serene courtesy, a civility which is not servile, will be a good introduction into any society.

And it is well to have that philosophical spirit which puts the best possible interpretation upon the conduct of others. Be not in haste to consider yourself neglected. Self-respect does not easily receive an insult. A lady who is fully aware of her own respectability, who has always lived in the best society, is never afraid to bow or call first, or to introduce the people whom she may desire should know each other. She perhaps presumes on her position, but it is very rare that such a person offends; for tact is almost always the concomitant of social success.

There has been a movement lately towards the stately bows and courtesies of the past in our recent importation of Old-World fashions. A lady silently courtesies when introduced, a gentleman makes a deep bow without speaking. We have had the custom of hand-shaking--and a very good custom it is--but perhaps the latest fashion in ceremonious introduction forbids it. If a gentleman carries his crush hat, and a lady her fan and a bouquet, hand-shaking may not be perfectly convenient. However, if a lady or gentleman extends a hand, it should be taken cordially. Always respond to the greeting in the key-note of the giver.

CHAPTER V

VISITING.

No term admits of a wider interpretation than this; no subject is capable of a greater number of subdivisions. The matter of formal visiting has led to the writing of innumerable books. The decay of social visiting is a cause of regret to all the old-fashioned people who remember how agreeable it was; but our cities have grown too large for it, and in our villages the population changes too quickly. The constant effort to make the two systems shake hands, to add cordiality to formality, and to provide for all the forced conditions of a rapidly growing and constantly changing society, these are but a few of the difficulties attending this subject.

The original plan of an acquaintance in a formal city circle was to call once or twice a year on all one's friends personally, with the hope and the remote expectation of finding two or three at home. When society was smaller in New York, this was possible, but it soon grew to be impossible, as in all large cities. This finally led to the establishment of a reception day which held good all winter. That became impossible and tiresome, and was narrowed down to four Tuesdays, perhaps, in one month; that resolved itself into one or two five-o'clock teas; and then again, if a lady got lame or lazy or luxurious, even the last easy method of receiving her friends became too onerous, and cards were left or sent in an envelope.

Now, according to the strict rules of etiquette, one card a year left at the door, or one sent in an envelope, continues the acquaintance. We can never know what sudden pressure of calamity, what stringent need of economy, what exigencies of work, may prompt a lady to give up her visiting for a season. Even when there is no apparent cause, society must ask no questions, but must acquiesce in the most good-natured view of the subject.

Still, there must be uniformity. We are not pleased to receive Mrs. Brown's card by post, and then to meet her making a personal visit to our next neighbor. We all wish to receive our personal visits, and if a lady cannot call on all her formal acquaintances once, she had better call on none.

If she gives one reception a year and invites all her "list," she is then at liberty to refrain from either calling or sending a card, unless she is asked to a wedding or dinner, a ladies' lunch or a christening, or receives some very particular invitation which she must return by an early personal call--the very formal and the punctilious say within a week, but that is often impossible.

And if a lady have a day, the call should be made on that day; it is rude to ignore the intimation. One should try to call on a reception day. But here in a crowded city another complication comes in. If a lady have four Thursdays in January and several other ladies have Thursdays, it may be impossible to reach all those ladies on their reception day. There is nothing for it, then, but to good-naturedly apologize, and to regret that calling hours are now reduced to between four and six in large cities.

Some people have too many acquaintances. If they hope to do anything in the world but drive about and leave cards, they must exonerate themselves from blame by giving a reception, having a day or an evening for receiving, and then trust to the good-nature of society, or its forgetfulness, which is about the same thing, to excuse them.

Happy those ladies who can give up an evening a week to their friends; that rubs out the score on the social slate, besides giving a number of people a chance to spend a very agreeable hour in that society which gathers around a hospitable lamp.

The danger of this kind of hospitality is that it is abused by bores, who are too apt to congregate in numbers, and to wear out the lady of the house by using her parlor as a spot where they are safe from the rain and cold and free to bestow their tediousness on anybody, herself included. Then a lady after committing herself to a reception evening often wishes to go out herself. It requires unselfishness to give up an evening to that large circle, some of whom forget it, some go elsewhere, some come too often, and sometimes, alas! no on e calls. These are the drawbacks of an "evening at home." However, it is a laudable custom; one could wish it were more common.

No one can forget the eloquent thanks of such men as Horace Walpole, and other persons of distinction, to the Misses Berry, in London, who kept up their evening receptions for sixty years. But, from the trials of those who have too much visiting, we turn to the people who have all the means and *how?*

appliances of visiting and no one to visit.

The young married woman who comes to New York, or any other large city, often passes years of loneliness before she has made her acquaintances. She is properly introduced, we will say by her mother-in-law or some other friend, and then, after a round of visits in which she has but, perhaps, imperfectly apprehended the positions and names of her new acquaintances, she has a long illness, or she is called into mourning, or the cares of the nursery surround her, and she is shut out from society until it has forgotten her; and when she is ready to emerge, it is difficult for her to find her place again in the visiting-book. If she is energetic and clever, she surmounts this difficulty by giving a series of receptions, or engaging in charities, or working on some committee, making herself of use to society in some way; and thus picks up her dropped stitches. But some young women are without the courage and tact to do this thing; they wait, expecting that society will find them out, and, taking them up, will do all the work and leave them to accept or refuse civilities as they please. Society never does this; it has too much on its hands; a few conspicuously beautiful and gifted people may occasionally receive such an ovation, but it is not for the rank and file.

Every young woman should try to make at least one personal visit to those who are older than herself, and she should show charity towards those who do not return this visit immediately. Of course, she has a right to be piqued if her visit be persistently ignored; and she should not press herself upon a cold or indifferent acquaintance, but she should be slow to wrath; and if she is once invited to the older lady's house, it is worth a dozen calls so far as the intention of civility is concerned.

It is proper to call in person, or to leave a card, after an acquaintance has lost a relative, after an engagement is announced, after a marriage has taken place, after a return from Europe, and of course after an invitation has been extended; but, as society grows larger and larger, the first four visits may be omitted, and cards sent if it is impossible to pay the visits personally. Most ladies in large cities are invisible except on their days; in this way alone can they hope to have any time for their own individual tastes, be these what they may--china painting, authorship, embroidery, or music. So the formal visiting gets to be a mere matter of card-leaving; and the witty author who suggested that there should be a "clearing-house for cards," and who hailed the Casino at Newport as a good institution for the same, was not without genius. One hates to lose time in this world while greasing the machinery, and the formal, perfunctory card-leaving is little else.

Could we all have abundant leisure and be sure to find our friends at home, what more agreeable business than visiting? To wander from one pleasant interior to another, to talk a little harmless gossip, to hear the last _mot_, the best piece of news, to see one's friends, their children, and the stranger within their gates--all this is charming; it is the Utopia of society; it would be the apotheosis of visiting--if there were such a thing!

Unfortunately, it is impossible. There may be here and there a person of such exalted leisure that he can keep his accounts to society marked in one of those purple satin manuals stamped "Visites," and make the proper marks every day under the heads of "address," "received," "returned visits," and "reception days," but he is a rara avis.

Certain rules are, however, immutable. A first call from a new acquaintance should be speedily returned. These are formal calls, and should be made in person between the hours of four and six in New York and other large cities. Every town has its own hours for receiving, however. When calling for the first time on several ladies not mother and daughters in one family, a card should be left on each. In the first call of the season, a lady leaves her own card and those of her husband, sons, and daughters.

A lady has a right to leave her card without asking for the lady of the house if it is not her day, or if there is any reason--such as bad weather, pressure of engagements, or the like--which renders time an important matter.

If ladies are receiving, and she is admitted, the visitor should leave her husband's cards for the gentlemen of the family on the hall table. Strangers staying in town who wish to be called upon should send their cards by post, with address attached, to those whom they would like to see. There is no necessity of calling after a tea or general reception if one has attended the festivity, or has left or sent a card on that day.

For reception days a lady wears a plain, dark, rich dress, taking care, however, never to be overdressed at home. She rises when her visitors enter, and is careful to seat her friends so that she can have a word with each. If this is impossible, she keeps her eye on the recent arrivals to be sure to speak to every one. She is to be forgiven if she pays more attention to the aged, to some distinguished stranger, or to some one who has the still higher claim of misfortune, or to one of a modest and shrinking temperament, than to one young, gay, fashionable, and rich. If she neglects these fortunate visitors they will not feel it; if she bows low to them and neglects the others, she betrays that she is a snob. If a lady is not sure that she is known by name to her hostess, she should not fail to pronounce her own name. Many ladies send their cards to the young brides who have come into a friend's family, and yet who are without personal acquaintance. Many, alas! forget faces, so that a name quickly pronounced is a help. In the event of an exchange of calls between two ladies who have never met (and this has gone on for years in New York, sometimes until death has removed one forever), they should take an early opportunity of speaking to each other at some friend's house; the younger should approach the elder and introduce herself; it is always regarded as a kindness; or the one who has received the first attention should be the first to speak.

It is well always to leave a card in the hall even if one is received, as it assists the lady's memory in her attempts to return these civilities. Cards of condolence must be returned by a mourning-card sent in an envelope at such reasonable time after the death of a relative as one can determine again to take up the business of society. When the separate card of a lady is left, with her reception day printed in one corner, two cards of her husband should be left, one for the lady, the other for the master, of the house; but after the first call of the season, it is not necessary to leave the husband's card, except after a dinner invitation. It is a convenience, although not a universal custom, to have the joint names of husband and wife, as "Dr. and Mrs. J. B. Watson," printed on one card, to use as a card of condolence or congratulation, but not as a visiting-card. These cards are used as "P. P. C." cards, and can be sent in an envelope by post. Society is rapidly getting over its prejudice against sending cards by post. In Europe it is always done, and it is much safer. Etiquette and hospitality have been reduced to a system in the Old World. It would be much more convenient could we do that here. Ceremonious visiting is the machinery by which an acquaintance is kept up in a circle too large for social visiting; but every lady should try to make one or two informal calls each winter on intimate friends. These calls can be made in the morning in the plainest walking-dress, and are certainly the most agreeable and flattering of all visits.

CHAPTER VI

INVITATIONS, ACCEPTANCES, AND REGRETS.

The engraving of invitation-cards has become the important function of more than one enterprising firm in every city, so that it seems unnecessary to say more than that the most plain and simple style of engraving the necessary words is all that is requisite.

The English ambassador at Rome has a plain, stiff, unglazed card of a large size, on which is engraved,

Sir Augustus and Lady Paget request the pleasure of _____ company on Thursday evening, November fifteenth, at ten o'clock. The favor of an answer is requested.

The lady of the house writes the name of the invited guest in the blank space left before the word "company." Many entertainers in America keep these blanks, or half-engraved invitations, always on hand, and thus save themselves the trouble of writing the whole card.

Sometimes, however, ladies prefer to write their own dinner invitations. The formula should always be,

Mr. and Mrs. Henry Brown request the pleasure of Mr. and Mrs. Jones's company at dinner. November fifteenth, at seven o'clock, 132 Blank St. West.

These invitations should be immediately answered, and with a peremptory acceptance or a regret. Never enter into any discussion or prevision with a dinner invitation. Never write, saying "you will come if you do not have to leave town," or that you will "try to come," or, if you are a married pair, that you will "one of you come." Your hostess wants to know exactly who is coming and who isn't, that she may arrange her table accordingly. Simply say,

Mr. and Mrs. James Jones accept with pleasure the polite invitation of Mr.

and Mrs. Henry Brown for dinner on November fifteenth, at seven o'clock.

Or if it is written in the first person, accept in the same informal manner, but quickly and decisively.

After having accepted a dinner invitation, if illness or any other cause interfere with your going to the dinner, send all immediate note to your hostess, that she may fill your place. Never selfishly keep the place open for yourself if there is a doubt about your going. It has often made or marred the pleasure of a dinner-party, this hesitancy on the part of a guest to send in time to her hostess her regrets, caused by the illness of her child, or the coming on of a cold, or a death in the family, or any other calamity. Remember always that a dinner is a most formal affair, that it is the highest social compliment, that its happy fulfilment is of the greatest importance to the hostess, and that it must be met in the same formal spirit. It precludes, on her part, the necessity of having to make a first call if she be the older resident, although she generally calls first. Some young neophytes in society, having been asked to a dinner where the elderly lady who gave it had forgotten to enclose her card, asked if they should call afterwards. Of course they were bound to do so, although their hostess should have called or enclosed her card. However, one invitation to dinner is better than many cards as a social compliment.

We have been asked by many, "To whom should the answer to an invitation be addressed?" If Mr. and Mrs. Brown invite you, answer Mr. and Mrs. Brown. If Mrs. John Jones asks you to a wedding, answer Mrs. John Jones. Another of our correspondents asks, "Shall I respond to the lady of the house or to the bride if asked to a wedding?" This seems so impossible a confusion that we should not think of mentioning so self-evident a fact had not the doubt arisen. One has nothing to say to the bride in answering such an invitation; the answer is to be sent to the hostess, who writes.

Always carefully observe the formula of your invitation, and answer it exactly. As to the card of the English ambassador, a gentleman should write: "Mr. Algernon Gracie will do himself the honor to accept the invitation of Sir Augustus and Lady Paget." In America he would be a trifle less formal, saying, "Mr. Algernon Gracie will have much pleasure in accepting the polite invitation of Mr. and Mrs. Henry Brown." We notice that on all English cards the "R.S.V.P." is omitted, and that a plain line of English script is engraved, saying, "The favor of an answer is requested."

In this country the invitations to a dinner are always in the name of both host and hostess, but invitations to a ball, "at home," a tea, or garden-party, are in the name of the hostess alone. At a wedding the names of both host and hostess are given. And if a father entertains for his daughters, he being a widower, his name appears alone for her wedding; but if his eldest daughter presides over his household, his and her name appear together for dinners, receptions, and "at homes." Many widowed fathers, however, omit the names of their daughters on the invitation. A young lady at the head of her father's house may, if she is no longer very young, issue her own cards for a tea. It is never proper for very young ladies to invite gentlemen in their own name to visit at the house, call on them, or to come to dinner. The invitation must come from the father, mother, or chaperon.

At the Assembly, Patriarchs', Charity ball, or any public affair, the word "ball" is used, but no lady invites you to a "ball" at her own house. The words "At Home," with "Cotillion" or "Dancing" in one corner, and the hour and date, alone are necessary. If it is to be a small, informal dance, the word "Informal" should be engraved in one corner. Officers of the army and navy giving a ball, members of the hunt, bachelors, members of a club, heads of committees, always "request the pleasure," or, "the honor of your company." It is not proper for a gentleman to describe himself as "at home;" he must "request the pleasure." A rich bachelor of Utopia who gave many entertainments made this mistake, and sent a card--"Mr. Horatio Brown. At Home. Tuesday, November fourteenth. Tea at four"--to a lady who had been an ambassadress. She immediately replied: "Mrs. Rousby is very glad to hear that Mr. Horatio Brown is at home--she hopes that he will stay there; but of what possible consequence is that to Mrs. Rousby?" This was a piece of rough wit, but it told the young man of his mistake. Another card, issued with the singular formula, "Mrs. Ferguson hopes to see Mrs. Rousby at the church," on the occasion of the wedding of a daughter, brought forth the rebuke, "Nothing is so deceitful as human hope," The phrase is an improper one. Mrs. Ferguson should have "requested the pleasure."

In asking for an invitation to a ball for friends, ladies must be cautious not to intrude too far, or to feel offended if refused. Often a hostess has a larger list than she can fill, and she is not able to ask all whom she would wish to invite. Therefore a very great discretion is to be observed on the part of those who ask a favor. A lady may always request an invitation for distinguished strangers, or for a young dancing man if she can answer for him in every way, but rarely for a married couple, and almost never for a couple living in the same city, unless newly arrived.

Invitations to evening or day receptions are generally "at home" cards. A lady may use her own visiting cards for five-o'clock tea. For other entertainments, "Music," "Lawn-tennis," "Garden-party," "Readings and Recitals," may be engraved in one corner, or written in by the lady herself.

As for wedding invitations, they are almost invariably sent out by the parents of the bride, engraved in small script on note-paper. The style can always be obtained of a fashionable engraver. They should be sent out a fortnight before the wedding-day, and are not to be answered unless the guests are requested to attend a "sit-down" breakfast, when the answer must be as explicit as to a dinner. Those who cannot attend the wedding send or leave their visiting-cards either on the day of the wedding or soon after. Invitations to a luncheon are generally written by the hostess on note-paper, and should be rather informal, as luncheon is an informal meal. However, nowadays ladies' luncheons have become such grand, consequential, and expensive affairs, that invitations are engraved and sent out a fortnight in advance, and answered immediately. There is the same etiquette as at dinner observed at these formal luncheons. There is such a thing, however, as a "stand-up" luncheon--a sort of reception with banquet, from which one could absent one's self without being missed.

Punctuality in keeping all engagements is a feature of a well-bred character, in society as well as in business, and it cannot be too thoroughly insisted upon.

In sending a "regret" be particular to word your note most respectfully. Never write the word "regrets" on your card unless you wish to insult your hostess. Send a card without any pencilling upon it, or write a note, thus: "Mrs. Brown regrets that a previous engagement will deprive her of the pleasure of accepting the polite invitation of Mrs. Jones."

No one should, in the matter of accepting or refusing an invitation, economize his politeness. It is better to err on the other side. Your friend has done his best in inviting you.

The question is often asked us, "Should invitations be sent to people in mourning?" Of course they should. No one would knowingly intrude on a house in which there is or has been death within a month; but after that, although it is an idle compliment, it is one which must be paid; it is a part of the machinery of society. As invitations are now directed by the hundreds by hired amanuenses, a lady should carefully revise her list, in order that no names of persons deceased may be written on her cards; but the members of the family who remain, and who have suffered a loss, should be carefully remembered, and should not be pained by seeing the name of one who has departed included in the invitations or wedding-cards. People in deep mourning are not invited to dinners or luncheons, but for weddings and large entertainments cards are sent as a token of remembrance and compliment. After a year of mourning the bereaved family should send out cards with a narrow black edge to all who have remembered them.

Let it be understood that in all countries a card sent by a private hand in an envelope is equivalent to a visit. In England one sent by post is equivalent to a visit, excepting after a dinner. Nothing is pencilled on a card sent by post, except the three letters "P.P.C." No such words as "accepts," "declines," "regrets" should be written on a card. As much ill-will is engendered in New York by the loss of cards for large receptions and the like, some of which the messenger-boys fling into the gutter, it is a thousand pities that we cannot agree to send all invitations by mail. People always get letters that are sent by post, particularly those which they could do without. Why should they not get their more interesting letters that contain invitations? It is considered thoroughly respectful in England, and as our people are fond of copying that stately etiquette, why should they not follow this sensible part of it?

It is in every sense as complimentary to send a letter by the post as by the dirty fingers of a hired messenger. Very few people in this country can afford to send by their own servants, who, again, rarely find the right address.

CHAPTER VII

CARDS OF COMPLIMENT, COURTESY, CONDOLENCE, AND CONGRATULATION.

A distinguished lady of New York, on recovering from a severe illness, issued a card which is a new departure. In admiring its fitness and the need which has existed for just such a card, we wonder that none of us have before invented something so compact and stately, pleasing and proper--that her thought had not been our thought. It reads thus, engraved in elegant script, plain and modest: "Mrs. _____ presents her compliments and thanks for recent kind inquiries." This card, sent in an envelope which bears the family crest as a seal, reached all those who had left cards and inquiries for a useful and eminent member of society, who lay for weeks trembling between life and death.

This card is an attention to her large circle of anxious friends which only a kind-hearted woman would have thought of, and yet the thought was all; for after that the engraver and the secretary could do the rest, showing what a labor-saving invention it is to a busy woman who is not yet sufficiently strong to write notes to all who had felt for her severe suffering. The first joy of convalescence is of gratitude, and the second that we have created an interest and compassion among our friends, and that we were not alone as we struggled with disease. Therefore we may well recommend that this card should become a fashion. It meets a universal want.

This may be called one of the "cards of compliment"--a phase of card-leaving to which we have hardly reached in this country. It is even more, it is a heartfelt and friendly blossom of etiquette, "just out," as we say of the apple-blossoms.

Now as to the use of it by the afflicted: why would it not be well for persons who have lost a friend also to have such a card engraved? "Mr. R____ begs to express his thanks for your kind sympathy in his recent bereavement," etc. It would save a world of letter-writing to a person who does not care to write letters, and it would be a very pleasant token to receive when all other such tokens are impossible. For people leave their cards on a mourner, and never know whether they have been received or not. Particularly is this true of apartment-houses; and when people live in hotels, who knows whether the card ever reaches its destination? We generally find that it has not done so, if we have the courage to make the inquiry.

Those cards which we send by a servant to make the necessary inquiries for a sick friend, for the happy mother and the new-born baby, are essentially "cards of compliment." In excessively ceremonious circles the visits of ceremony on these occasions are very elaborate--as at the Court of Spain, for instance; and a lady of New York was once much amused at receiving the card of a superb Spanish official, who called on her newly arrived daughter when the latter was three days old, leaving a card for the "new daughter." He of course left a card for the happy mamma, and did not ask to go farther than the door, but he came in state.

In England the "family" were wont to send christening cards after a birth, but this has never been the fashion in this country, and it is disappearing in England. The complimentary card issued for such events is now generally an invitation to partake of caudle--a very delicious porridge made of oatmeal and raisins, brandy, spices, and sugar, and formally served in the lady's chamber before the month's seclusion is broken. It will be remembered that Tom Thumb was dropped into a bowl of fermity, which many antiquarians suppose to have been caudle. Nowadays a caudle party is a very gay, dressy affair, and given about six weeks after young master or mistress is ready to be congratulated or condoled with on his or her entrance upon this mundane sphere. We find in English books of etiquette very formal directions as to these cards of compliment. "Cards to inquire after friends during illness must be left in person, and not sent by post. On a lady's visiting-card must be written above the printed name, 'To inquire,' and nothing else should be added to these words."

For the purpose of returning thanks, printed cards are sold, with the owner's name written above the printed words. These printed cards are generally sent by post, as they are despatched while the person inquired after is still an invalid. These cards are also used to convey the intelligence of the sender's recovery. Therefore they would not be sent while the person was in danger or seriously ill. But this has always seemed to us a very poor and. business-like way of returning "kind inquiries." The printed card looks cheap. Far better the engraved and carefully prepared card of Mrs. _____, which has the effect of a personal compliment.

We do not in this country send those hideous funeral or memorial cards which are sold in England at every stationer's to apprise one's friends of a death in the family. There is no need of this, as the newspapers spread the sad intelligence.

There is, however, a very elaborate paper called a "_faire part_," issued in both England and France after a death, in which the mourner announces to you the lamented decease of some person connected with him. Also on the occasion of a marriage, these elaborate papers, engraved on a large sheet of letter-paper, are sent to all one's acquaintances in England and on the Continent.

Visits of condolence can begin the week after the event which occasions them. Personal visits are only made by relatives or very intimate friends, who will of course be their own judges of the propriety of speaking fully of the grief which has desolated the house. The cards are left at the door by the person inquiring for the afflicted persons, and one card is as good as half a dozen. It is not necessary to deluge a mourning family with cards. These cards need not be returned for a year, unless our suggestion be followed, and the card engraved as we have indicated, and then sent by post. It is not yet a fashion, but it is in the air, and deserves to be one.

Cards of congratulation are left in person, and if the ladies are at home the visitor should go in, and be hearty in his or her good wishes. For such visits a card sent by post would, among intimate friends, be considered cold-blooded. It must at least be left in person.

Now as to cards of ceremony. These are to be forwarded to those who have sent invitations to weddings, carefully addressed to the person who invites you; also after an entertainment to which you have been asked, within a week after a dinner (this must be a personal visit), and on the lady's "day," if she has one; and we may add here that if on making a call a lady sees that she is not recognized, she should hasten to give her name. (This in answer to many inquiries.) Only calls of pure ceremony are made by handing in cards, as at a tea or general reception, etc. When cards have been left once in the season they need not be left again.

Under the mixed heads of courtesy and compliment should be those calls made to formally announce a betrothal. The parents leave the cards of the betrothed pair, with their own, on all the connections and friends of the two families. This is a formal announcement, and all who receive this intimation should make a congratulatory visit if possible.

As young people are often asked without their parents, the question arises, What should the parents do to show their sense of this attention? They should leave or send their cards with those of their children who have received the invitation. These are cards of courtesy. Cards ought not to be left on the daughters of a family without also including the parents in courteous formality. Gentlemen, when calling on any number of ladies, send in only one card, and cards left on a reception day where a person is visiting are not binding on the visitor to return. No separate card is left on a guest on reception days.

When returning visits of ceremony, as the first visit after a letter of introduction, or as announcing your arrival in town or your intended departure, one may leave a card at the door without inquiring for the lady.

Attention to these little things is a proof at once of self-respect and of respect for one's friends. They soon become easy matters of habit, and of memory. To the well-bred they are second nature. No one who is desirous of pleasing in society should neglect them.

A lady should never call on a gentleman unless professionally or officially. She should knock at his door, send in her card, and be as ceremonious as possible, if lawyer, doctor, or clergyman. On entering a crowded drawing-room it may be impossible to find the hostess at once, so that in many fine houses in New York the custom of announcing the name has become a necessary fashion. It is impossible to attempt to be polite without cultivating a good memory. The absent or self-absorbed person who forgets names and faces, who recalls unlucky topics, confuses relationships, speaks of the dead as if they were living, or talks about an unlucky adventure in the family, who plunges into personalities, who metaphorically treads on a person's toes, will never succeed in society. He must consider his "cards of courtesy."

The French talk of "la politesse du foyer." They are full of it. Small sacrifices, little courtesies, a kindly spirit, insignificant attentions, self-control, an allowance for the failings of others--these go to make up the elegance of life. True politeness has its roots very deep. We should not cultivate politeness merely from a wish to please, but because we would consider the feelings and spare the time of others. Cards of compliment and courtesy, therefore, save time as well as express a kindly remembrance. Everything in our busy world--or "whirl," as some people call it--that does these two things is a valuable discovery.

A card of courtesy is always sent with flowers, books, bonbonnieres, game, sweetmeats, fruits--any of the small gifts which are freely offered among intimate friends. But in acknowledging these gifts or attentions a card is not a sufficient return. Nor is it proper to write "regrets" or "accepts" on a card. A note should be written in either case.

A card of any sort must be scrupulously plain. Wedding cards should be as simple and unostentatious as possible.

The ceremony of paying visits and of leaving cards has been decided by the satirist as meaningless, stupid, and useless; but it underlies the very structure of society. Visits of form, visits of ceremony, are absolutely necessary. You can hardly invite people to your house until you have called and have left a card. And thus one has a safeguard against intrusive and undesirable acquaintances. To stop an acquaintance, one has but to stop leaving cards. It is thus done quietly but securely.

Gentlemen who have no time to call should be represented by their cards. These may well be trusted to the hands of wife, mother, daughter, sister, but should be punctiliously left.

The card may well be noted as belonging only to a high order of development. No monkey, no "missing link," no Zulu, no savage, carries a card. It is the tool of civilization, its "field-mark and device." It may be improved; it may be, and has been, abused; but it cannot be dispensed with under our present environment.

CHAPTER VIII

THE ETIQUETTE OF WEDDINGS.

Scarcely a week passes during the year that the fashionable journals do not publish "answers to correspondents" on that subject of all others most interesting to young ladies, the etiquette of weddings. No book can tell the plain truth with sufficient emphasis, that the etiquette at a grand wedding is always the same. The next day some one writes to a newspaper again,

"Shall the bridegroom wear a dress-coat at the hour of eleven A.M., and who pays for the wedding-cards?" The wedding of to-day in England has "set the fashion" for America. No man ever puts on a dress-coat before his seven-o'clock dinner, therefore every bridegroom is dressed in a frock-coat and light trousers of any pattern he pleases; in other words, he wears a formal morning dress, drives to the church with his best man, and awaits the arrival of the bride in the vestry-room. He may wear gloves or not as he chooses. The best man is the intimate friend, sometimes the brother, of the groom. He accompanies him to the church, as we have said, follows him to the altar, stands at his right hand a little behind him, and holds his hat during the marriage-service. After that is ended he pays the clergyman's fee, accompanies, in a coup‚ by himself, the bridal party home, and then assists the ushers to introduce friends to the bridal pair.

The bridegroom is allowed to make what presents he pleases to the bride, and to send something in the nature of a fan, a locket, a ring, or a bouquet to the bridesmaids; he has also to buy the wedding-ring, and, of course, he sends a bouquet to the bride; but he is not to furnish cards or carriages or the wedding-breakfast; this is all done by the bride's family. In England the groom is expected to drive the bride away in his own carriage, but in America even that is not often allowed.

The bride meantime is dressed in gorgeous array, generally in white satin, with veil of point-lace and orange blossoms, and is driven to the church in a carriage with her father, who gives her away. Her mother and other relatives having preceded her take the front seats. Her bridesmaids should also precede her, and await her in the chancel of the church.

The ushers then proceed to form the procession with which almost all city weddings are begun. The ushers first, two and two; then the bridesmaids, two and two; then some pretty children--bridesmaids under ten; and then the bride, leaning on her father's right arm. Sometimes the child bridesmaids precede the others. As the cortege reaches the lowest altar-step the ushers break ranks and go to the right and left; the bridesmaids also separate, going to the right and left, leaving a space for the bridal pair. As the bride reaches the lowest step the bridegroom advances, takes her by her right hand, and conducts her to the altar, where they both kneel. The clergyman, being already in his place, signifies to them when to rise, and then proceeds to make the twain one.

The bridal pair walk down the aisle arm-in-arm, and are immediately conducted to the carriage and driven home; the rest follow. In some cases, but rarely in this country, a bridal register is signed in the vestry.

Formerly brides removed the whole glove; now they adroitly cut the finger of the left-hand glove, so that they can remove that without pulling off the whole glove for the ring. Such is a church wedding, performed a thousand times alike. The organ peals forth the wedding-march, the clergyman pronounces the necessary vows to slow music, or not, as the contracting parties please. Music, however, adds very much to this ceremony. In a marriage at home, the bridesmaids and best man are usually dispensed with. The clergyman enters and faces the company, the bridal pair follow and face him. After the ceremony the clergyman retires, and the wedded pair receive congratulations.

An attempt has been made in America to introduce the English fashion of a wedding-breakfast. It is not as yet acclimated, but it is, perhaps, well to describe here the proper etiquette. The gentlemen and ladies who are asked to this breakfast should be apprised of that honor a fortnight in advance, and should accept or decline immediately, as it has all the formality of a dinner, and seats are, of course, very important. On arriving at the house where the breakfast is to be held, the gentlemen leave their hats in the hall, but ladies do not remove their bonnets. After greeting the bride and bridegroom, and the father and mother, the company converse for a few moments until breakfast is announced. Then the bride and groom go first, followed by the bride's father with the groom's mother, then the groom's father with the bride's mother, then the best man with the first bridesmaid, then the bridesmaids with attendant gentlemen, who have been invited for this honor, and then the other invited guests, as the bride's mother has arranged. Coffee and tea are not offered, but bouillon, salads, birds, oysters, and other hot and cold dishes, ices, jellies, etc., are served at this breakfast, together with champagne and other wines, and finally the wedding-cake is set before the bride, and she cuts a slice.

The health of the bride and groom is then proposed by the gentleman chosen for this office, generally the father of the groom, and responded to by the father of the bride. The groom is sometimes expected to respond, and he proposes the health of the bridesmaids, for which the best man returns thanks. Unless all are unusually happy speakers, this is apt to be awkward, and "stand-up" breakfasts are far more commonly served, as the French say, en buffet. In the first place, the possibility of asking more people commends this latter practice, and it is far less trouble to serve a large, easy collation to a number of people standing about than to furnish what is really a dinner to a number sitting down.

Wedding presents are sent any time within two months before the wedding, the earlier the better, as many brides like to arrange their own tables artistically, if the presents are shown. Also, all brides should write a personal note thanking each giver for his gift, be it large or small.

All persons who send gifts should be invited to the wedding and to the reception, although the converse of this proposition does not hold true; for not all who are asked to the wedding are expected to send gifts.

Wedding presents have now become almost absurdly gorgeous. The old fashion, which was started among the frugal Dutch, of giving the young couple their household gear and a sum of money with which to begin, has now degenerated into a very bold display of wealth and ostentatious generosity, so that friends of moderate means are afraid to send anything. Even the cushion on which a wealthy bride in New York was lately expected to kneel was so elaborately embroidered with pearls that she visibly hesitated to press it with her knee at the altar. Silver and gold services, too precious to be trusted to ordinary lock and key, are displayed at the wedding and immediately sent off to some convenient safe. This is one of the necessary and inevitable overgrowths of a luxury which we have not yet learned to manage. In France they do things better, those nearest of kin subscribing a sum of money, which is sent to the bride's mother, who expends it in the bridal trousseau, or in jewels or silver, as the bride pleases.

So far has this custom transcended good taste that now many persons of refined minds hesitate to show the presents.

After giving an hour and a half to her guests, the bride retires to change her dress; generally her most intimate friends accompany her. She soon returns in her travelling-dress, and is met at the foot of the stairs by the groom, who has also changed his dress. The father, mother, and intimate friends kiss the bride, and, as the happy pair drive off, a shower of satin slippers and rice follows them. If one slipper alights on the top of the carriage, luck is assured to them forever.

Wedding-cake is no longer sent about. It is neatly packed in boxes; each guest takes one, if she likes, as she leaves the house.

Wedding-favors made of white ribbon and artificial flowers are indispensable in England, but America has had the good taste to abjure them until lately. Such ornaments are used for the horses' ears and the servants' coats in this country. Here the groom wears a boutonniere of natural flowers.

A widow should never be accompanied by bridesmaids, or wear a veil or orange-blossoms at her marriage. She should at church wear a colored silk and a bonnet. She should be attended by her father, brother, or some near friend.

It is proper for her to remove her first wedding-ring, as the wearing of that cannot but be painful to the bridegroom.

If married at home, the widow bride may wear a light silk and be bonnetless, but she should not indulge in any of the signs of first bridal.

It is an exploded idea that of allowing every one to kiss the bride. It is only meet that the near relatives do that.

The formula for wedding-cards is generally this:

Mr. and Mrs. Brown request the pleasure of your company at the wedding of their daughter Maria to John Stanley, at Ascension Church, on Tuesday, November fifteenth, at two o'clock.

These invitations are engraved on note-paper.

If friends are invited to a wedding-breakfast or a reception at the house, that fact is stated on a separate card, which is enclosed in the same envelope.

Of course in great cities, with a large acquaintance, many are asked to the church and not to the house. This fact should never give offence.

The smaller card runs in this fashion:

Reception at 99 B Street, at half-past two.

To these invitations the invited guests make no response save to go or to leave cards. All invited guests, however, are expected to call on the young couple and to invite them during the year.

Of course there are quieter weddings and very simple arrangements as to serving refreshments: a wedding-cake and a decanter of sherry often are alone offered to the witnesses of a wedding.

Many brides prefer to be married in travelling-dress and hat, and leave immediately, without congratulations.

The honey-moon in our busy land is usually only a fortnight in the sky, and some few bridal pairs prefer to spend it at the quiet country house of a friend, as is the English fashion. But others make a hurried trip to Niagara, or to the Thousand Islands, or go to Europe, as the case may be. It is extraordinary that none stay at home; in beginning a new life all agree that a change of place is the first requisite.

After the return home, bridal dinners and parties are offered to the bride, and she is treated with distinction for three months. Her path is often strewed with flowers from the church to her own door, and it is, metaphorically, so adorned during the first few weeks of married life. Every one hastens to welcome her to her new condition, and she has but to smile and accept the amiable congratulations and attentions which are showered upon her. Let her parents remember, however, in sending cards after the wedding, to let the bride's friends know where she can be found in her married estate.

Now as to the time for the marriage. There is something exquisitely poetical in the idea of a June wedding. It is the very month for the softer emotions and for the wedding journey. In England it is the favorite month for marriages. May is considered unlucky, and in an old almanac of 1678 we find the following notice: "Times prohibiting marriage: Marriage comes in on the 13th day of January and at Septuagesima Sunday; it is out again until Low Sunday, at which time it comes in again and goes not out until Rogation Sunday. Thence it is forbidden until Trinity Sunday, from whence it is unforbidden until Advent Sunday; but then it goes out and comes not in again until the 18th of January next following."

Our brides have, however, all seasons for their own, excepting May, as we have said, and Friday, an unlucky day. The month of roses has very great recommendations. The ceremony is apt to be performed in the country at a pretty little church, which lends its altar-rails gracefully to wreaths, and whose Gothic windows open upon green lawns and trim gardens. The bride and her maids can walk over the delicate sward without soiling their slippers, and an opportunity offers for carrying parasols made entirely of flowers. But if it is too far to walk, the bride is driven to church in her father's carriage with him alone, her mother, sisters, and bridesmaids having preceded her. In England etiquette requires that the bride and groom should depart from the church in the groom's carriage. It is strict etiquette there that the groom furnish the carriage with which they return to the wedding-breakfast and afterwards depart in state, with many wedding-favors on the horses' heads, and huge white bouquets on the breasts of coachman and footman.

It is in England, also, etiquette to drive with four horses to the place where the honey-moon is to be spent; but in America the drive is generally to the nearest railway-station.

Let us give a further sketch of the duties of the best man. He accompanies the groom to the church and stands near him, waiting at the altar, until the bride arrives; then he holds the groom's hat. He signs the register afterwards as witness, and pays the clergyman's fee, and then follows the bridal procession out of the church, joining the party at the house, where he still further assists the groom by presenting the guests. The bridesmaids sometimes form a line near the door at a June wedding, allowing the bride to walk through this pretty alley-way to the church.

The bridegroom's relatives sit at the right of the altar or communion rails, thus being on the bridegroom's right hand, and those of the bride sit on the left, at the bride's left hand. The bridegroom and best man stand on the clergyman's left hand at the altar. The bride is taken by her right hand by the groom, and of course stands on his left hand; her father stands a little behind her. Sometimes the female relatives stand in the chancel with the bridal group, but this, can only happen in a very large church; and the rector must arrange this, as in high churches the marriages take place outside the chancel.

After the ceremony is over the clergyman bends over and congratulates the young people. The bride then takes the left arm of the groom, and passes down the aisle, followed by her bridesmaids and the ushers.

Some of our correspondents have no good asked us what the best man is doing at this moment? Probably waiting in the vestry, or, if not, he hurries down a side aisle, gets into a carriage, and drives to the house where the wedding reception is to be held.

October is a good month for both city and country weddings. In our climate, the brilliant October days, not too warm, are admirable for the city guests, who are invited to a country place for the wedding, and certainly it is a pleasant season for the wedding journey. Travelling costumes for brides in England are very elegant, even showy. Velvet, and even light silks and satins, are used; but in our country plain cloth and cashmere costumes are more proper and more fashionable.

For weddings in families where a death has recently occurred, all friends, even the widowed mother, should lay aside their mourning for the ceremony, appearing in colors. It is considered unlucky and inappropriate to wear black at a wedding. In our country a widowed mother appears at her daughter's wedding in purple velvet or silk; in England she wears deep cardinal red, which is considered, under these circumstances, to be mourning, or proper for a person who is in mourning.

We should add that ushers and groomsmen are unknown at an English wedding. The sexton of the church performs the functions which are attended to here by ushers.

Note.--The young people who are about to be married make a list together as to whom cards should be sent, and all cards go from the young lady's family. No one thinks it strange to get cards for a wedding. A young lady should write a note of thanks to every one who sends her a present before she leaves home; all her husband's friends, relatives, etc., all her own, and to people whom she does not know these notes should especially be written, as their gifts may be prompted by a sense of kindness to her parents or her _fianc‚_, which she should recognize. It is better taste to write these notes on note-paper than on cards. It is not necessary to send cards to each member of a family; include them all under the head of "Mr. and Mrs. Brown and family." It would be proper for a young lady to send her cards to a physician under whose care she has been if she was acquainted with him socially, but it is not expected when the acquaintance is purely professional. A fashionable and popular physician would be swamped with wedding-cards if that were the custom. If, however, one wishes to show gratitude and remembrance, there would be no impropriety in sending cards to such a gentleman.

CHAPTER IX

"WHO PAYS FOR THE CARDS?"

We have received a number of letters from our correspondents asking whether the groom pays for the wedding cards. This question we have answered so often in the negative that we think it well to explain the philosophy of the etiquette of weddings, which is remotely founded on the early savage history of mankind, and which bears fruit in our later and more complex civilization, still reminding us of the past. In early and in savage days the man sought his bride heroically, and carried her off by force. The Tartar still does this, and the idea only was improved in patriarchal days by the purchase of the bride by the labor of her husband, or by his wealth in flocks and herds. It is still a theory that the bride is thus carried off. Always, therefore, the idea has been cherished that the bride is something carefully guarded, and the groom is looked upon as a sort of friendly enemy, who comes to take away the much-prized object from her loving and jealous family. Thus the long-cherished theory bears fruit in the English ceremonial, where the only carriage furnished by the groom is the one in which he drives the bride away to the spending of the honeymoon. Up to that time he has had no rights of proprietorship. Even this is not allowed in America among fashionable people, the bride's father sending them in his own carriage on the first stage of their journey. It is not etiquette for the groom to furnish anything for his own wedding but the ring and a bouquet for the bride, presents for the bridesmaids and the best man, and some token to the ushers. He pays the clergyman.

He should not pay for the cards, the carriages, the entertainment, or anything connected with the wedding. This is decided in the high court of etiquette. That is the province of the family of the bride, and should be insisted upon. If they are not able to do this, there should be no wedding and no cards. It is better for a portionless girl to go to the altar in a travelling dress, and to send out no sort of invitations or wedding cards, than to allow the groom to pay for them. This is not to the disparagement of the rights of the groom. It is simply a proper and universal etiquette.

At the altar the groom, if he is a millionaire, makes his wife his equal by saying, "With all my worldly goods I thee endow;" but until he has uttered these words she has no claim on his purse for clothes, or cards, or household furnishing, or anything but those articles which come under the head of such gifts as it is a lover's province to give.

A very precise, old-time aristocrat of New York broke her daughter's engagement to a gentleman because he brought her a dress from Paris. She said, if he did not know enough not to give her daughter clothes while she was under her roof, he should not have her. This is an exaggerated feeling, but the principle is a sound one. The position of a woman is so delicate, the relations of engaged people so uncertain, that it would bring about an awkwardness if the gentleman were to pay for the shoes, the gowns, the cards of his betrothed.

Suppose, as was the case twice last winter, that an engagement of marriage is broken after the cards are out. Who is to repay the bridegroom if he has paid for the cards? Should the father of the bride send him a check? That would be very insulting, yet a family would feel nervous about being under pecuniary indebtedness to a discarded son-in-law. The lady can return her ring and the gifts her lover has made her; they have suffered no contact that will injure them. But she could not return shoes or gowns or bonnets.

It is therefore wisely ordered by etiquette that the lover be allowed to pay for nothing that could not be returned to him without loss, if the engagement were dissolved, even on the wedding morning.

Of course in primitive life the lover may pay for his lady-love, as we will say in the case of a pair of young people who come together in a humble station. Such marriages are common in America, and many of these pairs have mounted to the very highest social rank. But they must not attempt anything which is in imitation of the etiquette of fashionable life unless they can do it well and thoroughly.

Nothing is more honorable than a marriage celebrated in the presence only of father, mother, and priest. Two young people unwilling or unable to have splendid dresses, equipages, cards, and ceremony, can always be married this way, and go to the Senate or White House afterwards. They are not hampered by it hereafter. But the bride should never forget her dignity. She should never let the groom pay for cards, or for anything, unless it is the marriage license, wherever it is needful in this country, and the clergyman's fee. If she does, she puts herself in a false position.

A very sensible observer, writing of America and its young people, and the liberty allowed them, says "the liberty, or the license, of our youth will have to be curtailed. As our society becomes complex and artificial, like older societies in Europe, our children will be forced to approximate to them in status, and parents will have to waken to a sense of their responsibilities."

This is a remark which applies at once to that liberty permitted to engaged couples in rural neighborhoods, where the young girl is allowed to go on a journey at her lover's expense. A girl's natural protectors should know better than to allow this. They know that her purity is her chief attraction to man, and that a certain coyness and virginal freshness are the dowry she should bring her future husband. Suppose that this engagement is broken off. How will she be accepted by another lover after having enjoyed the hospitality of the first? Would it not always make a disagreeable feeling between the two men, although No. 2 might have perfect respect for the girl?

Etiquette may sometimes make blunders, but it is generally based on a right principle, and here it is undoubtedly founded in truth and justice. In other countries this truth is so fully realized that daughters are guarded by the vigilance of parents almost to the verge of absurdity. A young girl is never allowed to go out alone, and no man is permitted to enter the household until his character has undergone the closest scrutiny. Marriage is a unique contract, and all the various wrongs caused by hasty marriages, all the troubles before the courts, all the divorces, are multiplied by the carelessness of American parents, who, believing, and truly believing, in the almost universal purity of their daughters, are careless of the fold, not remembering the one black sheep.

This evil of excessive liberty and of the loose etiquette of our young people cannot be rooted out by laws. It must begin at the hearth-stone, Family life must be reformed; young ladies must be brought up with greater strictness. The bloom of innocence should not be brushed off by careless hands. If a mother leaves her daughter matronless, to receive attentions without her dignified presence, she opens the door to an unworthy man, who may mean marriage or not. He may be a most unsuitable husband even if he does mean marriage. If he takes the young lady about, paying for her cab hire, her theatre tickets, and her journeyings, and then drops her, whom have they to thank but themselves that her bloom is brushed off, that her character suffers, that she is made ridiculous, and marries some one whom she does not love, for a home.

Men, as they look back on their own varied experience, are apt to remember with great respect the women who were cold and distant. They love the fruit which hung the highest, the flower which was guarded, and which did not grow under their feet in the highway. They look back with vague wonder that they were ever infatuated with a fast girl who matured into a vulgar woman.

And we must remember what a fatal effect upon marriage is the loosing of the ties of respect. Love without trust is without respect, and if a lover has not respected his _fianc‚e_, he will never respect his wife.

It is the privilege of the bride to name the wedding day, and of her father and mother to pay for her trousseau. After the wedding invitations are issued she does not appear in public.

The members of the bride's family go to the church before the bride; the bridegroom and his best man await them at the altar.

The bride comes last, with her father or brother, who is to give her away. She is joined at the altar step by her _fianc‚_, who takes her hand, and then she becomes his for life.

All these trifles mean much, as any one can learn who goes through with the painful details of a divorce suit.

Now when the circle of friends on both sides is very extensive, it has of late become customary to send invitations to some who are not called to the wedding breakfast to attend the ceremony in church. This sometimes takes the place of issuing cards. No one thinks of calling on the newly married who has not received either an invitation to the ceremony at church or cards after their establishment in their new home.

Now one of our correspondents writes to us, "Who pays for the _after_-cards?" In most cases these are ordered with the other cards, and the bride's mother pays for them. But if they are ordered after the marriage, the groom may pay for these as he would pay for his wife's ordinary expenses. Still, it is stricter etiquette that even these should be paid for by the bride's family.

People who are asked to the wedding send cards to the house if they cannot attend, and in any case send or leave cards within ten days after, unless they are in very deep mourning, when a dispensation is granted them.

The etiquette of a wedding at home does not differ at all from the etiquette of a wedding in church with regard to cards. A great confusion seems to exist in the minds of some of our correspondents as to whom they shall send their return cards on being invited to a wedding. Some ask: "Shall I send them to the bride, as I do not know her mother?" Certainly not; send them to whomsoever invites you. Afterwards call on the bride or send her cards, but the first and important card goes to the lady who gives the wedding.

The order of the religious part of the ceremony is fixed by the church in which it occurs. The groom must call on the rector or clergyman, see the organist, and make what arrangements the bride pleases, but, we repeat, all _expenses_, excepting the fee to the clergyman, are borne by the bride's family.

The sexton should see to it that the white ribbon is stretched across the aisle, that the awning and carpet are in place, and it would be well if the police regulations could extend to the group of idlers who crowd around the church door, to the great inconvenience of the guests.

A wedding invitation requires no answer, unless it be to a sit-down wedding breakfast. Cards left afterwards are all-sufficient. The separate cards of the bride and groom are no longer included in the invitation. Nothing black in the way of dress but the gentlemen's coats is admissible at a wedding.

CHAPTER X

WEDDINGS AFTER EASTER.

We may expect a great deal of color in the coming bridal trousseau, beginning at the altar. The bridesmaids have thus lost one chance of distinguishing themselves by a different and a colored dress. But although some eccentric brides may choose to be married in pink, we cannot but believe, from the beautiful dresses which we have seen, that the greater number will continue to be wedded in white; therefore dressmakers need not turn pale.

And all our brides may rejoice that they are not French brides. It is very troublesome to be married in France, especially if one of the high contracting parties be a foreigner. A certificate of baptism is required, together with that of the marriage of the father and mother, and a written consent of the grandfather and grandmother, if either is alive and the parents dead. The names of the parties are then put up on the door of the _mairie_, or mayor's office, for eleven days.

In England there are four ways of getting married. The first is by special license, which enables two people to be married at any time and at any place; but this is very expensive, costing fifty pounds, and is only obtainable through an archbishop. Then there is the ordinary license, which can be procured either at Doctors' Commons or through a clergyman, who must also be a surrogate, and resident in the diocese where the marriage is to take place; both parties must swear that they are of age, or, if minors, that they have the consent of their parents. But to be married by banns is considered the most orthodox as well as the most economical way of proceeding. The banns must be published in the church of the parish in which the lady lives for three consecutive Sundays prior to the marriage, also the same law holds good for the gentleman, and the parties must have resided fifteen days in the parish. Or the knot may be tied at a licensed chapel, or at the office of a registrar, notice being given three weeks previously.

We merely quote these safeguards against imprudent marriages to show our brides how free they are. And perhaps, as we sometimes find, they are too free; there is danger that there may be too much ease in tying the knot that so many wish untied later, judging from the frequency of divorce.

However, we will not throw a damper on that occasion which for whirl and bustle and gayety and excitement is not equalled by any other day in a person's life. The city wedding in New York is marked first by the arrival of the caterer, who comes to spread the wedding breakfast; and later on by the florist, who appears to decorate the rooms, to hang the floral bell, or to spread the floral umbrella, or to build a grotto of flowers in the bow-window where the happy couple shall stand. Some of the latest freaks in floral fashion cause a bower of tall-growing ferns to be constructed, the ferns meeting over the bridal pair. This is, of course, supposing that the wedding takes place at home. Then another construction is a house entirely of roses, large enough to hold the bride and bridegroom. This is first built of bamboo or light wood, then covered thick with roses, and is very beautiful and almost too fragrant. If some one had not suggested "bathing-house," as he looked at this floral door to matrimony, it would have been perfect. It also looks a little like a confessional. Perhaps a freer sweep is better for both bride and groom. There should not be a close atmosphere, or too many overfragrant flowers; for at a home wedding, however well the arrangements have been anticipated, there is always a little time spent in waiting for the bride, a few presents arrive late, and there is always a slight confusion, so that the mamma is apt to be nervous and flushed, and the bride agitated.

A church wedding involves a great deal more trouble with carriages for the bridesmaids and for the family, and for the bride and her father, who must go together to the church.

Fortunately there is no stern law, if every one is late at church, for the hour appointed, as in England. There the law would read, "The rite of marriage is to be performed between the hours of 8 A.M. and noon, upon pain of suspension and felony with fourteen years' transportation." Such is the stern order to the officiating priests.

The reason for this curious custom and the terrible penalty awaiting its infringement is traceable, it is said, to the wrongs committed on innocent parties by the "hedge" parsons. Also, alas! because our English ancestors were apt to be drunk after midday, and unable to take an oath.

Here the guests arrive first at the church. The groom emerges from the vestry, supported by his best man, and then the organ strikes up the Wedding March.

Two little girls, beautifully dressed in Kate Greenaway hats and white gowns, and with immense sashes, carrying bouquets, come in first; then the bridesmaids, who form an avenue. Then the bride and her father walk up to the altar, where the groom claims her, and her father steps back. The bride stands on the left hand of the bridegroom; her first bridesmaid advances nearly behind her, ready to receive the glove and bouquet. After the ceremony is over, the bride and groom walk down the aisle first, and the children follow; after them the bridesmaids, then the ushers, then the father and mother, and so on. Sometimes the ushers go first, to be ready to cloak the bride, open the doors, keep back the people, and generally preserve order.

The signing of the register in the vestry is not an American custom, but it is now the fashion to have a highly illuminated parchment certificate signed by the newly married pair, with two or three witnesses, the bridesmaids, the best man, the father and mother, and so on, generally being the attesting parties.

If a sit-down wedding breakfast has been arranged, it occurs about half an hour after the parties return from church. An attempt is being made to return to the manners of the past, and for the bridegroom (_… la_ Sir Charles Grandison) to wait on the guests with a napkin on his arm. This often makes much amusement, and breaks in on the formality. Of course his waiting is very much of a sinecure and a joke.

The table for a wedding breakfast of this sort should be of a horseshoe shape. But for a city wedding, where many guests are to be invited in a circle which is forever widening, this sort of an exclusive breakfast is almost impossible, and a large table is generally spread, where the guests go in uninvited, and are helped by the waiters.

Eight bridesmaids is a fashionable number; and the bride has, of course, the privilege of choosing the dresses. The prettiest toilettes we have seen were of heliotrope gaze over satin; and again clover red, lighted up with white lace. The bonnets were of white chip, with feathers of red, for this last dress; broad hats of yellow satin, with yellow plumes, will surmount the heliotrope bridesmaids. One set of bridesmaids will wear Nile-green dresses, with pink plumes in their coiffures; another set, probably those with the pink bride, will be in white satin and silver.

A bride's dress has lately been ornamented with orange blossoms and lilacs. The veil was fastened on with orange flowers; the corsage bouquet was of orange flowers and lilacs mixed; the lace over-dress was caught up with lilac sprays; the hand bouquet wholly of lilacs; The gardener's success in producing these dwarf bushes covered with white lilacs has given us the beautiful flower in great perfection. Cowslips are to be used as corsage and hand bouquets for bridesmaids' dresses, the dresses being of pale blue surah, with yellow satin Gainsborough hats, and yellow plumes. White gloves and shoes are proper for brides. The white undressed kid or Swedish glove will be the favorite; and high princesse dresses with long sleeves are still pronounced the best style.

As for wedding presents, great favor is shown to jewelry and articles somewhat out of the common. Vases of costly workmanship, brass wine-coolers, enamelled glass frames, small mirrors set in silver, belt clasps, pins of every sort of conceit for the hair, choice old Louis Treize silver boxes of curious design, and watches, even old miniatures, are all of the order of things most desired. So many of our spring brides are going immediately to Europe that it seems absurd to load them down with costly dinner sets, or the usual lamps and pepper-casters. These may come later. How much prettier to give the bride something she can wear!

Wedding presents, if shown, will be in the second-story front room, spread on tables and surrounded by flowers. Some brides will give an afternoon tea the day before to show the presents to a few intimate friends. Each present will bear the name of the giver on his or her card.

One bride intends to make a most original innovation. Instead of going immediately out of town, she will remain at home and attend the Bachelors' Ball, in the evening, leaving for Philadelphia at three in the morning. At several of the church weddings the guests are only bidden there; there will be no reception.

Widows who are to be married again should be reminded that they can neither have wedding favors nor wear a veil or orange blossoms. A widow bride should wear a bonnet, she should have no bridesmaids, and a peach-blossom silk or velvet is a very pretty dress. At a certain up-town wedding all the gentlemen will wear a wedding favor excepting the groom. He always wears only a flower.

Wedding favors should be made of white ribbon and silver leaves. Large bouquets of white flowers should ornament the ears of the horses and the coats of the coachmen and footmen.

It is a matter of taste whether the bride wears her gloves to the altar or whether she goes up with uncovered hands. "High-Church" brides prefer the latter custom, The bride carries a prayer-book, if she prefers, instead of a bouquet. The Holy Communion is administered to the married pair if they desire it.

One correspondent inquires, "Who should be asked to a wedding?" We should say all your visiting list, or none. There is an unusual feeling about being left out at a wedding, and no explanation that it is "a small and not general invitation" seems to satisfy those who are thus passed over. It is much better to offend no one on so important an occasion.

Wedding cards and wedding stationery have not altered at all. The simple styles are the best. The bridal linen should be marked with the maiden name of the bride.

If brides could only find out some way to let their friends know where they are to be found after marriage it, would be a great convenience.

The newest style of engagement ring is a diamond and a ruby, or a diamond and a sapphire, set at right angles or diagonally. Bangles with the bridal monogram set in jewels are very pretty, and a desirable ornament for the bridesmaids' gifts, serving as a memento and a particularly neat ornament. They seem to have entirely superseded the locket. The bride's name cut in silver or gold serves for a lace pin, and is quite effective.

CHAPTER XI

SUMMER WEDDINGS.

A new fashion in the engraving of the wedding note-paper is the first novelty of the early summer wedding. The card is entirely discarded, and sheets of note-paper, with the words of the invitation in very fine running script, are now universally used, without crests or ciphers. We are glad to see that the very respectful form of invitation, "Mr. and Mrs. John H. Brown request the honor of your presence," etc., is returning to fashionable favor. It never should have gone out. Nothing is more self-respecting than respect, and when we ask our friends to visit us we can well afford to be unusually courteous. The brief, curt, and not too friendly announcement, "Mr. and Mrs. John H. Brown request your presence," etc., etc., may well yield to the much more elegant and formal compliment.

From high social authority in New York we have an invitation much simpler and more cordial, also worthy of imitation: "Mr. and Mrs. Winslow

Appleblossom request the pleasure of your company at the wedding reception of their daughter, on Tuesday afternoon June the sixteenth." This is without cards or names, presuming that the latter will follow later on.

Another very comprehensive and useful announcement of a wedding, from a lady living out of town, conveys, however, on one sheet of paper the desired information of where to find the bride:

_Mrs. Seth Osborne announces the marriage of her daughter Margu‚rite to Mr. Joseph Wendon, on Wednesday, September the ninth, at Bristol, Connecticut.

At Home after January first, at 758 Wood Street._

This card of announcement is a model of conciseness, and answers the oft-repeated question, "Where shall we go to find the married couple next winter?"

In arranging the house for the spring wedding the florists have hit upon a new device of having only one flower in masses; so we hear of the apple-blossom wedding, the lilac wedding, the lily wedding, the rose wedding and the daffodil wedding, the violet wedding, and the daisy wedding. So well has this been carried out that at a recent daisy wedding the bride's lace and diamond ornaments bore the daisy pattern, and each bridesmaid received a daisy pin with diamond centre.

This fashion of massing a single flower has its advantages when that flower is the beautiful feathery lilac, as ornamental as a plume; but it is not to be commended when flowers are as sombre as the violet, which nowadays suggests funerals. Daffodils are lovely and original, and apple-blossoms make a hall in a Queen Anne mansion very decorative. No one needs to be told that roses look better for being massed, and it is a pretty conceit for a bride to make the flower which was the ornament of her wedding her flower for life.

The passion for little girls as bridesmaids receives much encouragement at the spring and summer weddings. One is reminded of the children weddings of the fifteenth century, as these darlings, wearing Kate Greenaway hats, walk up the aisle, preceding the bride. The young brother of the bride, a mere boy, who, in the fatherless condition of his sister, recently gave her away, also presented a touching picture. It has become a fashion now to invoke youth as well as age to give the blessings once supposed to be alone at the beck and call of those whom Time had sanctified.

The bridal dresses are usually of white satin and point lace, a preference for tulle veils being very evident. A pin for the veil, with a diamond ornament, and five large diamonds hanging by little chains, makes a very fine effect, and is a novelty. The groom at a recent wedding gave cat's-eyes set round with diamonds to his ushers for scarf pins, the cat's-eye being considered a very lucky stone.

The ushers and the groom wear very large boutonnieres of stephanotis and gardenias, or equally large bunches of lilies-of-the-valley, in their button-holes.

At one of the country weddings of the spring a piper in full Scotch costume discoursed most eloquent music on the lawn during the wedding ceremony. This was a compliment to the groom, who is a captain in a Highland regiment.

A prevailing fashion for wedding presents is to give heavy pieces of furniture, such as sideboards, writing-tables, cabinets, and pianos.

A favorite dress for travelling is heliotrope cashmere, with bonnet to match. For a dark bride nothing is more becoming than dark blue tailormade with white vest and sailor collar. Gray cashmere with steel passementerie has also been much in vogue. A light gray mohair, trimmed with lace of the same color, was also much admired.

We have mentioned the surroundings of the brides, but have not spoken of the background. A screen hung with white and purple lilacs formed the background of one fair bride, a hanging curtain of Jacque-minot roses formed the appropriate setting of another. Perhaps the most regal of these floral screens was one formed of costly orchids, each worth a fortune. One of the most beautiful of the spring wedding dresses was made of cream-white satin over a tulle petticoat, the tulle being held down by a long diagonal band of broad pearl embroidery, the satin train trimmed with bows of ribbon in true-lovers' knots embroidered in seed-pearls; a shower of white lilacs trimmed one side of the skirt.

Another simple dress was made of white silk, trimmed with old Venetian point, the train of striped ivory point and white satin depending _… la_ Watteau from the shoulders, and fastened at the point of the waist. At the side three large pleats formed a drapery, which was fringed with orange-blossoms.

From England we hear of the most curious combinations as to travelling-dresses. Biscuit-colored canvas, embroidered around the polonaise in green and gold, while the skirt is edged with a broad band of green velvet. The new woollen laces of all colors make a very good effect in the "going-away dress" of a bride.

We are often asked by summer brides whether they should wear bonnets or round hats for their travelling-dress. We unhesitatingly say bonnets. A very pretty wedding bonnet is made of lead-colored beads without foundation, light and transparent; strings of red velvet and a bunch of red plums complete this bonnet. Gold-colored straw, trimmed with gold-brown velvet and black net, makes a pretty travelling-bonnet. Open-work black straw trimmed with black lace and red roses, very high in the crown, with a "split front," is a very becoming and appropriate bonnet for a spring costume.

A pretty dress for the child bridemaids is a pink faille slip covered with dotted muslin, not tied in at the waist, and the broadest of high Gainsborough hats of pale pink silk with immense bows, from the well-known pictures of Gainsborough's pretty women.

But if a summer bride must travel in a bonnet, there is no reason that her trousseau should not contain a large Leghorn hat, the straw caught up on the back in long loops, the spaces between filled in with bows of heliotrope ribbon. The crown should be covered with white ostrich tips. This is a very becoming hat for a lawn party.

It would be a charming addition to our well-known and somewhat worn-out Wedding-March, always played as the bride walks up the aisle, if a chorus of choir boys would sing an epithalamium, as is now done in England. These fresh young voices hailing the youthful couple would be in keeping with the child bridesmaids and the youthful brothers. Nay, they would suggest those frescoes of the Italian villas where Hymen and Cupid, two immortal boys, always precede the happy pair.

It is a pleasant part of weddings everywhere that the faithful domestics who have loved the bride from childhood are expected to assist by their presence at the ceremony, each wearing a wedding favor made by the fair hand of the bride herself. An amusing anecdote is told of a Yorkshire coachman, who, newly arrived in America, was to drive the bride to church. Not knowing him, particularly as he was a new addition to the force, the bride sent him his favor by the hands of her maid. But Yorkshire decided stoutly against receiving such a vicarious offering, and remarked, "Tell she I'd rather 'ave it from she." And so "she" was obliged to come down and affix the favor to his livery coat, or he would have resigned the "ribbons." The nurses, the cook, the maids, and the men-servants in England always expect a wedding favor and a small gratuity at a wedding, and in this country should be remembered by a box of cake, and possibly by a new dress, cap, or bonnet, or something to recall the day.

The plan of serving the refreshments at a buffet all through the reception retains its place as the most convenient and appropriate of forms. The wedding breakfast, where toasts are drunk and speeches made, is practicable in England, but hardly here, where we are not to the manner born. The old trained domestics who serve such a feast can not be invented at will in America, so that it is better to allow our well-filled tables to remain heavily laden, as they are, with dainties which defy competition, served by a corps of waiters.

The pretty plan of cutting the bride cake and hunting for a ring has been long exploded, as the bridesmaids declare that it ruins their gloves, and that in these days of eighteen buttons it is too much trouble to take off and put on a glove for the sake of finding a ring in a bit of greasy pastry. However, it might supplement a wedding supper.

CHAPTER XII

AUTUMN WEDDINGS.

The first thing which strikes the eye of the fortunate person who is invited to see the bridal gifts is the predominance of silver-ware. We have now passed the age of bronze and that of brass, and silver holds the first place of importance. Not only the coffee and tea sets, but the dinner sets and the whole furniture of the writing-table, and even brooms and brushes, are made with repouss‚ silver handles--the last, of course, for the toilette, as for dusting velvet, feathers, bonnets, etc.

The oxidized, ugly, discolored silver is not so fashionable as it was, and the beautiful, bright, highly polished silver, with its own natural and unmatchable color, has come in. The salvers afford a splendid surface for a monogram, which is now copied from the old Dutch silver, and bears many a true-lovers' knot, and every sort and kind of ornamentation; sometimes even a little verse, or posy, as it was called in olden time. One tea-caddy at a recent wedding bore the following almost obsolete rhyme, which Corydon might have sent to Phyllis in pastoral times:

"My heart to you is given; Oh do give yours to me: We'll lock them up together, And throw away the key."

It should be added that the silver tea-caddy was in the shape of a heart, and that it had a key. Very dear to the heart of a housewife is the tea-caddy which can be locked.

Another unique present was a gold tea scoop of ancient pattern, probably once a baby's pap spoon. There were also apostle-spoons, and little silver canoes and other devices to hold cigarettes and ashes; little mysterious boxes for the toilette, to hold the tongs for curling hair, and hair-pins; mirror frames, and even chair-backs and tables--all of silver.

Several beautiful umbrellas, with all sorts of handles, recalled the anecdote of the man who said he first saw his wife in a storm, married her in a storm, lived with her in a hurricane, but buried her in pleasant weather; parasols with jewelled handles, and beautiful painted fans, are also favorite offerings to the newly married.

Friends conspire to make their offerings together, so that there may be no duplicates, and no pieces in the silver service which do not match. This is a very excellent plan. Old pieces like silver tankards, Queen Anne silver, and the ever beautiful Baltimore workmanship, are highly prized.

It is no longer the fashion to display the presents at the wedding. They are arranged in an upper room, and shown to a few friends of the bride the day before the ceremony. Nor is it the fashion for the bride to wear many jewels. These are reserved for her first appearance as a married woman.

Clusters of diamond stars, daisies, or primroses that can be grouped together are now favorite gifts. In this costly gift several friends join again, as in the silver presentation. Diamond bracelets that can be used as necklaces are also favorite presents. All sorts of vases, bits of china, cloisonn‚, clocks (although there is not such a stampede of clocks and lamps as a few years ago), choice etchings framed, and embroidered table-cloths, doyleys, and useful coverings for bureau and wash-stands, are in order.

The bride now prefers simplicity in her dress--splendid and costly simplicity. An elegant white-satin and a tulle veil, the latter very full, the former extremely long and with a sweeping train, high corsage, and long sleeves, long white gloves, and perhaps a flower in the hair--such is the latest fashion for an autumn bride. The young ladies say they prefer that their magnificence should wait for the days after marriage, when their jewels can be worn. There is great sense in this, for a bride is interesting enough when she is simply attired.

The solemnization of the marriage should be in a church, and a high ecclesiastical functionary should be asked to solemnize it. The guests are brought in by the ushers, who, by the way, now wear pearl-colored kid-gloves, embroidered in black, as do the groom and best man. The front seats are reserved for the relatives and intimate friends, and the head usher has a paper on which are written the names of people entitled to these front seats. The seats thus reserved have a white ribbon as a line of demarcation. Music should usher in the bride.

The fashion of bridesmaids has gone out temporarily, and one person, generally a sister, alone accompanies the bride to the altar as her female aid. The bride, attended by her father or near friend, comes in last, after the ushers. After her mother, sister, and family have preceded her, these near relatives group themselves about the altar steps. Her sister, or one bridesmaid, stands near her at the altar rail, and kneels with her and the bridegroom, as does the best man. The groom takes his bride from the hand of her father or nearest friend, who then retires and stands a little behind the bridal pair. He must be near enough to respond quickly when he hears the words, "Who giveth this woman to be married to this man?" The bride and groom walk out together after the ceremony, followed by the nearest relatives, and proceed to the home where the wedding breakfast is served. Here the bridal pair stand under an arch of autumn-leaves, golden-rod, asters, and other seasonable flowers, and receive their friends, who are presented by the ushers.

The father and mother do not take any stated position on this occasion, but mingle with the guests, and form a part of the company. In an opulent countryhouse, if the day is fine, little tables are set out on the lawn, the ladies seat themselves around, and the gentlemen carry the refreshments to them; or the piazzas are beautifully decorated with autumn boughs and ferns, flowers, evergreens, and the refreshments are served there. If it is a bad day, of course the usual arrangements of a crowded buffet are in order; there is no longer a "sit-down" wedding breakfast; it does not suit our American ideas, as recent experiments have proved. We have many letters asking if the gentlemen of the bride's family should wear gloves. They should, and, as we have indicated, they should be of pearl-colored kid, embroidered in the seams with black.

The one bridesmaid must be dressed in colors. At a recent very fashionable wedding the bridesmaid wore bright buttercup yellow, a real Directoire dress, white lace skirt, yellow bodice, hat trimmed with yellow--a very picturesque, pretty costume. The silk stockings and slippers were of yellow, the hat of Leghorn, very large, turned up at one side, yellow plumes, and long streamers of yellow-velvet ribbon. Yellow is now esteemed a favorite color and a fortunate one. It once was deemed the synonym for envy, but that has passed away.

The carrying of an ivory prayer-book was found to be attended with inconvenience, therefore was discontinued. Still, if a young lady wishes to have her prayer-book associated with her vows at the altar, she can properly carry it. Brides are, however, leaving their bouquets at home, as the immense size of a modern bouquet interfered with the giving and taking of the ring.

A very pretty bit of ornamentation for an autumn wedding is the making of a piece of tapestry of autumn leaves to hang behind the bride as she receives. This can be done by sewing the leaves on a piece of drugget on which some artist has drawn a clever sketch with chalk and charcoal. We have seen some really elaborate and artistic groups done in this way by earnest and unselfish girl friends. Romeo and Juliet, Hamlet and Ophelia, Tristan and Iseult, can thus be made to serve as decorations.

The walls of the church can, of course, be exquisitely decorated with palms in an Oriental pattern, flowers, and leaves. The season is one when nature's bounty is so profuse that even the fruits can be pressed into service. Care should be taken not to put too many tuberoses about, for the perfume is sickening to some.

The engagement ring should be worn on the third finger of the left hand. It should have a solitaire stone--either a diamond or a colored stone. Colored stones and diamonds, set diagonally, as a sapphire and a diamond, are also worn; but not a pearl, as, according to the German idea, "pearls are tears for a bride." The wedding ring is entirely different, being merely a plain gold ring, not very wide nor a square band, as it was a few years since, and the engagement ring is worn as a guard above the wedding ring. It is not usual for the bride expectant to give a ring to her intended husband, but many girls like to give an engagement gift to their betrothed. Inside the engagement ring is the date of the engagement and the initials of each of the contracting parties. The wedding ring has the date of the marriage and the initials.

If the marriage takes place at home, the bride and groom enter together, and take their place before the clergyman, who has already entered; then come the father and mother and other friends. A pair of hassocks should be arranged for the bridal pair to kneel upon, and the father should be near to allow the clergyman to see him when he asks for his authority.

For autumn weddings nothing is so pretty for the travelling-dress as a tailor-made costume of very light cloth, with sacque to match for a cold day. No travelling-dress should of itself be too heavy, as our railway carriages are kept so very warm.

We have been asked to define the meaning of the word "honeymoon." It comes from the Germans, who drank mead, or metheglin--a beverage made of honey--for thirty days after the wedding.

The bride-cake is no longer cut and served at weddings; the present of cake in boxes has superseded that. At the wedding breakfast the ices are now packed in fancy boxes, which bear nuptial mottoes and orange-blossoms and violets on their surfaces. As the ring is the expressive emblem of the perpetuity of the compact, and as the bride-cake and customary libations form significant symbols of the nectar sweets of matrimony, it will not do to banish the cake altogether, although few people eat it, and few wish to carry it away.

Among the Romans, June was considered the most propitious month for marriage; but with the Anglo-Saxons October has always been a favorite and auspicious season. We find that the festival has always been observed in very much the same way, whether druidical, pagan, or Christian.

We have been asked, Who shall conduct the single bridesmaid to the altar? It should be the brother of the groom, her own _fianc‚_, or some chosen friend--never the best man; he does not leave his friend the groom until he sees him fairly launched on that hopeful but uncertain sea whose reverses and whose smiles are being constantly tempted.

"That man must lead a happy life Who is directed by a wife. Who's freed from matrimonial claims Is sure to suffer for his pains."

This is a "posy" for some October silver.

CHAPTER XIII

BEFORE THE WEDDING AND AFTER.

The reception of an engaged girl by the family of her future husband should be most cordial, and no time should be lost in giving her a warm welcome. It is the moment of all others when she will feet such a welcome most gratefully, and when any neglect will be certain to give her the keenest unhappiness.

It is the fashion for the mother of the groom to invite both the family of the expectant bride and herself to a dinner as soon as possible after the formal announcement of the engagement. The two families should meet and should make friendships at once. This is important.

It is to these near relatives that the probable date of the wedding-day is first whispered, in time to allow of much consultation and preparation in the selection of wedding gifts. In opulent families each has sometimes given the young couple a silver dinner service and much silver besides, and the rooms of the bride's father's house look like a jeweller's shop when the presents are shown. All the magnificent ormolu ornaments for the chimney-piece, handsome clocks and lamps, fans in large quantities, spoons, forks by the hundred, and of late years the fine gilt ornaments, furniture, camel's-hair shawls, bracelets--all are piled up in most admired confusion. And when the invitations are out, then come in the outer world with their more hastily procured gifts; rare specimens of china, little paintings, ornaments for the person--all, all are in order.

A present is generally packed where it is bought, and sent with the giver's card from the shop to the bride directly. She should always acknowledge its arrival by a personal note written by herself. A young bride once gave mortal offence by not thus acknowledging her gifts. She said she had so many that she could not find time to write the notes, which was naturally considered boastful and most ungracious.

Gifts which owe their value to the personal taste or industry of the friend who sends are particularly complimentary. A piece of embroidery, a painting, a water-color, are most flattering gifts, as they betoken a long and predetermined interest.

No friend should be deterred from sending a small present, one not representing a money value, because other and richer people can send a more expensive one. Often the little gift remains as a most endearing and useful souvenir.

As for showing the wedding gifts, that is a thing which must be left to individual taste. Some people disapprove of it, and consider it ostentatious; others have a large room devoted to the display of the presents, and it is certainly amusing to examine them.

As for the conduct of the betrothed pair during their engagement, our American mammas are apt to be somewhat more lenient in their views of the liberty to be allowed than are the English. With the latter, no young lady is allowed to drive alone with her _fianc‚_; there must be a servant in attendance. No young lady must visit in the family of her _fianc‚_, unless he has a mother to receive her. Nor is she allowed to go to the theatre alone with him, or to travel under his escort, to stop at the same hotel, or to relax one of those rigid rules which a severe chaperon would enforce; and it must be allowed that this severe and careful attention to appearances is in the best taste.

As for the engagement-ring, modern fashion prescribes a diamond solitaire, which may range in price from two hundred and fifty to two thousand dollars. The matter of presentation is a secret between the engaged pair.

Evening weddings do not differ from day weddings essentially, except that the bridegroom wears evening dress.

If the wedding is at home, the space where the bridal party is to stand is usually marked off by a ribbon, and the clergyman comes down in his robes before the bridal pair; they face him, and he faces the company. Hassocks are prepared for them to kneel upon. After the ceremony the clergyman retires, and the bridal party take his place, standing to receive their friends' congratulations.

Should there be dancing at a wedding, it is proper for the bride to open the first quadrille with the best man, the groom dancing with the first bridesmaid. It is not, however, very customary for a bride to dance, or for dancing to occur at an evening wedding, but it is not a bad old custom.

After the bridal pair return from their wedding-tour, the bridesmaids each give them a dinner or a party, or show some attention, if they are so situated that they can do so. The members of the two families, also, each give a dinner to the young couple.

It is now a very convenient and pleasant custom for the bride to announce with her wedding-cards two or more reception days during the winter after her marriage, on which her friends can call upon her. The certainty of finding a bride at home is very pleasing. On these occasions she does not wear her wedding-dress, but receives as if she had entered society as one of its members. The wedding trappings are all put away, and she wears a dark silk, which may be as handsome as she chooses. As for wearing her wedding-dress to balls or dinners after her marriage, it is perfectly proper to do so, if she divests herself of her veil and her orange-blossoms.

The bride should be very attentive and conciliatory to all her husband's friends, They will look with interest upon her from the moment they hear of the engagement, and it is in the worst taste for her to show indifference to them.

Quiet weddings, either in church or at the house, are very much preferred by some families. Indeed, the French, from whom we have learned many-- and might learn more--lessons of grace and good taste, infinitely prefer them.

For a quiet wedding the bride dresses in a travelling dress and bonnet, and departs for her wedding-tour. It is the custom in England, as we have said, for the bride and groom to drive off in their own carriage, which is dressed with white ribbons, the coach-man and groom wearing white bouquets, and favors adorning the horses' ears, and for them to take a month's honeymoon. There also the bride (if she be Hannah Rothschild or the Baroness Burdett-Coutts) gives her bridesmaids very elegant presents, as a locket or a bracelet, while the groom gives the best man a scarf-pin or some gift. The American custom is not so universal. However, either bride or groom gives something to the bridesmaid and a scarf-pin to each usher. Thus a wedding becomes a very expensive and elaborate affair, which quiet and economical people are sometimes obliged to avoid.

After the marriage invitations are issued, the lady does not appear in public.

The period of card-leaving after a wedding is not yet definitely fixed. Some authorities say ten days, but that in a crowded city, and with an immense acquaintance, would be quite impossible.

If only invited to the church, many ladies consider that they perform their whole duty by leaving a card sometime during the winter, and including the young couple in their subsequent invitations. Very rigorous people call, however, within ten days, and if invited to the house, the call is still more imperative, and should be made soon after the wedding.

But if a young couple do not send their future address, but only invite one to a church-wedding, there is often a very serious difficulty in knowing where to call, and the first visit must be indefinitely postponed until they send cards notifying their friends of their whereabouts.

Wedding invitations require no answer. But people living at a distance, who cannot attend the wedding, should send their cards by mail, to assure the hosts that the invitation has been received. The usual form for wedding-cards is this:

Mr. and Mrs. Theodore Chapman request your presence at the marriage of their daughter, on Wednesday evening, November fourth, at eight o'clock. Grace Church.

The card of the young lady, that of her intended husband, and another card to the favored--

At Home after the ceremony, 7 East Market Street--

is also enclosed.

People with a large acquaintance cannot always invite all their friends, of course, to a wedding reception, and therefore invite all to the church. Sometimes people who are to give a small wedding at home request an answer to the wedding invitation; in that case, of course, an answer should be sent, and people should be very careful not to ignore these flattering invitations. Any carelessness is inexcusable when so important an event is on the tapis. Bridesmaids, if prevented by illness or sudden bereavement from officiating, should notify the bride as soon as possible, as it is a difficult thing after a bridal cort‚ge is arranged to reorganize it.

As to the wedding-tour, it is no longer considered obligatory, nor is the seclusion of the honey-moon demanded. A very fashionable girl who married an Englishman last summer at Newport returned in three days to take her own house at Newport, and to receive and give out invitations. If the newly married pair thus begin house-keeping in their own way, they generally issue a few "At Home" cards, and thereby open an easy door for future hospitalities. Certainly the once perfunctory bridal tour is no longer deemed essential, and the more sensible fashion exists of the taking of a friend's house a few miles out of town for a month.

If the bridal pair go to a watering-place during their early married days, they should be very careful of outward display of tenderness.

Such exhibitions in the cars or in public places as one often sees, of the bride laying her head on her husband's shoulder, holding hands, or kissing, are at once vulgar and indecent. All public display of an affectionate nature should be sedulously avoided. The affections are too sacred for such outward showing, and the lookers-on are in a very disagreeable position. The French call love-making _l'...... deux_, and no egotism is agreeable. People who see a pair of young doves cooing in public are apt to say that a quarrel is not far off. It is possible for a lover to show every attention, every assiduity, and not to overdo his demonstrations. It is quite possible for the lady to be fond of her husband without committing the slightest offence against good taste.

The young couple are not expected, unless Fortune has been exceptionally kind, to be immediately responsive in the matter of entertainments. The outer world is only too happy to entertain them. Nothing can be more imprudent than for a young couple to rush into expenditures which may endanger their future happiness and peace of mind, nor should they feel that they are obliged at once to return the dinners and the parties given to them. The time will come, doubtless, when they will be able to do so.

But the announcement of a day on which the bride will receive her friends is almost indispensable. The refreshments on these occasions should not exceed tea and cake, or, at the most, punch, tea, chocolate, and cakes, which may stand on a table at one end of the room, or may be handed by a waiter. Bouillon, on a cold day of winter, is also in order, and is perhaps the most serviceable of all simple refreshments. For in giving a "four-o'clock tea," or several day receptions, a large entertainment is decidedly vulgar.

CHAPTER XIV

GOLD, SILVER, AND TIN WEDDINGS.

Very few people have the golden opportunity of living together for fifty years in the holy estate of matrimony. When they have overcome in so great a degree the many infirmities of the flesh, and the common incompatibility of tempers, they deserve to be congratulated, and to have a wedding festivity which shall be as ceremonious as the first one, and twice as impressive. But what shall we give them?

The gifts of gold must be somewhat circumscribed, and therefore the injunction, so severe and so unalterable, which holds good at tin and silver weddings, that no presents must be given of any other metal than that designated by the day, does not hold good at a golden wedding. A card printed in gold letters, announcing that John Anderson and Mary Brown were married, for instance, in 1830, and will celebrate their golden wedding in 1880, is generally the only golden manifestation. One of the cards recently issued reads in this way:

1831. 1881.

Mr. and Mrs. John Anderson, At Home November twenty-first, 1881, Golden Wedding, 17 Carmichael Street, at eight o'clock.

All done in gold, on white, thick English paper, that is nearly all the exhibition of gold necessary at a golden wedding, unless some friend gives the aged bride a present of jewellery. The bride receives her children and grandchildren dressed in some article which she wore at her first wedding, if any remain. Sometimes a veil, or a handkerchief, or a fan, scarcely ever the whole dress, has lasted fifty years, and she holds a bouquet of white flowers. A wedding-cake is prepared with a ring in it, and on the frosting is the date, and the monogram of the two, who have lived together so long.

These golden weddings are apt to be sad. It is not well for the old to keep anniversaries--too many ghosts come to the feast. Still, if people are happy enough to wish to do so, there can be no harm in it. Their surroundings may possibly surpass their fondest dreams, but as it regards themselves, the contrast is painful. They have little in common with bridal joys, and unless it is the wish of some irrepressible descendant, few old couples care to celebrate the golden wedding save in their hearts. If they have started at the foot of the ladder, and have risen, they may not wish to remember their early struggles; if they have started high, and have gradually sunk into poverty or ill health, they certainly do not wish to photograph those better days by the fierce light of an anniversary, It is only the very exceptionally good, happy, and serene people who can afford to celebrate a golden wedding.

Far otherwise with the silver wedding, which comes in this country while people are still young, in the very prime of life, With much before them, and when to stop midway to take an account of one's friends and one's blessings is a wise and a pleasant thing. The cards are issued, printed in silver, somewhat in this style:

1856. 1881.

_Mr. and Mrs. Carter request the pleasure of your company on Wednesday, October the twenty-seventh, at eight o'clock. Silver Wedding.

John Carter. Sarah Smith._

Such, at least, is one form. Many people do not, however, add their names at the end; while, again, some go even farther; and transcribe the marriage notice from the newspaper of the period.

Gifts of silver being comparatively inexpensive, and always useful, almost all friends who are invited send a gift of silver-ware, marked "Silver Wedding" or, still better, marked with an appropriate motto, and the initials of the pair, engraved in a true-lover's knot.

In old Dutch silver these pretty monograms and the lover's knot are very common. This was probably put upon the original wedding silver, and we know that the art was studied by such men as Albrecht Drer, Benvenuto Cellini, and Rubens, for we find among their drawings many monograms and such devices. It adds very much to the beauty of a piece of silver to bear such engraving, and it is always well to add a motto, or a "posy," as the bid phrase has it, thus investing the gift with a personal interest, in our absence of armorial bearings. Since many pretty ornaments come in silver, it is possible to vary the gifts by sometimes presenting flacons (a pendant flacon for the _chatelaine_: some very artistic things come in this pretty ornament now, with colored plaques representing antique figures, etc.). Sometimes a costly intaglio is sunk in silver and set as a pin. Clocks of silver, bracelets, statuary in silver, necklaces, picture-frames, and filigree pendants hanging to silver necklaces which resemble pearls; beautiful jewel-cases and boxes for the toilet; dressing-cases well furnished with silver; hand-mirrors set in fretted silver; bracelets, pendant seals, and medallions in high relief--all come now for gifts in the second precious metal. A very pretty gift was designed by a young artist for his mother on the celebration of her silver wedding. It was a monogram and love-knot after the fashion of the seventeenth century, and made, when joined, a superb belt-clasp, each little ornament of the relief repeating the two dates. Mantle clasps of solid silver ornamented with precious stones, and known in the Middle Ages as _fermillets_, are pretty presents, and these ornaments can be also enriched with gold and enamel without losing their silver character. Chimerical animals and floral ornaments are often used in enriching these agrafes.

Mirrors set in silver are very handsome for the toilet-table; also, brushes and combs can be made of it. All silver is apt to tarnish, but a dip in water and ammonia cleans it at once, and few people now like the white foamy silver; that which has assumed a gray tint is much more admired. Indeed, artistic jewellers have introduced the hammered silver, which looks like an old tin teapot, and to the admirers of the real silver tint is very ugly; but it renders the wearing of a silver _chƒtelaine_ very much easier, for the chains and ornaments which a lady now wears on her belt are sure to grow daily into the fashion. Silver parasol handles are also very fashionable. We have enlarged upon this subject of gifts of silver in answer to several questions as to what it is proper to give at a silver wedding. Of course the wealthy can send pitchers, vases, vegetable dishes, soup tureens, and waiters. All the beautiful things which are now made by our silversmiths are tempting to the purse. There are also handsome silver necklaces, holding old and rare coins, and curious watches of silver, resembling fruits, nuts, and animals. The farther back we go in the history of silver-ware, the better models we are sure to obtain.

As for the entertainment, it includes the inevitable cake, of course, and the bride puts the knife into it as she did twenty-five years ago. The ring is eagerly sought for. Then a large and plentiful repast is offered, exactly like that of any reception-table. Champagne is in order, healths are drunk, and speeches made at most of these silver weddings.

Particularly delightful are silver weddings which are celebrated in the country, especially if the house is large enough to hold a number of guests. Then many a custom can be observed of peculiar significance and friendliness; everybody can help to prepare the feast, decorate the house with flowers, and save the bride from those tearful moments which come with any retrospect. All should try to make the scene a merry one, for there is no other reason for its celebration.

Tin weddings, which occur after ten years have passed over two married heads, are signals for a general frolic. Not only are the usual tin utensils which can be used for the kitchen and household purposes offered, but fantastic designs and ornaments are gotten up for the purpose of raising a laugh. One young bride received a handsome check from her father-in-law, who labelled it "Tin," and sent it to her in a tin pocket-book elaborately constructed for the purpose. One very pretty tin fender was constructed for the fireplace of another, and was not so ugly. A tin screen, tin chandeliers, tin fans, and tin tables have been offered. If these serve no other purpose, they do admirably for theatrical properties later, if the family like private plays, etc., at home.

Wooden weddings occur after five years of marriage, and afford the bride much refurnishing of the kitchen, and nowadays some beautiful presents of wood-carving. The wooden wedding, which was begun in jest with a step-ladder and a rolling-pin several years ago, now threatens to become a very splendid anniversary indeed, since the art of carving in wood is so popular, and so much practised by men and women. Every one is ready for a carved box, picture-frame, screen, sideboard, chair, bureau, dressing-table, crib, or bedstead. Let no one be afraid to offer a bit of wood artistically carved. Everything is in order but wooden nutmegs; they are ruled out.

At one of the golden weddings of the Rothschilds we read of such presents as a solid gold dinner service; a chased cup of Benvenuto Cellini in solid gold, enriched with precious stones; a box, with cover of gold, in the early

Renaissance, with head of Marie de Medicis in oxidized gold; of rings from Cyprus, containing sapphires from the tombs of the Crusaders; of solid crystals cut in drinking cups, with handles of gold; of jade goblets set in gold saucers; of singing-birds in gold; and of toilet appliances, all in solid gold, not to speak of chains, rings, etc. This is luxury, and as such to be commended to those who can afford it. But it must entail great inconvenience. Gold is so valuable that a small piece of it goes a great way, and even a Rothschild would not like to leave out a gold dressing-case, lest it might tempt the most honest of waiting-women.

No doubt some of our millionaire Americans can afford such golden wedding-presents, but of course they are rare, and even if common, would be less in keeping than some less magnificent gifts. Our republican simplicity would be outraged and shocked at seeing so much coin of the realm kept out of circulation.

There are, however, should we wish to make a present to a bride of fifty years' standing, many charming bits of gold jewellery very becoming, very artistic, and not too expensive for a moderate purse. There are the delicate productions of Castellani, the gold and enamel of Venice, the gold-work of several different colors which has become so artistic; there are the modern antiques, copied from the Phoenician jewellery found at Cyprus--these made into pins for the cap, pendants for the neck, rings and bracelets, boxes for the holding of small sweetmeats, so fashionable many years ago, are pretty presents for an elderly lady. For a gentleman it is more difficult to find souvenirs. We must acknowledge that it is always difficult to select a present for a gentleman. Unless he has as many feet as Briareus had hands, or unless he is a centipede, he cannot wear all the slippers given to him; and the shirt-studs and sleeve-buttons are equally burdensome. Rings are now fortunately in fashion, and can be as expensive as one pleases. But one almost regrets the disuse of snuff, as that gave occasion for many beautiful boxes. It would be difficult to find, however, such gold snuffboxes as were once handed round among monarchs and among wealthy snuffers. The giving of wedding-presents has had to endure many changes since its first beginning, which was a wise and generous desire to help the young pair to begin house-keeping. It has become now an occasion of ostentation. So with the gifts at the gold and silver weddings. They have almost ceased to be friendly offerings, and are oftener a proof of the giver's wealth than of his love.

No wonder that some delicate-minded people, wishing to celebrate their silver wedding, cause a line to be printed on their invitations, "No presents received."

Foreigners have a beautiful custom, which we have not, of remembering every fˆte day, every birthday, every saint's day, in a friend's calendar. A bouquet, a present of fruit, a kind note, a little celebration which costs nothing, occurs in every family on papa's birthday or mamma's fˆte day. But as we have nothing of that sort, and as most people prefer that, as in the case of the hero of the _Pirates_, a birthday shall only come once in four years, it is well for us to celebrate the tin, silver, and golden weddings.

The twentieth anniversary of one's wedding is never celebrated. It is considered very unlucky to do so. The Scotch think one or the other will die within the year if the twentieth anniversary is even alluded to.

CHAPTER XV

THE ETIQUETTE OF BALLS.

A hostess must not use the word "ball" on her invitation-cards. She may say,

_Mrs. John Brown requests the pleasure of the company of Mr. and Mrs. Amos Smith on Thursday evening, November twenty-second, at nine o'clock.

Dancing. R.S.V.P._

Or,

_Mrs. John Brown At Home Thursday evening, November twenty-second, at nine o'clock.

Cotillion at ten. R. S. V. P._

But she should not indicate further the purpose of her party. In New York, where young ladies are introduced to society by means of a ball at Delmonico's, the invitation is frequently worded,

_Mr. and Mrs. Amos Smith request the pleasure of your company Thursday evening, November twenty-second, at nine o'clock.

Delmonico' s._

The card of the young debutante is sometimes (although not always) enclosed.

If these invitations are sent to new acquaintances, or to strangers in town, the card of the gentleman is enclosed to gentlemen, that of both the gentleman and his wife to ladies and gentlemen, if it is a first invitation.

A ballroom should be very well lighted, exceedingly well ventilated, and very gayly dressed. It is the height of the gayety of the day; and although dinner calls for handsome dress, a ball demands it. Young persons of slender figure prefer light, diaphanous dresses; the chaperons can wear heavy velvet and brocade. Jewels are in order. A profusion of flowers in the hands of the women should add their brightness and perfume to the rooms. The great number of bouquets sent to a d‚butante is often embarrassing. The present fashion is to have them hung, by different ribbons, on the arm, so that they look as if almost a trimming to the dress.

Gentlemen who have not selected partners before the ball come to their hostess and ask to be presented to ladies who will dance with them. As a hostess cannot leave her place while receiving, and people come at all hours to a ball, she generally asks two or three well-known society friends to receive with her, who will take this part of her duty off her hands, for no hostess likes to see "wall-flowers" at her ball: she wishes all her young people to enjoy themselves. Well-bred young men always say to the hostess that they beg of her to introduce them to ladies who may be without partners, as they would gladly make themselves useful to her. After dancing with a lady, and walking about the room with her for a few times, a gentleman is at perfect liberty to take the young lady back to her chaperon and plead another engagement.

A great drawback to balls in America is the lack of convenience for those who wish to remain seated. In Europe, where the elderly are first considered, seats are placed around the room, somewhat high, for the chaperons, and at their feet sit the debutantes. These red-covered sofas, in two tiers, as it were, are brought in by the upholsterer (as we hire chairs for the crowded musicales or readings so common in large cities), and are very convenient. It is strange that all large halls are not furnished with them, as they make every one comfortable at very little expense, and add to the appearance of the room. A row of well-dressed ladies, in velvet, brocade, and diamonds, some with white hair, certainly forms a very distinguished background for those who sit at their feet.

Supper is generally served all the evening from a table on which flowers, fruits, candelabra, silver, and glass are displayed, and which is loaded with hot oysters, boned turkey, salmon, game _pƒt‚s_, salads, ices, jellies, and fruits, from the commencement of the evening. A hot supper, with plentiful cups of bouillon, is served again for those who dance the german.

But if the hostess so prefer, the supper is not served until she gives the word, when her husband leads the way with the most distinguished lady present, the rest of the company following. The hostess rarely goes in to supper until every one has been served. She takes the opportunity of walking about her ballroom to see if every one is happy and attended to. If she does go to supper, it is in order to accompany some distinguished guest--like the President, for instance. This is, however, a point which may be left to the tact of the hostess.

A young lady is not apt to forget her ballroom engagements, but she should be sure not to do so. She must be careful not to offend one gentleman by refusing to dance with him, and then accepting the offer of another. Such things, done by frivolous girls, injure a young man's feelings unnecessarily, and prove that the young lady has not had the training of a gentlewoman. A young man should not forget if he has asked a young lady for the german. He must send her a bouquet, and be on hand to dance with her. If kept away by sickness, or a death in his family, he must send her a note before the appointed hour.

It is not necessary to take leave of your hostess at a ball. All that she requires of you is to bow to her on entering, and to make yourself as agreeable and happy as you can while in her house.

Young men are not always as polite as they should be at balls. They ought, if well-bred, to look about, and see if any lady has been left unattended at supper, to ask if they can go for refreshments, if they can lead a lady to a seat, go for a carriage, etc. It is not an impertinence for a young man thus to speak to a lady older than himself, even if he has not been introduced; the roof is a sufficient introduction for any such purpose.

The first persons asked to dance by the young gentlemen invited to a house should be the daughters of the house. To them and to their immediate relatives and friends must the first attentions be paid.

It is not wise for young ladies to join in every dance, nor should a young chaperon dance, leaving her proteg‚e sitting. The very bad American custom of sending several young girls to a ball with a very young chaperon-- perhaps one of their number who has just been married--has led to great vulgarity in our American city life, not to say to that general misapprehension of foreigners which offends without correcting our national vanity. A mother should endeavor to attend balls with her daughters, and to stay as long as they do. But many mothers say, "We are not invited: there is not room for us." Then her daughters should not accept. It is a very poor American custom not to invite the mothers. Let a lady give two or three balls, if her list is so large that she can only invite the daughters. If it be absolutely necessary to limit the invitations, the father should go with the daughters, for who else is to escort them to their carriage, take care of them if they faint, or look to their special or accidental wants? The fact that a few established old veterans of society insist upon "lagging superfluous on the stage" should not deter ladies who entertain from being true to the ideas of the best society, which certainly are in favor of chaperonage.

A lady should not overcrowd her rooms. To put five hundred people into a hot room, with no chairs to rest in, and little air to breathe, is to apply a very cruel test to friendship. It is this impossibility of putting one's "five hundred dear friends" into a narrow house which has led to the giving of balls at public rooms--an innovation which shocked a French woman of rank who married an American. "You have no safeguard for society in America," she observed, "but your homes. No aristocracy, no king, no courts, no traditions, but the sacred one of home. Now, do you not run great risks when you abandon your homes, and bring out your girls at a hotel?" There is something in her wise remarks; and with the carelessness of chaperonage in cities which are now largely populated by irresponsible foreigners the dangers increase.

The first duty of a gentleman on entering a ballroom is to make his bow to the lady of the house and to her daughters; he should then strive to find his host--a very difficult business sometimes. Young men are to be very much censured, however, who do not find out their host, and insist on being presented to him. Paterfamilias in America is sometimes thought to hold a very insignificant place in his own house, and be good for nothing but to draw checks. This is indicative of a very low social condition, and no man invited to a gentleman's house should leave it until he has made his bow to the head thereof.

It is proper for intimate friends to ask for invitations for other friends to a ball, particularly for young gentlemen who are "dancing men." More prudence should be exercised in asking in behalf of ladies, but the hostess has always the privilege of saying that her list is full, if she does not wish to invite her friends' friends. No offence should be taken if this refusal be given politely. In a majority of luxurious houses a tea-room is open from the beginning to the end of a ball, frequently on the second story, where bouillon, tea, coffee, and macaroons are in order, or a plate of sandwiches, or any such light refreshment, for those who do not wish a heavy supper. A large bowl of iced lemonade is also in this room--a most grateful refreshment after leaving a hot ballroom.

The practice of putting crash over carpets has proved so unhealthy to the dancers, on account of the fine fuzz which rises from it in dancing, that it is now almost wholly abandoned; and parquet floors are becoming so common, and the dancing on them is so much more agreeable in every way, that ladies have their heavy parlor carpets taken up before a ball rather than lay a crash.

A smoking-room, up or down stairs, is set apart for the gentlemen, where, in some houses, cigars and brandy and effervescent waters are furnished. If this provision be not made, it is the height of indelicacy for gentlemen to smoke in the dressing-rooms.

The bad conduct of young men at large balls, where they abuse their privileges by smoking, getting drunk at supper, eating unreasonably, blockading the tables, and behaving in an unseemly manner, even coming to blows in the supper-rooms, has been dwelt upon in the annals of the past, which annals ever remain a disgrace to the young fashionables of any city. Happily, such breaches of decorum are now so rare that there is no need to touch upon them here.

Many of our correspondents ask the embarrassing question, "Who is it proper to invite to a first ball?" This is a question which cannot be answered in a general way. The tact and delicacy of the host must decide it.

At public balls there should be managers, ushers, stewards, and, if possible, a committee of ladies to receive. It is very much more conducive to the elegance of a ball if there be a recognized hostess, or committee of hostesses: the very aspect of the room is thus improved. And to a stranger from another city these ladies should be hospitable, taking care that she be introduced and treated with suitable attention.

An awning and carpet should be placed at the front entrance of a house in which a ball is to be given, to protect the guests against the weather and the gaze of the crowd of by-standers who always gather in a great city to see the well-dressed ladies alight. Unfortunately, in a heavy rain these awnings are most objectionable; they are not water-proof, and as soon as they are thoroughly wet they afford no protection whatever.

The cotillion styled the German was first danced by the German court just after the battle of Waterloo, probably at the ball at Aix-la-Chapelle given to the allied sovereigns. Favors are given merely to promote enjoyment and to give variety. It is not necessary that people be matrimonially engaged to dance it. One engages his partner for it as for any other dance. It had been fashionable in Europe many years before it came to this country, but has been danced here for over forty years, first coming out at Washington.

CHAPTER XVI

FASHIONABLE DANCING.

The return to quadrilles at some of the latest balls at Delmonico's in the winter of 1884 was an important epoch in the history of dancing, reiterating the well-known proverb of the dressmakers that everything comes round in fifty years. Fashion seems to be perennial in this way, for it is almost fifty years--certainly forty--since the quadrille was at the height of fashion. In Germany, where they dance for dancing's sake, the quadrille was long ago voted rococo and stiff. In England and at court balls it served always as a way, a dignified manner, for sovereigns and people of inconveniently high rank to begin a ball, to open a festivity, and it had a sporadic existence in the country and at Washington even during the years when the Lancers, a much livelier dance, had chased it away from the New York balls for a long period of time.

The quadrille is a stately and a conversational dance. The figures are accurate, and every one should know them well enough to respond to the voice of the leader. But inasmuch as the figures are always calling one away from his partner, the first law is to have a large supply of small-talk, so that, on rejoining, a remark and a smile may make up for lost time. A calm, graceful carriage, the power to make an elegant courtesy, are necessary to a lady. No one in these days takes steps; a sort of galop is, however, allowed in the rapid figures of the quadrille. A defiant manner, sometimes assumed by a bashful man, is out of place, although there are certain figures which make a man feel rather defiant. One of these is where he is obliged, as _cavalier seul_, to advance to three ladies, who frequently laugh at him. Then a man should equally avoid a boisterous demeanor in a quadrille; not swinging the lady round too gayly. It is never a romping dance, like the Virginia reel, for instance.

All people are apt to walk through a quadrille slowly, to music, until they come to the "ladies' chain" or the "promenade." It is, however, permissible to add a little swinging-step and a graceful dancing-movement to this stately promenade. A quadrille cannot go on evenly if any confusion arises from the ignorance, obstinacy, or inattention of one of the dancers. It is proper, therefore, if ignorant of the figures, to consult a dancing-master and to learn them. It is a most valuable dance, as all ages, sizes, and conditions of men and women can join in it. The young, old, stout, thin, lazy, active, maimed, or single, _without loss of caste_, can dance a quadrille. No one looks ridiculous dancing a quadrille. It is decidedly easier than the German, makes a break in a _tˆte-…-tˆte_ conversation, and enables a gentleman to be polite to a lady who may not be a good dancer for waltz or polka. The morality of round dances seems now to be little questioned. At any rate, young girls in the presence of their mothers are not supposed to come to harm from their enjoyment. Dancing is one of the oldest, the most historical, forms of amusement. Even Socrates learned to dance. There is no longer an excommunication on the waltz, that dance which Byron abused.

In England the _valse … deux temps_ is still the most fashionable, as it always will be the most beautiful, of dances. Some of the critics of all countries have said that only Germans, Russians, and Americans can dance it. The Germans dance it very quickly, with a great deal of motion, but render it elegant by slacking the pace every now and then. The Russians waltz so quietly, on the contrary, that they can go round the room holding a brimming glass of champagne without spilling a drop. This evenness in waltzing is very graceful, and can only be reached by long practice, a good ear for music, and a natural gracefulness. Young Americans, who, as a rule, are the best dancers in the world, achieve this step to admiration. It is the gentleman's duty in any round dance to guide his fair companion gracefully; he must not risk a collision or the chance of a fall. A lady should never waltz if she feels dizzy. It is a sign of disease of the heart, and has brought on death. Neither should she step flat-footed, and make her partner carry her round; but must do her part of the work, and dance lightly and well, or not at all. Then, again, neither should her partner waltz on the tip of his toes, nor lift his partner too much off the floor; all should be smooth, graceful, delicate.

The American dance of the season is, however, the polka--not the old-fashioned "heel and toe," but the step, quick and gay, of the Sclavonic nationalities. It may be danced slowly or quickly. It is always, however, a spirited step, and the music is undoubtedly pretty. The dancing-masters describe the step of a polka as being a "hop, three glides, and a rest," and the music is two-four time. In order to apply the step to the music one must make it in four-eight time, counting four to each measure of the music, each measure taking about a second of time by the watch. The polka redowa and the polka mazourka are modifications of this step to different times.

The galop is another fashionable dance this winter. It is very easy, and is danced to very quick music; it is inspiriting at the end of a ball.

The minuet de la cour was first danced in the ancient province of Poitou,

France. In Paris, in 1653, Louis XIV., who was passionately fond of it, danced it to perfection. In 1710, Marcel, the renowned dancing-master, introduced it into England. Then it went out for many years, until Queen Victoria revived it at a _bal costum‚_ at Buckingham Palace in 1845. In New York it was revived and ardently practised for Mrs. W. K. Vanderbilt's splendid fancy ball in 1883, and it was much admired. There seems no reason why the grace, the dignity, the continuous movement; the courtesy, the _pas grace_, the skilfully-managed train, the play with the fan, should not commend this elegant dance to even our republican dancers; but it has not been danced this winter. It is possibly too much trouble. A dancing-master worked all winter to teach it to the performers of the last season.

To make a courtesy (or, as we are fond of saying, a _curtsy_) properly is a very difficult art, yet all who dance the quadrille must learn it. To courtesy to her partner the lady steps off with the right foot, carrying nearly all her weight upon it, at the same time raising the heel of the left foot, thus placing herself in the second position, facing her partner, counting one. She then glides the left foot backward and across till the toe of the left foot is directly behind the right heel, the feet about one half of the length of the foot apart. This glide commences on the ball of the left foot, and terminates with both feet flat upon the floor, and the transfer of the weight to the backward foot. The bending of the knees and the casting down of the eyes begin with the commencement of the glide with the left foot, and the genuflection is steadily continued until the left foot reaches the position required, counting _two_; then, without changing the weight from the backward foot, she gradually rises, at the same time raising the forward heel and lifting the eyes, until she recovers her full height, counting _three_; and finally transfers the weight to the forward foot, counting four. Such is the elaborate and the graceful courtesy. It should be studied with a master.

The "German" (the "Cotillon," as the French call it) is, however, and probably long will be, the most fashionable dance in society. It ends every ball in New York, Washington, Boston, Philadelphia, and Newport; it is a part of the business of life, and demands consummate skill in its leadership. Any number may join in it; it often reaches twice around a large ballroom. All the couples in it are regarded as introduced to each other. No lady can refuse to dance with any gentleman who is brought to her in the German. So long as she remains in the charmed circle she must dance with any one in it.

Therefore the German must only be introduced at select assemblies, not at a public ball. The leader opens the German by motioning to certain couples to make a tour de valse round the room.

Many of our correspondents write to ask us what are the latest and the favorite figures in the German. This is a difficult question to answer, as the leader always has his own favorite figures. The German generally begins with _l'avant trois double_, which may be generally described thus: the leader, having performed the tour de valse with his partner, leaves her, and brings forward two other ladies; his lady brings forward two other gentlemen; the two trios place themselves opposite each other, then forward and back, and each gentleman with the lady in front of him performs a tour de valse. Should the company be large, two or more couples may start together, each couple choosing other ladies and gentlemen in the same manner as the first couple. Then comes La Chaise after the tour de valse. The leader places his partner in a chair in the centre of the room; he then brings forward two gentlemen and presents them to the lady, who chooses one of them, after which he seats the gentleman who is rejected, and brings to him two ladies; he also selects a partner, and the leader dances with the refused lady to her place. This figure may be danced by any number of couples.

Les Drapeaux is a favorite figure. Five or six duplicate sets of small flags of national or fancy devices must be in readiness. The leader takes a flag of each pattern, and his partner takes the duplicate. They perform a tour de valse. The conductor then presents his flags to five or six ladies, and his partner presents the corresponding flags to as many gentlemen. The gentlemen then seek the ladies having the duplicates, and with them perform a _tour de valse_, waving the flags as they dance. Repeated by all the couples.

Les Bouquets brings in the favors. A number of small bouquets and boutonnieres are placed upon a table or in a basket. The first couple perform a _tour de valse_; they then separate. The gentleman takes a bouquet, and the lady a boutonniere. They now select new partners, to whom they present the bouquet and boutonniere, the lady attaching the boutonniere to the gentleman's coat. They perform a tour de valse with their new partners. Repeated by all the couples. Other favors are frequently substituted for bouquets and boutonnieres, such as rosettes, miniature flags, artificial butterflies, badges, sashes, bonbons, little bells (the latter being attached to small pieces of ribbon and pinned to the coat or dress), scarf-pins, bangles, fans, caps, imitation antique coins, breastpins, lace pins, lockets; and even gifts of great value, such as shawls, scarfs, vases, picture-frames, writing-desks, and chairs (represented, of course, by tickets) have been this winter introduced in the german. But the cheap, light, fantastic things are the best, and contribute more to the amusement of the company.

Some of the figures of the German border on the romp. One of these is called La Corde. A rope is stretched by the leading couple across the room, and the gentlemen jump over it to reach their partners. Much amusement is occasioned by the tripping of gentlemen who are thrown by the intentional raising of the rope. After all have reached their partners they perform a _tour de valse_, and regain their seats. This is a figure not to be commended. Still less is the figure called Les Masques. The gentlemen put on masques resembling "Bully Bottom" and other grotesque faces and heads of animals. They raise these heads above a screen, the ladies choosing partners without knowing them; the gentlemen remain en masque until the termination of the tour de valse. This figure was danced at Delmonico's and at the Brunswick last winter, and the mammas complained that the fun grew rather too fast and furious. Les Rubans is a very pretty figure. Six ribbons, each about a yard in length, and of various colors, are attached to one end of a stick about twenty-four inches in length, also a duplicate set of ribbons, attached to another stick, must be in readiness. The first couple perform a _tour de valse_, then separate; the gentleman takes one set of ribbons, and stops successively in front of the ladies whom he desires to select to take part in the figure; each of these ladies rises and takes hold of the loose end of the ribbon; the first lady takes the other set of ribbons, bringing forward the six gentlemen in the same manner. The first couple conduct the ladies and gentlemen towards each other, and each gentleman dances with the lady holding the ribbon duplicate of his own; the first gentleman dances with his partner.

We might go on indefinitely with these figures, but have no more space. The position of a dancer should be learned with the aid of a teacher. The upper part of the body should be quiet; the head held in a natural position, neither turned to one side nor the other; the eyes neither cast down nor up. The gentleman should put his arm firmly around a lady's waist, not holding her too close, but firmly holding her right hand with his left one; the lady turns the palm of her right hand downward; her right arm should be nearly straight, but not stiff. The gentleman's left arm should be slightly bent, his elbow inclined slightly backward. It is very inelegant, however--indeed, vulgar--to place the joined hands against the gentleman's side or hip; they should be kept clear of the body. The step should be in unison; if the gentleman bends his right elbow too much, he draws the lady's left shoulder against his right, thereby drawing the lady too close. The gentleman's right shoulder and the lady's left should be as far apart as the other shoulders. If a gentleman does not hold his partner properly, thereby causing her either to struggle to be free or else to dance wildly for want of proper support, if he permits himself and partner to collide with other couples, he cannot be considered a good dancer.

CHAPTER XVII

LETTERS AND LETTER-WRITING.

The person who can write a graceful note is always spoken of with phrases of commendation. The epistolary art is said to be especially feminine, and the novelists and essayists are full of compliments to the sex, which is alternately praised and objurgated, as man feels well or ill. Bulwer says: "A woman is the genius of epistolary communication. Even men write better to a woman than to one of their own sex. No doubt they conjure up, while writing, the loving, listening face, the tender, pardoning heart, the ready tear of sympathy, and passionate confidences of heart and brain flow rapidly from the pen." But there is no such thing now as an "epistolary style." Our immediate ancestors wrote better and longer letters than we do. They covered three pages of large letter-paper with crow-quill handwriting, folded the paper neatly, tucked one edge beneath the other (for there were no envelopes), and then sealed it with a wafer or with sealing-wax. To send one of these epistles was expensive--twenty-five cents from New York to Boston. However, the electric telegraph and cheap postage and postal-cards may have been said, in a way, to have ruined correspondence in the old sense; lovers and fond mothers doubtless still write long letters, but the business of the letter-writer proper is at an end. The writing of notes has, however, correspondingly increased; and the last ten years have seen a profuse introduction of emblazoned crest and cipher, pictorial design, and elaborate monogram in the corners of ordinary note-paper. The old illuminated missal of the monks, the fancy of the Japanese, the ever-ready taste of the French, all have been exhausted to satisfy that always hungry caprice which calls for something new.

The frequency with which notes upon business and pleasure must fly across a city and a continent has done away, also, with the sealing-wax, whose definite, red, clear, oval was a fixture with our grandfathers, and which is still the only elegant, formal, and ceremonious way acknowledged in England, of sealing a letter.

There were, however, serious objections to the use of wax in this country, which were discovered during the early voyages to California. The intense heat of the Isthmus of Panama melted the wax, and letters were irretrievably glued together, to the loss of the address and the confusion of the postmaster. So the glued envelope--common, cheap, and necessary--became the almost prevailing fashion for all notes as well as letters.

The taste for colored note-paper with flowers in the corner was common among the belles of thirty years ago--the "rose-colored and scented _billet-doux_" is often referred to in the novels of that period. But colored note-paper fell into disuse long ago, and for the last few years we have not seen the heavy tints. A few pale greens, grays, blues, and lilacs have, indeed, found a place in fashionable stationery, and a deep coffee-colored, heavy paper had a little run about three years ago; but at the present moment no color that is appreciable is considered stylish, unless it be only a creamy white.

A long truce is at last bidden to the fanciful, emblazoned, and colored monogram; the crest and cipher are laid on the shelf, and ladies have simply the address of their city residence, or the name of their country place, printed in one corner (generally in color), or, latest device of fashion, a fac-simile of their initials, carefully engraved, and dashed across the corner of the note-paper. The day of the week, also copied from their own handwriting, is often impressed upon the square cards now so much in use for short notes, or on the note-paper.

There is one fashion which has never changed, and will never change, which is always in good taste, and which, perhaps, would be to-day the most perfect of all styles, and that is, good, plain, thick, English notepaper, folded square, put in a square envelope, and sealed with red sealing-wax which bears the imprint of the writer's coat of arms. No one can make any mistake who uses such stationery as this in any part of the world. On such paper and in such form are ambassadors' notes written; on such paper and in such style would the Princess Louise write her notes.

However, there is no law against the monogram. Many ladies still prefer it, and always use the paper which has become familiar to their friends. It is, however, a past rather than a present fashion.

The plan of having all the note-paper marked with the address is an admirable one, for it effectually reminds the person who receives the note where the answer should be sent--information of which some ladies forget the importance, and which should always be written, if not printed, at the head of a letter. It also gives a stylish finish to the appearance of the note-paper, is simple, unpretending, and useful.

The ink should invariably be black. From the very superior, lasting qualities of a certain purple fluid, which never became thick in the inkstand, certain ladies, a few years ago, used the purple and lilac inks very much. But they are not elegant; they are not in fashion; the best note-writers do not use them. The plain black ink, which gives the written characters great distinctness, is the only fashionable medium.

Every lady should study to acquire an elegant, free, and educated hand; there is nothing so useful, so sure to commend the writer everywhere, as such a chirography; while a cramped, poor, slovenly, uneducated, unformed handwriting is sure to produce the impression upon the reader that those qualities are more or less indicative of the writer's character. The angular English hand is at present the fashion, although less legible and not more beautiful than the round hand. We cannot enter into that great question as to whether or not handwriting is indicative of character; but we hold that a person's notes are generally characteristic, and that a neat, flowing, graceful hand, and a clean sheet, free from blots, are always agreeable to the eye. The writer of notes, also, must carefully discriminate between the familiar note and the note of ceremony, and should learn how to write both.

Custom demands that we begin all notes in the first person, with the formula of "My dear Mrs. Smith," and that we close with the expressions, "Yours cordially," "Yours with much regard," etc. The laws of etiquette do not permit us to use numerals, as 3, 4, 5, but demand that we write out _three, four, five_. No abbreviations are allowed in a note to a friend, as, "Sd be glad to see you;" one must write out, "I should be glad to see you." The older letter-writers were punctilious about writing the first word of the page below the last line of the page preceding it. The date should follow the signing of the name.

A great and very common mistake existing among careless letter-writers is the confusion of the first and third persons; as a child would write, "Miss Lucy Clark will be happy to come to dinner, but I am going somewhere else." This is, of course, wildly ignorant and improper.

A note in answer to an invitation should be written in the third person, if the invitation be in the third person. No abbreviations, no visible hurry, but an elaborate and finished ceremony should mark such epistles. For instance, an acceptance of a dinner invitation must be written in this form:

Mr. and Mrs. Cadogan have great pleasure in accepting the polite invitation of Mr. and Mrs. Sutherland for dinner on the seventeenth inst., at seven o'clock. 18 Lombard Square. July sixth.

One lady in New York was known to answer a dinner invitation simply with the words, "Come with pleasure." It is unnecessary to add that she was never invited again.

It is impossible to give persons minute directions as to the style of a note, for that must be the outgrowth of years of careful education, training, and good mental powers. "To write a pretty note" is also somewhat of a gift. Some young men and young girls find it very easy, others can scarcely acquire the power. It is, however, absolutely necessary to strive for it.

In the first place, arrange your ideas, know what you want to say, and approach the business of writing a note with a certain thoughtfulness. If it is necessary to write it hastily, summon all your powers of mind, and try to make it brief, intelligible, and comprehensive.

Above all things, spell correctly. A word badly spelled stands out like a blot on a familiar or a ceremonious note.

Do not send a blurred, blotted, slovenly note to any one; it will remain to call up a certain prejudice against you in the mind of the recipient. The fashion is not now, as it once was, imperative that a margin be left around the edge of the paper. People now write all over the paper, and thus abolish a certain elegance which the old letters undoubtedly possessed. But postage is a consideration, and all we can ask of the youthful letter-writers is that they will not cross their letters. Plaid letters are the horror of all people who have not the eyes of a hawk.

No letter or note should be written on ruled paper. To do so is both inelegant and unfashionable, and savors of the school-room. Every young person should learn to write without lines.

The square cards are much used, and are quite large enough for the transmission of all that a lady ordinarily wishes to say in giving or accepting an invitation. The day of the week and the address are often printed on the card.

Square envelopes have also driven the long ones from the table of the elegant note-writer, and the custom of closing all ceremonious notes with sealing-wax is still adhered to by the most fastidious. It would be absurd, however, to say that it is nearly as common as the more convenient habit of moistening the gummed envelope, but it is far more elegant, and every young person should learn how to seal a note properly. To get a good impression from an engraved stone seal, anoint it lightly with linseed-oil, to keep the wax from adhering; then dust it with rouge powder to take off the gloss, and press it quickly, but firmly, on the melted wax.

Dates and numerical designations, such as the number of a house, may be written in Arabic figures, but quantities should be expressed in words. Few abbreviations are respectful. A married lady should always be addressed with the prefix of her husband's Christian name.

In this country, where we have no titles, it is the custom to abbreviate everything except the title of "Reverend," which we always give to the clergy. But it would be better if we made a practice of giving to each person his special title, and to all returned ambassadors, members of Congress, and members of the Legislature the title of "Honorable." The Roman Catholic clergy and the bishops of the Episcopal and Methodist churches should be addressed by their proper titles, and a note should be, like a salutation, infused with respect. It honors the writer and the person to whom it is written, while a careless letter may injure both.

CHAPTER XVIII

COSTLY THY HABIT.

We are often asked as to the appropriate dress to be worn at afternoon tea, at balls, at dinners, christenings, etc.

Neatness and simple elegance should always characterize a lady, and after that she may be as expensive as she pleases, if only at the right time. And we may say here that simplicity and plainness characterize many a rich woman in a high place; and one can always tell a real lady from an imitation one by her style of dress. Vulgarity is readily seen even under a costly garment. There should be harmony and fitness, and suitability as to age and times and seasons. Every one can avoid vulgarity and slovenliness; and in these days, when the fashions travel by telegraph, one can be la mode_.

French women have a genius for dress. An old or a middle-aged woman understands how to make the best of herself in the assorting and harmonizing of colors; she never commits the mistake of making herself too youthful. In our country we often see an old woman bedizened like a _Figurante_, imagining that she shall gain the graces of youth by borrowing its garments. All this aping of youthful dress "multiplies the wrinkles of old age, and makes its decay more conspicuous."

For balls in this country, elderly women are not expected to go in low neck unless they wish to, so that the chaperon can wear a dress such as she would wear at a dinner--either a velvet or brocade, cut in Pompadour shape, with a profusion of beautiful lace. All her ornaments should match in character, and she should be as unlike her charge as possible. The young girls look best in light gossamer material, in tulle, crepe, or tarlatan, in pale light colors or in white, while an elderly, stout woman never looks so badly as in low-necked light-colored silks or satins, Young women look well in natural flowers; elderly women, in feathers and jewelled head-dresses.

If elderly women with full figure wear low-necked dresses, a lace shawl or scarf, or something of that sort, should be thrown over the neck; and the same advice might be given to thin and scrawny figures. A lady writes to us as to what dress should be worn at her child's christening. We should advise a high-necked dark silk; it may be of as handsome material as she chooses, but it should be plain and neat in general effect. No woman should overdress in her own house; it is the worst taste. All dress should correspond to the spirit of the entertainment given. Light-colored silks, sweeping trains, bonnets very gay and garnished with feathers, lace parasols, and light gloves, are fit for carriages at the races, but they are out of place for walking in the streets. They may do for a wedding reception, but they are not fit for a picnic or an excursion. Lawn parties, flower shows, and promenade concerts, should all be dressed for in a gay, bright fashion; and the costumes for these and for yachting purposes may be as effective and coquettish as possible; but for church, for readings, for a morning concert, for a walk, or a morning call on foot, a tailor-made costume, with plain, dark hat, is the most to be admired. Never wear a "dressy" bonnet in the street.

The costumes for picnics, excursions, journeys; and the sea-side should be of a strong fabric, simple cut, and plain color. Things which will wash are better for our climate. Serge, tweed, and piqu‚ are the best.

A morning dress for a late breakfast may be as luxurious as one pleases. The modern fashion of imitation lace put on in great quantities over a foulard or a gingham, a muslin or a cotton, made up prettily, is suitable for women of all ages; but an old "company dress" furbished up to do duty at a watering-place is terrible, and not to be endured.

It has been the fashion this season to wear full-dress at weddings. The bride and her maids have appeared with low neck and short sleeves in the cold morning air at several fashionable churches. The groom at the same time wearing morning costume. It is an era of low necks. The pendulum of fashion is swinging that way. We have spoken of this before, so only record the fact that the low neck will prevail in many summer evening dresses as well as for morning weddings.

The very tight fashion of draping skirts should make all women very careful as to the way they sit down. Some Frenchman said he could tell a gentleman by his walk; another has lately said that he can tell a lady by the way she sits down. A woman is allowed much less freedom of posture than a man. He may change his position as he likes, and loll or lounge, cross his legs, or even nurse his foot if he pleases; but a woman must have grace and dignity; in every gesture she must be "ladylike." Any one who has seen a great actress like Modjeska sit down will know what an acquired grace it is.

A woman should remember that she "belongs to a sex which cannot afford to be grotesque." There should never be rowdiness or carelessness.

The mania for extravagant dress on the stage, the _pieces des robes_, is said to be one of the greatest enemies of the legitimate drama. The leading lady must have a conspicuous display of elaborate gowns, the latest inventions of the modistes. In Paris these stage costumes set the fashions, and bonnets and caps and gowns become individualized by their names. They look very well on the wearers, but they look very badly on some elderly, plain, middle-aged, stout woman who has adopted them.

Plain satins and velvet, rich and dark brocades, made by an artist, make any one look well. The elderly woman should be able to move without effort or strain of any kind; a black silk well made is indispensable; and even "a celebrity of a by-gone day" may be made to look handsome by a judicious but not too brilliant toilette.

The dress called "complimentary mourning," which is rather a contradiction in terms, is now made very elegant and dressy. Black and white in all the changes, and black bugles and bead trimming, all the shades of lilac and of purple, are considered by the French as proper colors and trimmings in going out of black; while for full mourning the English still preserve the cap, weepers, and veil, the plain muslin collar and cuffs, the crape dress, large black silk cloak, crape bonnet and veil.

Heavy, ostentatious, and expensive habiliments are often worn in mourning, but they are not in the best taste. The plain-surfaced black silks are commendable.

For afternoon tea in this country the hostess generally wears a handsome high-necked gown, often a combination of stamped or brocaded velvet, satin, and silk. She rarely wears what in England is called a "tea-gown," which is a semi-loose garment. For visiting at afternoon teas no change is made from the ordinary walking dress, unless the three or four ladies who help receive come in handsome reception dresses. A skirt of light brocade with a dark velvet over-dress is very much worn at these receptions, and if made by a French artist is a beautiful dress. These dark velvets are usually made high, with a very rich lace ruff.

The high Medicean collar and pretty Medicean cap of velvet are in great favor with the middle-aged ladies of the present day, and are a very becoming style of dress for the opera. The present fashion of full dress at the opera, while it may not improve the music, certainly makes the house look very pretty and stately.

Too many dresses are a mistake, even for an opulent woman. They get out of fashion, and excepting for a girl going out to many balls they are entirely unnecessary. A girl who is dancing needs to be perpetually renewed, for she should be always fresh, and the "wear and tear" of the cotillion is enormous. There is nothing so poor as a dirty, faded, and patched-up ball-dress; the dancer had better stay at home than wear such.

The fashion of sleeves should be considered. A stout woman looks very badly in a loose sleeve of hanging lace which only reaches the elbow. It makes the arm look twice as large. She should wear, for a thin sleeve, black lace to the wrist, with bands of velvet running down, to diminish the size of the arm. All those lace sleeves to the elbow, with drops of gold, or steel trimming, or jets, are very unbecoming; no one but the slight should wear them.

Tight lacing is also very unbecoming to those who usually adopt it--women of thirty-eight or forty who are growing a little stout. In thus trussing themselves up they simply get an unbecoming redness of the face, and are not the handsome, comfortable-looking creatures which Heaven intended they should be. Two or three beautiful women well known in society killed themselves last year by tight lacing. The effect of an inch less waist was not apparent enough to make this a wise sacrifice of health and ease of breathing.

At a lady's lunch party, which is always an occasion for handsome dress, and where bonnets are always worn, the faces of those who are too tightly dressed always show the strain by a most unbecoming flush; and as American rooms are always too warm, the suffering must be enormous.

It is a very foolish plan, also, to starve one's self, or "_bant_," for a graceful thinness; women only grow wrinkled, show crow's-feet under the eyes, and look less young than those who let themselves alone.

A gorgeously dressed woman in the proper place is a fine sight. A well-dressed woman is she who understands herself and her surroundings.

CHAPTER XIX

DRESSING FOR DRIVING.

No one who has seen the coaching parade in New York can have failed to observe the extraordinary change which has come over the fashion in dress for this conspicuous occasion. Formerly ladies wore black silks, or some dark or low-toned color in woollen or cotton or silk; and a woman who should have worn a white dress on top of a coach would, ten years ago, have been thought to make herself undesirably conspicuous.

Now the brightest colored and richest silks, orange, blue, pink, and lilac dresses, trimmed with lace flounces, dinner dresses, in fact--all the charming confections of Worth or Piugat--are freely displayed on the coach-tops, with the utmost graciousness, for every passer-by to comment on. The lady on the top of a coach without a mantle appears very much as she would at a full-dress ball or dinner. She then complains that sometimes ill-natured remarks float up from the gazers, and that the ladies are insulted. The fashion began at Longchamps and at Ascot, where, especially at the former place, a lady was privileged to sit in her victoria, with her lilac silk full ruffled to the waist, in the most perfect and aristocratic seclusion. Then the fast set of the Prince of Wales took it up, and plunged into rivalry in dressing for the public procession through the London streets, where a lady became as prominent an object of observation as the Lord Mayor's coach. It has been taken up and developed in America until it has reached a climax of splendor and, if we may say so, inappropriateness, that is characteristic of the following of foreign fashions in this country. How can a white satin, trimmed with lace, or an orange silk, be the dress in which a lady should meet the sun, the rain, or the dust of a coaching expedition? Is it the dress in which she feels that she ought to meet the gaze of a mixed assemblage in a crowded hotel or in a much frequented thoroughfare? What change of dress can there be left for the drawing-room?

We are glad to see that the Princess of Wales, whose taste seems to be as nearly perfect as may be, has determined to set her pretty face against this exaggerated use of color. She appeared recently in London, on top of a coach, in a suit of navy-blue flannel. Again, she and the Empress of Austria are described as wearing dark, neat suits of _drap d''‚t‚_, and also broadcloth dresses. One can see the delicate figures and refined features of these two royal beauties in this neat and inconspicuous dress, and, when they are contrasted with the flaunting pink and white and lace and orange dresses of those who are not royal, how vulgar the extravagance in color becomes!

Our grandmothers travelled in broadcloth riding-habits, and we often pity them for the heat and the distress which they must have endured in the heavy, high-fitting, long-sleeved garments; yet we cannot but think they would have looked better on top of a coach than their granddaughters--who should remember, when they complain of the rude remarks, that we have no aristocracy here whose feelings the mob is obliged to respect, and that the plainer their dress the less apt they will be to hear unpleasant epithets applied to them. In the present somewhat aggressive Amazonian fashion, when a woman drives a man in her pony phaeton (he sitting several inches below her), there is no doubt much audacity unintentionally suggested by a gay dress. A vulgar man, seeing a lady in white velvet, Spanish lace, a large hat--in what he considers a "loud" dress--does not have the idea of modesty or of refinement conveyed to his mind by the sight; he is very apt to laugh, and to say something not wholly respectful. Then the lady says, "With how little respect women are treated in large cities, or at Newport, or at Saratoga!" Were she more plainly dressed, in a dark foulard or an inconspicuous flannel or cloth dress, with her hat simply arranged, she would be quite as pretty and better fitted for the matter she has in hand, and very much less exposed to invidious comment. Women dress plainly enough when tempting the "salt-sea wave," and also when on horseback. Nothing could be simpler than the riding-habit, and yet is there any dress so becoming? But on the coach they should not be too fine.

Of course, women can dress as they please, but if they please to dress conspicuously they must be ready to take the consequences. A few years ago no lady would venture into the street unless a mantle or a scarf covered her shoulders. It was a lady-like precaution. Then came the inglorious days of the "tied-backs," a style of dress most unbecoming to the figure, and now happily no more. This preposterous fashion had, no doubt, its influence on the manners of the age.

Better far, if women would parade their charms, the courtly dresses of those beauties of Bird-cage Walk, by St. James's Park, where "Lady Betty Modish" was born--full, long, bouffant brocades, hair piled high, long and graceful scarfs, and gloves reaching to the elbow. Even the rouge and powder were a mask to hide the cheek which did or did not blush when bold eyes were fastened upon it. Let us not be understood, however, as extolling these. The nineteenth-century beauty mounts a coach with none of these aids to shyness. No suggestion of hiding any of her charms occurs to her. She goes out on the box seat without cloak or shawl, or anything but a hat on the back of her head and a gay parasol between her and a possible thunder-storm. These ladies are not members of an acclimatization society. They cannot bring about a new climate. Do they not suffer from cold? Do not the breezes go through them? Answer, all ye pneumonias and diphtherias and rheumatisms!

There is no delicacy in the humor with which the funny papers and the caricaturists treat these very exaggerated costumes. No delicacy is required. A change to a quieter style of dress would soon abate this treatment of which so many ladies complain. Let them dress like the Princess of Wales and the Empress of Austria, when in the conspicuous high-relief of the coach, and the result will be that ladies, married or single, will not be subjected to the insults of which so many of them complain, and of which the papers are full after every coaching parade.

Lady riders are seldom obliged to complain of the incivility of a passer-by. Theirs are modest figures, and, as a general thing nowadays, they ride well. A lady can alight from her horse and walk about in a crowded place without hearing an offensive word: she is properly dressed for her exercise.

Nor, again, is a young lady in a lawn-tennis suit assailed by the impertinent criticisms of a mixed crowd of by-standers. Thousands play at Newport, Saratoga, and other places of resort, with thousands looking on, and no one utters a word of rebuke. The short flannel skirt and close Jersey are needed for the active runner, and her somewhat eccentric appearance is condoned. It is not considered an exhibition or a show, but a good, healthy game of physical exercise. People feel an interest and a pleasure in it. It is like the old-fashioned merry-making of the May-pole, the friendly jousts of neighbors on the common play-ground of the neighborhood, with the dances under the walnut-trees of sunny Provence. The game is an invigorating one, and even those who do not know it are pleased with its animation. We have hitherto neglected that gymnastic culture which made the Greeks the graceful people they were, and which contributed to the cultivation of the mind.

Nobody finds anything to laugh at in either of these costumes; but when people see a ball-dress mounted high on a coach they are very apt to laugh at it; and women seldom come home from a coaching parade without a tingling cheek and a feeling of shame because of some comment upon their dress and appearance. A young lady drove up, last summer, to the Ocean House at Newport in a pony phaeton, and was offended because a gentleman on the piazza said, "That girl has a very small waist, and she means us to see it." Who was to blame? The young lady was dressed in a very conspicuous manner: she had neither mantle nor jacket about her, and she probably did mean that her waist should be seen.

There is a growing objection all over the world to the hour-glass shape once so fashionable, and we ought to welcome it as the best evidence of a tendency towards a more sensible form of dress, as well as one more conducive to health and the wholesome discharge of a woman's natural and most important functions. But if a woman laces herself into a sixteen-inch belt, and then clothes herself in brocade, satin, and bright colors, and makes herself conspicuous, she should not object to the fact that men, seeing her throw aside her mantle, comment upon her charms in no measured terms. She has no one to blame but herself.

We might add that by this over-dressing women deprive themselves of the advantage of contrast in style. Lace, in particular, is for the house and for the full-dress dinner or ball. So are the light, gay silks, which have no fitness of fold or of texture for the climbing of a coach. If bright colors are desired, let ladies choose the merinos and nuns' veilings for coaching dresses; or, better still, let them dress in dark colors, in plain and inconspicuous dresses, which do not seem to defy both dust and sun and rain as well. On top of a coach they are far more exposed to the elements than when on the deck of a yacht.

Nor, because the fast set of the Prince of Wales do so in London, is there any reason why American women should appear on top of a coach dressed in red velvet and white satin. Let them remember the fact that the Queen had placed Windsor Castle at the disposal of the Prince for his use during Ascot week, but that when she learned that two somewhat conspicuous American beauties were expected, she rescinded the loan and told the Prince to entertain his guests elsewhere.

CHAPTER XX

INCONGRUITIES OF DRESS.

We are all aware of the value of a costume, such as the dress of the Pompadour era: the Swiss peasant's bodice, the Normandy cap, the faldetta of the Maltese, the Hungarian national dress, the early English, the Puritan square-cut, the Spanish mantilla, the Roman scarf and white cap--all these come before us; and as we mention each characteristic garment there steps out on the canvas of memory a neat little figure, in which every detail from shoe to head-dress is harmonious.

No one in his wildest dreams, however, could set out with the picture of a marquise, and top it off with a Normandy cap. Nor could he put powder on the dark hair of the jaunty little Hungarian. The beauty of these costumes is seen in each as a whole, and not in the parts separately. The marquise must wear pink or blue, or some light color; she must have the long waist, the square-cut corsage, the large hoop, the neat slipper, with rosette and high heel, the rouge and patches to supplement her powdered hair, or she is no marquise.

The Swiss peasant must have the short skirt, the white chemisette, the black velvet bodice, the cross and ribbon, the coarse shoes, and the head-dress of her canton; the Normandy peasant her dark, striking dress, her high-heeled, gold-buckled shoe, and her white apron; the Hungarian her neat, military scarlet jacket, braided with gold, her scant petticoat and military boot, her high cap and feather. The dress of the English peasant, known now as the "Mother Hubbard" hat and cloak, very familiar to the students of costumes as belonging to the countrywomen of Shakspeare's time, demands the short, bunched-up petticoat and high-heeled, high-cut shoes to make it perfect.

We live in an age, however, when fashion, irrespective of artistic principle, mixes up all these costumes, and borrows a hat here and a shoe there, the effect of each garment, diverted from its original intention, being lost.

If "all things by their season seasoned are," so is all dress (or it should be) seasonable and comprehensive, congruous and complete. The one great secret of the success of the French as artists and magicians of female costume is that they consider the entire figure and its demands, the conditions of life and of luxury, the propriety of the substance, and the needs of the wearer. A lady who is to tread a velvet carpet or a parqueted floor does not need a wooden shoe; she needs a satin slipper or boot. Yet in the modern drawing-room we sometimes see a young lady dancing in a heavy Balmoral boot which is only fitted for the bogs and heather of a Scotch tramp. The presence of a short dress in a drawing-room, or of a long train in the street, is part of the general incongruity of dress.

The use of the ulster and the Derby hat became apparent on English yachts, where women learned to put themselves in the attitude of men, and very properly adopted the storm jib; but, if one of those women had been told that she would, sooner or later, appear in this dress in the streets of London, she would have been shocked.

In the days of the French emigration, when highborn ladies escaped on board friendly vessels in the harbor of Honfleur, many of them had on the long-waisted and full-skirted overcoats of their husbands, who preferred to shiver rather than endure the pain of seeing their wives suffer from cold. These figures were observed by London tailors and dress-makers, and out of them grew the English pelisse which afterwards came into fashion. On a stout Englishwoman the effect was singularly absurd, and many of the early caricatures give us the benefit of this incongruity; for although a small figure looks well in a pelisse, a stout one never does. The Englishwoman who weighs two or three hundred pounds should wear a sacque, a shawl, or a loose cloak, instead of a tight-waisted pelisse. However, we are diverging. The sense of the personally becoming is still another branch of the great subject of dress. A velvet dress, for instance, demands for its trimmings expensive and real lace. It should not be supplemented by Breton or imitation Valenciennes. All the very pretty imitation laces are appropriate for cheap silks, poplins, summer fabrics, or dresses of light and airy material; but if the substance of the dress be of the richest, the lace should be in keeping with it.

So, also, in respect to jewellery: no cheap or imitation jewellery should be worn with an expensive dress. It is as foreign to good taste as it would be for a man to dress his head and body in the most fashionable of hats and coats, and his legs in white duck. There is incongruity in the idea.

The same incongruity applies to a taste for which our countrymen have often been blamed--a desire for the magnificent, A woman who puts on diamonds, real lace, and velvets in the morning at a summer watering-place is decidedly incongruous. Far better be dressed in a gingham, with Hamburg embroidery, and a straw hat with a handkerchief tied round it, now so pretty and so fashionable. She is then ready for the ocean or for the mountain drive, the scramble or the sail. Her boots should be strong, her gloves long and stout. She thus adapts her attire to the occasion. In the evening she will have an opportunity for the delicate boot and the trailing gauze or silk, or that deft combination of all the materials known as a "Worth Costume."

In buying a hat a woman should stand before a long Psyche glass, and see herself from head to foot. Often a very pretty bonnet or hat which becomes the face is absolutely dreadful in that wavy outline which is perceptible to those who consider the effect as a whole. All can remember how absurd a large figure looked in the round poke hat and the delicate Fanchon bonnet, and the same result is brought about by the round hat. A large figure should be topped by a Gainsborough or Rubens hat, with nodding plumes. Then the effect is excellent and the proportions are preserved.

Nothing can be more incongruous, again, than a long, slim, aesthetic figure with a head-gear so disproportionately large as to suggest a Sandwich-Islander with his head-dress of mats. The "aesthetic craze" has, however, brought in one improvement in costume. It is the epauletted sleeve, which gives expansion to so many figures which are, unfortunately, too narrow. All physiologists are speculating on the growing narrowness of chest in the Anglo-Saxon race. It is singularly apparent in America. To remedy this, some ingenious dress-maker devised a little puff at the top of the arm, which is most becoming. It is also well adapted to the "cloth of gold" costume of the days of Francis I., which modern luxury so much affects. It is a Frond sort of costume, this nineteenth-century dress, and can well borrow some of the festive features of the sixteenth and seventeenth centuries, if they be not incongruous. We, like those rich nobles and prosperous burghers, have lighted on piping times of peace; we have found a new India of our own; our galleons come laden with the spoils of all countries; we are rich, and we are able to wear velvet and brocade.

But we should be as true as they to the proprieties of dress. In the ancient burgher days the richest citizen was not permitted to wear velvet; he had his own picturesque collar, his dark-cloth suit, his becoming hat. He had no idea of aping the cian, with his long hat and feather. We are all patricians; we can wear either the sober suit or the gay one; but do let us avoid incongruity.

A woman, in dressing herself for an evening of festivity, should remember that, from her ear-rings to her fan, all must suggest and convey the idea of luxury. A wooden fan is very pretty in the morning at a watering-place, but it will not do in the evening. None of the modern _chƒtelaine_ arrangements, however ornamental, are appropriate for evening use. The _chƒtelaine_ meant originally the chain on which the lady of the house wore her keys; therefore its early association of usefulness remains: it is not luxurious in intention, however much modern fashion may have adorned it.

Many a fashion has, it is true, risen from a low estate. The Order of the Garter tells of a monarch's caprice; the shoe-buckle and the horseshoe have crept up into the highest rank of ornaments. But as it takes three generations to make a gentleman, so does it take several decades to give nobility to low-born ornament. We must not try to force things.

A part of the growing and sad incongruity of modern dress appears in the unavoidable awkwardness of a large number of bouquets. A belle cannot leave the insignia of belledom at home, nor can she be so unkind as to carry

Mr. Smith's flowers and ignore Mr. Brown's; so she appears with her arms and hands full, to the infinite detriment of her dress and general effect. Some arrangement might be devised whereby such trophies could be dragged in the train of the high-priestess of fashion.

A little reading, a little attention to the study of costume (a beautiful study, by-the-way), would soon teach a young woman to avoid the incongruous in dress. Some people have taste as a natural gift: they know how to dress from a consultation with their inner selves. Others, alas! are entirely without it. The people who make hats and coats and dresses for us are generally without any comprehension of the history of dress. To them the hat of the Roundhead and that of the Cavalier have the same meaning. To all people of taste and reading, however, they are very different, and all artists know that the costumes which retain their hold on the world have been preferred and have endured because of their fitness to conditions of climate and the grace and ease with which they were worn.

CHAPTER XXI

ETIQUETTE OF MOURNING.

There is no possibility of touching upon the subject of death and burial, and the conditions under which funerals should be conducted, without hurting some one's feelings. The Duke of Sutherland's attempt in England to do away with the dreadful shape which causes a shudder to all who have lost a friend-- that of the coffin--was called irreverent, because he suggested that the dead should be buried in wicker-work baskets, with fern-leaves for shrouds, so that the poor clay might the more easily return to mother earth. Those who favor cremation suffer again a still more frantic disesteem; and yet every one deplores the present gloomy apparatus and dismal observances of our occasions of mourning.

Death is still to the most Christian and resigned heart a very terrible fact, a shock to all who live, and its surroundings, do what we will, are painful. "I smell the mould above the rose," says Hood, in his pathetic lines on his daughter's death. Therefore, we have a difficulty to contend with in the wearing of black, which is of itself, to begin with, negatory of our professed belief in the resurrection. We confess the logic of despair when we drape ourselves in its gloomy folds. The dress which we should wear, one would think, might be blue, the color of the sky, or white, in token of light which the redeemed soul has reached.

Custom, which makes slaves of us all, has decreed that we shall wear black, as a mark of respect to those we have lost, and as a shroud for ourselves, protesting against the gentle ministration of light and cheerfulness with which our Lord ever strives to reach us. This is one side of the question; but, again, one word as to its good offices. A mourning dress does protect a woman while in deepest grief against the untimely gayety of a passing stranger. It is a wall, a cell of refuge. Behind a black veil she can hide herself as she goes out for business or recreation, fearless of any intrusion.

The black veil, on the other hand, is most unhealthy: it harms the eyes and it injures the skin. As it rubs against the nose and forehead it is almost certain to cause abrasions, and often makes an annoying sore. To the eyes enfeebled by weeping it is sure to be dangerous, and most oculists now forbid it.

The English, from whom we borrow our fashion in funeral matters, have a limitation provided by social law which is a useful thing. They now decree that crape shall only be worn six months, even for the nearest relative, and that the duration of mourning shall not exceed a year. A wife's mourning for her husband is the most conventionally deep mourning allowed, and every one who has seen an English widow will agree that she makes a "hearse" of herself. Bombazine and crape, a widow's cap; and a long; thick veil--such is the modern English idea. Some widows even have the cap made of black _crˆpe lisse_, but it is generally of white. In this country a widow's first mourning dresses are covered almost entirely with crape, a most costly and disagreeable material, easily ruined by the dampness and dust--a sort of penitential and self-mortifying dress, and very ugly and very expensive. There are now, however, other and more agreeable fabrics which also bear the dead black, lustreless look which is alone considered respectful to the dead, and which are not so costly as crape, or so disagreeable to wear. The Henrietta cloth and imperial serges are chosen for heavy winter dresses, while for those of less weight are tamise cloth, Bayonnaise, grenadine, nuns' veiling, and the American silk.

Our mourning usages are not overloaded with what may be called the pomp, pride, and circumstance of woe which characterize English funerals. Indeed, so overdone are mourning ceremonies in England--what with the hired mutes, the nodding plumes, the costly coffin, and the gifts of gloves and bands and rings, etc.--that Lady Georgiana Milnor, of Nunappleton, in York, a great friend of the Archbishop, wrote a book against the abuse, ordered her own body to be buried in a pine coffin, and forbade her servants and relatives to wear mourning. Her wishes were carried out to the letter. A black, cloth-covered casket with silver mountings is considered in the best taste, and the pall-bearers are given at most a white scarf and a pair of black gloves. Even this is not always done. At one time the traffic in these returned bands and gloves was quite a fortune to the undertaker. Mourning is very expensive, and often costs a family more than they can well afford; but it is a sacrifice that even the poorest gladly make, and those who can least afford it often wear the best mourning, so tyrannical is custom. They consider it--by what process of reasoning no one can understand, unless it be out of a hereditary belief that we hold in the heathen idea of propitiating the manes of the departed--an act of disrespect to the memory of the dead if the living are not clad in gloomy black.

However, our business is with the etiquette of mourning. Widows wear deep mourning, consisting of woollen stuffs and crape, for about two years, and sometimes for life, in America. Children wear the same for parents for one year, and then lighten it with black silk, trimmed with crape. Half-mourning gradations of gray, purple, or lilac have been abandoned, and, instead, combinations of black and white are used. Complimentary mourning is black silk without crape. The French have three grades of mourning--deep, ordinary, and half mourning. In deep mourning, woollen cloths only are worn; in ordinary mourning, silk and woollen; in half mourning, gray and violet. An American lady is always shocked at the gayety and cheerfulness of French mourning. In France, etiquette prescribes mourning for a husband for one year and six weeks--that is, six months of deep mourning, six of ordinary, and six weeks of half mourning. For a wife, a father, or a mother, six months--three deep and three half mourning; for a grandparent, two months and a half of slight mourning; for a brother or a sister, two months, one of which is in deep mourning; for an uncle or an aunt, three weeks of ordinary black. In America, with no fixity of rule, ladies have been known to go into deepest mourning for their own relatives or those of their husbands, or for people, perhaps, whom they have never seen, and have remained as gloomy monuments of bereavement for seven or ten years, constantly in black; then, on losing a child or a relative dearly loved, they have no extremity of dress left to express the real grief which fills their lives--no deeper black to go into. This complimentary mourning should be, as in the French custom, limited to two or three weeks. The health of a delicate child has been known to be seriously affected by the constant spectacle of his mother in deep mourning.

The period of a mourner's retirement from the world has been very much shortened of late. For one year no formal visiting is undertaken, nor is there any gayety in the house. Black is often worn for a husband or wife two years, for parents one year, and for brothers and sisters one year; a heavy black is lightened after that period. Ladies are beginning to wear a small black gauze veil over the face, and are in the habit of throwing the heavy crape veil back over the hat. It is also proper to wear a quiet black dress when going to a funeral, although this is not absolutely necessary.

Friends should call on the bereaved family within a month, not expecting, of course, to see them. Kind notes expressing sympathy are most welcome to the afflicted from intimate friends, and gifts of flowers, or any testimonial of sympathy, are thoughtful and appropriate. Cards and note-paper are now put into mourning by those who desire to express conventionally their regret for the dead; but very broad borders of black look like ostentation, and are in undoubted bad taste. No doubt all these things are proper enough in their way, but a narrow border of black tells the story of loss as well as an inch of coal-black gloom. The fashion of wearing handkerchiefs which are made with a two-inch square of white cambric and a four-inch border of black may well be deprecated. A gay young widow at Washington was once seen dancing at a reception, a few months after the death of her soldier husband, with a long black veil on, and holding in her black-gloved hand one of these handkerchiefs, which looked as if it had been dipped in ink. "She should have dipped it in blood," said a by-stander. Under such circumstances we learn how much significance is to be attached to the grief expressed by a mourning veil.

The mourning which soldiers, sailors, and courtiers wear has something pathetic and effective about it. A flag draped with crape, a gray cadet-sleeve with a black band, or a long piece of crape about the left arm of a senator, a black weed on a hat, these always touch us. They would even appear to suggest that the lighter the black, the more fully the feeling of the heart is expressed. If we love our dead, there is no danger that we shall forget them. "The customary suit of solemn black" is not needed when we can wear it in our hearts.

For lighter mourning jet is used on silk, and there is no doubt that it makes a very handsome dress. It is a singular fact that there is a certain comfort to some people in wearing very handsome black. Worth, on being asked to dress an American widow whom he had never seen, sent for her photograph, for he said that he wished to see "whether she was the sort of woman who would relish a becoming black."

Very elegant dresses are made with jet embroidery on crape--the beautiful soft French crape--but lace is never "mourning." Even the French, who have very light ideas on the subject, do not trim the most ornamental dresses with lace during the period of even second mourning, except when they put the woolen yak lace on a cloth cloak or mantilla. During a very dressy half mourning, however, black lace may be worn on white silk; but this is questionable. Diamond ornaments set in black enamel are allowed even in the deepest mourning, and also pearls set in black. The initials of the deceased, in black brilliants or pearls, are now set in lockets and sleeve-buttons, or pins. Gold ornaments are never worn in mourning.

White silk, embroidered with black jet, is used in the second stage of court mourning, with black gloves. Deep red is deemed in England a proper alternative for mourning black, if the wearer be called upon to go to a wedding during the period of the first year's mourning. At St. George's, Hanover Square, therefore, one may often see a widow assisting at the wedding of a daughter or a son, and dressed in a superb red brocade or velvet, which, directly the wedding is over, she will discard for her solemn black.

The question of black gloves is one which troubles all who are obliged to wear mourning through the heat of summer. The black kid glove is painfully warm and smutty, disfiguring the hand and soiling the handkerchief and face. The Swedish kid glove is now much more in vogue, and the silk glove is made with such neatness and with such a number of buttons that it is equally stylish, and much cooler and more agreeable.

Mourning bonnets are worn rather larger than ordinary bonnets. In England they are still made of the old-fashioned cottage shape, and are very useful in carrying the heavy veil and in shading the face. The Queen has always worn this style of bonnet. Her widow's cap has never been laid aside, and with her long veil of white falling down her back when she appears at court, it makes the most becoming dress that she has ever worn. For such a grief as hers there is something appropriate and dignified in her adherence to the mourning-dress. It fully expresses her sad isolation: for a queen can have no near friends. The whole English nation has sympathized with her grief, and commended her black dress. Nor can we criticise the grief which causes a mother to wear mourning for her children. If it be any comfort to her to wrap herself in crape, she ought to do so. The world has no right to quarrel with those who prefer to put ashes on their heads.

But for the mockery, the conventional absurdities, and the affectations which so readily lend themselves to caricature in the name of mourning, no condemnation can be too strong. There is a ghoul-like ghastliness in talking about "ornamental," or "becoming," or "complimentary" mourning. People of sense, of course, manage to dress without going to extremities in either direction. We see many a pale-faced mourner whose quiet mourning-dress tells the story of bereavement without giving us the painful feeling that crape is too thick, or bombazine too heavy, for comfort. Exaggeration is to be deprecated in mourning as in everything.

The discarding of mourning should be effected by gradations. It shocks persons of good taste to see a light-hearted young widow jump into colors, as if she had been counting the hours. If black is to be dispensed with, let its retirement be slowly and gracefully marked by quiet costumes, as the feeling of grief, yielding to the kindly influence of time, is shaded off into resignation and cheerfulness. We do not forget our dead, but we mourn for them with a feeling which no longer partakes of anguish.

Before a funeral the ladies of a family see no one but the most intimate friends. The gentlemen, of course, must see the clergyman and officials who manage the ceremony. It is now the almost universal practice to carry the remains to a church, where the friends of the family can pay the last tribute of respect without crowding into a private house. Pallbearers are invited by note, and assemble at the house of the deceased, accompanying the remains, after the ceremonies at the church, to their final resting-place. The nearest lady friends seldom go to the church or to the grave. This is, however, entirely a matter of feeling, and they can go if they wish. After the funeral only the members of the family return to the house, and it is not expected that a bereaved wife or mother will see any one other than the members of her family for several weeks.

The preparations for a funeral in the house are committed to the care of an undertaker, who removes the furniture from the drawing-room, filling all the space possible with camp-stools. The clergyman reads the service at the head of the coffin, the relatives being grouped around. The body, if not disfigured by disease, is often dressed in the clothes worn in life, and laid in an open casket, as if reposing on a sofa, and all friends are asked to take a last look. It is, however, a somewhat ghastly proceeding to try to make the dead look like the living. The body of a man is usually dressed in black. A young boy is laid out in his every-day clothes, but surely the young of both sexes look more fitly clad in the white cashmere robe.

The custom of decorating the coffin with flowers is a beautiful one, but has been, in large cities, so overdone, and so purely a matter of money, that now the request is generally made that no flowers be sent.

In England a lady of the court wears, for her parent, crape and bombazine (or its equivalent in any lustreless cloth) for three months. She goes nowhere during that period. After that she wears lustreless silks, trimmed with crape and jet, and goes to court if commanded. She can also go to concerts without violating etiquette, or to family weddings. After six months she again reduces her mourning to black and white, and can attend the "drawing-room" or go to small dinners. For a husband the time is exactly doubled, but in neither case should the widow be seen at a ball, a theatre, or an opera until after one year has elapsed.

In this country no person in mourning for a parent, a child, a brother, or a husband, is expected to be seen at a concert, a dinner, a party, or at any other place of public amusement, before three months have passed, After that one may be seen at a concert. But to go to the opera, or a dinner, or a party, before six months have elapsed, is considered heartless and disrespectful. Indeed, a deep mourning-dress at such a place is an unpleasant anomaly. If one choose, as many do, not to wear mourning, then they can go unchallenged to any place of amusement, for they have asserted their right to be independent; but if they put on mourning they must respect its etiquette, By many who sorrow deeply, and who regard the crape and solemn dress as a mark of respect to the dead, it is deemed almost a sin for a woman to go into the street, to drive, or to walk, for two years, without a deep crape veil over her face. It is a common remark of the censorious that a person who lightens her mourning before that time "did not care much for the deceased;" and many people hold the fact that a widow or an orphan wears her crape for two years to be greatly to her credit.

Of course, no one can say that a woman should not wear mourning all her life if she choose, but it is a serious question whether in so doing she does not injure the welfare and happiness of the living. Children, as we have said, are often strangely affected by this shrouding of their mothers, and men always dislike it.

Common-sense and common decency, however, should restrain the frivolous from engaging much in the amusements and gayeties of life before six months have passed after the death of any near friend. If they pretend to wear black at all, they cannot be too scrupulous in respecting the restraint which it imposes.

CHAPTER XXII

MOURNING AND FUNERAL USAGES.

Nothing in our country is more undecided in the public mind than the etiquette of mourning. It has not yet received that hereditary and positive character which makes the slightest departure from received custom so reprehensible in England. We have not the mutes, or the nodding feathers of the hearse, that still form part of the English funeral equipage; nor is the rank of the poor clay which travels to its last home illustrated by the pomp and ceremony of its departure. Still, in answer to some pertinent questions, we will offer a few desultory remarks, beginning with the end, as it were--the return of the mourner to the world.

n persons who have been in mourning wish to re-enter society, they should leave cards on all their friends and acquaintances, as an intimation that they are equal to the paying and receiving of calls. Until this intimation is given, society will not venture to intrude upon the mourner's privacy. In eases where cards of inquiry have been left, with the words "To inquire" written on the top of the card, these cards should be replied to by cards with "Thanks for kind inquiries" written upon them; but if cards for inquiry had not been left, this form can be omitted.

Of course there is a kind of complimentary mourning which does not necessitate seclusion--that which is worn out of respect to a husband's relative whom one may never have seen. But no one wearing a heavy crape veil should go to a gay reception, a wedding, or a theatre; the thing is incongruous. Still less should mourning prevent one from taking proper recreation: the more the heart aches, the more should one try to gain cheerfulness and composure, to hear music, to see faces which one loves: this is a duty, not merely a wise and sensible rule. Yet it is well to have some established customs as to visiting and dress in order that the gay and the heartless may in observing them avoid that which shocks every one--an appearance of lack of respect to the memory of the dead--that all society may move on in decency and order, which is the object and end of the study of etiquette.

A heartless wife who, instead of being grieved at the death of her husband, is rejoiced at it, should be taught that society will not respect her unless she pays to the memory of the man whose name she bears that "homage which vice pays to virtue," a commendable respect to the usages of society in the matter of mourning and of retirement from the world. Mourning garments have this use, that they are a shield to the real mourner, and they are often a curtain of respectability to the person who should be a mourner but is not. We shall therefore borrow from the best English and American authorities what we believe to be the most recent usages in the etiquette of mourning.

As for periods of mourning, we are told that a widow's mourning should last eighteen months, although in England it is somewhat lightened in twelve. For the first six months the dress should be of crape cloth, or Henrietta cloth covered entirely with crape, collar and cuffs of white crape, a crape bonnet with a long crape veil, and a widow's cap of white crape if preferred. In

America, however, widows' caps are not as universally worn as in England. Dull black kid gloves are worn in first mourning; after that gants de Suede or silk gloves are proper, particularly in summer. After six months' mourning the crape can be removed, and grenadine, copeau fringe, and dead trimmings used, if the smell of crape is offensive, as it is to some people. After twelve months the widow's cap is left off, and the heavy veil is exchanged for a lighter one, and the dress can be of silk grenadine, plain black gros-grain, or crape-trimmed cashmere with jet trimmings, and crˆpe lisse about the neck and sleeves.

All kinds of black fur and seal-skin are worn in deep mourning.

Mourning for a father or mother should last one year. During half a year should be worn Henrietta cloth or serge trimmed with crape, at first with black tulle at the wrists and neck. A deep veil is worn at the back of the bonnet, but not over the head or face like the widow's veil, which covers the entire person when down. This fashion is very much objected to by doctors, who think many diseases of the eye come by this means, and advise for common use thin nun's-veiling instead of crape, which sheds its pernicious dye into the sensitive nostrils, producing catarrhal disease as well as blindness and cataract of the eye. It is a thousand pities that fashion dictates the crape veil, but so it is. It is the very banner of woe, and no one has the courage to go without it. We can only suggest to mourners wearing it that they should pin a small veil of black tulle over the eyes and nose, and throw back the heavy crape as often as possible, for health's sake.

Jet ornaments alone should be worn for eighteen months, unless diamonds set as mementoes are used. For half-mourning, a bonnet of silk or chip, trimmed with crape and ribbon. Mourning flowers, and crˆpe lisse at the hands and wrists, lead the way to gray, mauve, and white-and-black toilettes after the second year.

Mourning for a brother or sister may be the same; for a stepfather or stepmother the same; for grandparents the same; but the duration may be shorter. In England this sort of respectful mourning only lasts three months.

Mourning for children should last nine months, The first three the dress should be crape-trimmed, the mourning less deep than that for a husband.

No one is ever ready to take off mourning; therefore these rules have this advantage--they enable the friends around a grief-stricken mother to tell her when is the time to make her dress more cheerful, which she is bound to do for the sake of the survivors, many of whom are perhaps affected for life by seeing a mother always in black. It is well for mothers to remember this when sorrow for a lost child makes all the earth seem barren to them.

We are often asked whether letters of condolence should be written on black-edged paper. Decidedly not, unless the writer is in black. The telegraph now flashes messages of respect and sympathy across sea and land like a voice from the heart. Perhaps it is better than any other word of sympathy, although all who can should write to a bereaved person. There is no formula possible for these letters; they must be left to the individual's good taste, and perhaps the simplest and least conventional are the best. A card with a few words pencilled on it has often been the best letter of condolence.

In France a long and deeply edged mourning letter or address, called a _faire part_, is sent to every one known to the family to advise them of a death. In this country that is not done, although some mention of the deceased is generally sent to friends in Europe who would not otherwise hear of the death.

Wives wear mourning for the relatives of their husbands precisely as they would for their own, as would husbands for the relatives of their wives. Widowers wear mourning for their wives two years in England; here only one year. Widowers go into society at a much earlier date than widows, it being a received rule that all gentlemen in mourning for relatives go into society very much sooner than ladies.

Ladies of the family attend the funeral of a relative if they are able to do so, and wear their deepest mourning. Servants are usually put in mourning for the head of the family--sometimes for any member of it. They should wear a plain black livery and weeds on their hats; the inside lining of the family carriage should also be of black.

The period of mourning for an aunt or uncle or cousin is of three months' duration, and that time at least should elapse before the family go out or into gay company, or are seen at theatres or operas, etc.

We now come to the saddest part of our subject, the consideration of the dead body, so dear, yet so soon to leave us; so familiar, yet so far away--the cast-off dress, the beloved clay. Dust to dust, ashes to ashes!

As for the coffin, it is simpler than formerly; and, while lined with satin and made with care, it is plain on the outside--black cloth, with silver plate for the name, and silver handles, being in the most modern taste. There are but few of the "trappings of woe." At the funeral of General Grant, twice a President, and regarded as the saviour of his country, there was a gorgeous catafalque of purple velvet, but at the ordinary funeral there are none of these trappings. If our richest citizen were to die to-morrow, he would probably be buried plainly. Yet it is touching to see with what fidelity the poorest creature tries to "bury her dead dacent." The destitute Irish woman begs for a few dollars for this sacred duty, and seldom in vain. It is a duty for the rich to put down ostentation in funerals, for it is an expense which comes heavily on those who have poverty added to grief.

In dressing the remains for the grave, those of a man are usually "clad in his habit as he lived." For a woman, tastes differ: a white robe and cap, not necessarily shroudlike, are decidedly unexceptionable. For young persons and children white cashmere robes and flowers are always most appropriate.

The late cardinal, whose splendid obsequies and whose regal "lying in state" were in keeping with his high rank and the gorgeous ceremonial of his Church, was strongly opposed to the profuse use of flowers at funerals, and requested that none be sent to deck his lifeless clay. He was a modest and humble man, and always on the right side in these things; therefore let his advice prevail. A few flowers placed in the dead hand, perhaps a simple wreath, but not those unmeaning memorials which have become to real mourners such sad perversities of good taste, such a misuse of flowers. Let those who can afford to send such things devote the money to the use of poor mothers who cannot afford to buy a coffin for a dead child or a coat for a living one.

In the course of a month after a death all friends of the deceased are expected to leave cards on the survivors, and it is discretionary whether these be written on or not. These cards should be carefully preserved, that, when the mourner is ready to return to the world, they may be properly acknowledged.

CHAPTER XXIII

LETTERS OF CONDOLENCE.

Probably no branch of the epistolary art has ever given to friendly hearts so much perplexity as that which has to do with writing to friends in affliction. It is delightful to sit down and wish anybody joy; to overflow with congratulatory phrases over a favorable bit of news; to say how glad you are that your friend is engaged or married, or has inherited a fortune, has written a successful book, or has painted an immortal picture. Joy opens the closet of language, and the gems of expression are easily found; but the fountain of feeling being chilled by the uncongenial atmosphere of grief, by the sudden horror of death, or the more terrible breath of dishonor or shame, or even by the cold blast of undeserved misfortune, leaves the individual sympathizer in a mood of perplexity and of sadness which is of itself a most discouraging frame of mind for the inditing of a letter.

And yet we sympathize with our friend: we desire to tell him so. We want to say, "My friend, your grief is my grief; nothing can hurt you that does not hurt me. I cannot, of course, enter into all your feelings, but to stand by and see you hurt, and remain unmoved myself, is impossible." All this we wish to say; but how shall we say it that our words may not hurt him a great deal more than he is hurt already? How shall we lay our hand so tenderly on that sore spot that we may not inflict a fresh wound? How can we say to a mother who bends over a fresh grave, that we regret the loss she has sustained in the death of her child? Can language measure the depth, the height, the immensity, the bitterness of that grief? What shall we say that is not trite and commonplace--even unfeeling? Shall we be pagan, and say that "whom the gods love die young," or Christian, and remark that "God does not willingly afflict the children of men?" She has thought of that, she has heard it, alas! often before--but too often, as she thinks now.

Shall we tell her what she has lost--how good, how loving, how brave, how admirable was the spirit which has just left the flesh? Alas! how well she knows that! How her tears well up as she remembers the silent fortitude, the heroic patience under the pain that was to kill! Shall we quote ancient philosophers and modern poets? They have all dwelt at greater or less length upon death and the grave. Or shall we say, in simple and unpremeditated words, the thoughts which fill our own minds?

The person who has to write this letter may be a ready writer, who finds fit expression at the point of his pen, and who overflows with the language of consolation--such a one needs no advice; but to the hundreds who do need help we would say that the simplest expressions are the best. A distant friend, upon one of these occasions, wrote a letter as brief as brief might be, but of its kind altogether perfect. It ran thus: "I have heard of your great grief, and I send you a simple pressure of the hand." Coming from a gay and volatile person, it had for the mourner great consolation; pious quotations, and even the commonplaces of condolence, would have seemed forced. Undoubtedly those persons do us great good, or they wish to, who tell us to be resigned-- that we have deserved this affliction; that we suffer now, but that our present sufferings are nothing to what our future sufferings shall be; that we are only entering the portals of agony, and that every day will reveal to us the magnitude of our loss. Such is the formula which certain persons use, under the title of "letters of condolence." It is the wine mixed with gall which they gave our Lord to drink; and as He refused it, so may we. There are, no doubt, persons of a gloomy and a religious temperament combined who delight in such phrases; who quote the least consolatory of the texts of Scripture; who roll our grief as a sweet morsel under their tongues; who really envy the position of chief mourner as one of great dignity and considerable consequence; who consider crape and bombazine as a sort of royal mantle conferring distinction. There are many such people in the world. Dickens and Anthony Trollope have put them into novels--solemn and ridiculous Malvolios; they exist in nature, in literature, and in art. It adds a new terror to death when we reflect that such persons will not fail to make it the occasion of letter-writing.

But those who write to us strongly and cheerfully, who do not dwell so much on our grief as on our remaining duties--they are the people who help us. To advise a mourner to go out into the sun, to resume his work, to help the poor, and, above all, to carry on the efforts, to emulate the virtues of the deceased--this is comfort. It is a very dear and consoling thing to a bereaved friend to hear the excellence of the departed extolled, to read and re-read all of the precious testimony which is borne by outsiders to the saintly life ended--and there are few so hard-hearted as not to find something good to say of the dead: it is the impulse of human nature; it underlies all our philosophy and our religion; it is the "stretching out of a hand," and it comforts the afflicted. But what shall we say to those on whom disgrace has laid its heavy, defiling hand? Is it well to write to them at all? Shall we not be mistaken for those who prowl like jackals round a grave, and will not our motives be misunderstood? Is not sympathy sometimes malice in disguise? Does not the phrase "I am so sorry for you!" sometimes sound like "I am so glad for myself?" Undoubtedly it does; but a sincere friend should not be restrained, through fear that his motive may be mistaken, from saying that he wishes to bear some part of the burden. Let him show that the unhappy man is in his thoughts, that he would like to help, that he would be glad to see him, or take him out, or send him a book, or at least write him a letter. Such a wish as this will hurt no one.

Philosophy--some quaint and dry bit of old Seneca, or modern Rochefoucauld--has often helped a struggling heart when disgrace, deserved or undeserved, has placed the soul in gyves of iron. Sympathetic persons, of narrow minds and imperfect education, often have the gift of being able to say most consolatory things. Irish servants, for instance, rarely hurt the feelings of a mourner. They burst out in the language of Nature, and, if it is sometimes grotesque, it is almost always comforting. It is the educated and conscientious person who finds the writing of a letter of condolence difficult.

Perhaps much of our dread of death is the result of a false education, and the wearing of black may after all be a mistake. At the moment when we need bright colors, fresh flowers, sunshine, and beauty, we hide ourselves behind crape veils and make our garments heavy with ashes; but as it is conventional it is in one way a protection, and is therefore proper. No one feels like varying the expressions of a grief which has the Anglo-Saxon seriousness in it, the Scandinavian melancholy of a people from whom Nature hides herself behind a curtain of night. To the sunny and graceful Greek the road of the dead was the Via Felice; it was the happy way, the gate of flowers; the tombs were furnished as the houses were, with images of the beloved, and the veriest trifles which the deceased had loved. One wonders, as the tomb of a child is opened on the road out of Tanagra, near Athens, and the toys and hobby-horse and little shoes are found therein, if, after all, that father and mother were not wiser than we who, like Constance, "stuff out his vacant garments with his form." Is there not something quite unenlightened in the persistence with which we connect death with gloom?

Our correspondents often ask us when a letter of condolence should be written? As soon as possible. Do not be afraid to intrude on any grief, It is generally a welcome distraction; to even the most morbid mourner, to read a letter; and those who are So stunned by grief as not to be able to write or to read will always have some willing soul near them who will read and answer for them.

The afflicted, however, should never be expected to answer letters, They can and should receive the kindest and the most prompt that their friends can indite, Often a phrase on which the writer has built no hope may be the airy-bridge over which the sorrowing soul returns slowly and blindly to peace and resignation. Who would miss the chance, be it one in ten thousand, of building such a bridge? Those who have suffered and been strong, those whom we love and respect, those who have the honest faith in human nature which enables them to read aright the riddle of this strange world, those who by faith walk over burning ploughshares and dread no evil, those are the people who write the best letters of condolence. They do not dwell on our grief, or exaggerate it, although they are evidently writing to us with a lump in the throat and a tear in the eye--they do not say so, but we feel it. They tell us of the certain influence of time, which will change our present grief into our future joy. They say a few beautiful words of the friend whom we have lost, recount their own loss in him in a few fitting words of earnest sympathy which may carry consolation, if only by the wish of the writer. They beg of us to be patient. God has brought life and immortality to light through death, and to those whom "he has thought worthy to endure," this thought may ever form the basis of a letter of condolence.

"Give me," said the dying Herder, "a great thought, that I may console myself with that." It is a present of no mean value, a great thought; and if every letter of condolence could bear with it one broad phrase of honest sympathy it would be a blessed instrumentality for carrying patience and resignation, peace and comfort, into those dark places where the sufferer is eating his heart out with grief, or where Rachel "weeps for her children, and will not be comforted, because they are not."

CHAPTER XXIV

CHAPERONS AND THEIR DUTIES.

It is strange that the Americans, so prone to imitate British customs, have been slow to adopt that law of English society which pronounces a chaperon an indispensable adjunct of every unmarried young woman.

The readers of "Little Dorrit" will recall the exceedingly witty sketch of Mrs. General, who taught her young ladies to form their mouths into a lady-like pattern by saying "papa, potatoes, prunes, and prism." Dickens knew very little of society, and cared very little for its laws, and his ladies and gentlemen were pronounced in England to be as great failures as his Little Nells and Dick Swivellers were successes; but he recognized the universality of chaperons. His portrait of Mrs. General (the first luxury which Mr. Dorrit allowed himself after inheriting his fortune) shows how universal is the necessity of a chaperon in English society, and on the Continent, to the proper introduction of young ladies, and how entirely their "style" depends upon their chaperon. Of course Dickens made her funny, of course he made her ridiculous, but he put her there. An American novelist would not have thought it worth mentioning, nor would an American papa with two motherless daughters have thought it necessary, if he travelled with them, to have a chaperon for his daughters.

Of course, a mother is the natural chaperon of her daughters, and if she understand her duties and the usages of society there is nothing further to be said. But the trouble is that many American mothers are exceedingly careless on this point. We need not point to the wonderful Mrs. Miller--Daisy's mother--in Henry James, Jr.'s, photograph of a large class of American matrons--a woman who loved her daughter, knew how to take care of her when she was ill, but did not know in the least how to take care of her when she was well; who allowed her to go about with young men alone, to "get engaged," if so she pleased, and who, arriving at a party after her daughter had appeared, rather apologized for coming at all. All this is notoriously true, and comes of our crude civilization. It is the transition state. Until we learn better, we must expect to be laughed at on the Pincian Hill, and we must expect English novelists to paint pictures of us which we resent, and French dramatists to write plays in which we see ourselves held up as savages.

Europeans have been in the habit of taking care of young girls, as if they were the precious porcelain of human clay. The American mamma treats her beautiful daughter as if she were a very common piece of delft indeed, and as if she could drift down the stream of life, knocking all other vessels to pieces, but escaping injury to herself.

Owing to the very remarkable and strong sense of propriety which American women innately possess--their truly healthy love of virtue, the absence of any morbid suspicion of wrong--this rule has worked better than any one would have dared hope. Owing, also, to the exceptionally respectful and chivalrous nature of American men, it has been possible for a young lady to travel unattended from Maine to Georgia, or anywhere within the new geographical limits of our social growth. Mr. Howells founded a romance upon this principle, that American women do not need a chaperon. Yet we must remember that all the black sheep are not killed yet, and we must also remember that propriety must be more attended to as we cease to be a young and primitive nation, and as we enter the lists of the rich, cultivated, luxurious people of the earth.

Little as we may care for the opinion of foreigners we do not wish our young ladies to appear in their eyes in a false attitude, and one of the first necessities of a proper attitude, one of the first demands of a polished society, is the presence of a chaperon. She should be a lady old enough to be the mother of her charge, and of unexceptionable manner. She must know society thoroughly herself, and respect its laws. She should be above the suspicion of reproach in character, and devoted to her work. In England there are hundreds of widows of half-pay officers--well-born, well-trained, well-educated women--who can be hired for money, as was Mrs. General, to play this part. There is no such class in America, but there is almost always a lady who will gladly perform the task of chaperoning motherless girls without remuneration.

It is not considered proper in England for a widowed father to place an unmarried daughter at the head of his house without the companionship of a resident chaperon, and there are grave objections to its being done here. We have all known instances where such liberty has been very bad for young girls, and where it has led to great scandals which the presence of a chaperon would have averted.

The duties of a chaperon are very hard and unremitting, and sometimes very disagreeable. She must accompany her young lady everywhere; she must sit in the parlor when she receives gentlemen; she must go with her to the skating-rink, the ball, the party, the races, the dinners, and especially to theatre parties; she must preside at the table, and act the part of a mother, so far as she can; she must watch the characters of the men who approach her charge, and endeavor to save the inexperienced girl from the dangers of a bad marriage, if possible. To perform this feat, and not to degenerate into a Spanish duenna, a dragon, or a Mrs. General--who was simply a fool--is a very difficult task.

No doubt a vivacious American girl, with all her inherited hatred of authority, is a troublesome charge. All young people are rebels. They dislike being watched and guarded. They have no idea what Hesperidean fruit they are, and they object to the dragon decidedly.

But a wise, well-tempered woman can manage the situation. If she have tact, a chaperon will add very much to the happiness of her young charge. She will see that the proper men are introduced; that her young lady is provided with a partner for the german; that she is asked to nice places; that she goes well dressed and properly accompanied; that she gives the return ball herself in handsome style.

"I owe," said a wealthy widower in New York, whose daughters all made remarkably happy marriages--"I owe all their happiness to Mrs. Constant, whom I was so fortunate as to secure as their chaperon. She knew society (which I did not), as if it were in her pocket. She knew exactly what girls ought to do, and she was so agreeable herself that they never disliked having her with them. She was very rigid, too, and would not let them stay late at balls; but they loved and respected her so much that they never rebelled, and now they love her as if she were really their mother."

A woman of elegant manners and of charming character, who will submit to the slavery--for it is little less--of being a chaperon, is hard to find; yet every motherless family should try to secure such a person. In travelling in Europe, an accomplished chaperon can do more for young girls than any amount of fortune. She has the thing they want--that is, knowledge. With her they can go everywhere--to picture-galleries, theatres, public and private balls, and into society, if they wish it. It is "etiquette" to have a chaperon, and it is the greatest violation of it not to have one.

If a woman is protected by the armor of work, she can dispense with a chaperon. The young artist goes about her copying unquestioned, but in society, with its different laws, she must be under the care of an older woman than herself.

A chaperon is indispensable to an engaged girl. The mother, or some lady friend, should always accompany a young one on her journeys to the various places of amusement and to the watering-places.

Nothing is more vulgar in the eyes of our modern society than for an engaged couple to travel together or to go to the theatre unaccompanied, as was the primitive custom. This will, we know, shock many Americans, and be called a "foolish following of foreign fashions." But it is true; and, if it were only for the "looks of the thing," it is more decent, more elegant, and more correct for the young couple to be accompanied by a chaperon until married. Society allows an engaged girl to drive with her _fianc‚_ in an open carriage, but it does not approve of his taking her in a close carriage to an evening party.

There are non-resident chaperons who are most popular and most useful. Thus, one mamma or elderly lady may chaperon a number of young ladies to a dinner, or a drive on a coach, a sail down the bay, or a ball at West Point. This lady looks after all her young charges, and attends to their propriety and their happiness. She is the guardian angel, for the moment, of their conduct. It is a care which young men always admire and respect--this of a kind, well-bred chaperon, who does not allow the youthful spirits of her charges to run away with them.

The chaperon, if an intelligent woman, and with the sort of social talent which a chaperon ought to have, is the best friend of a family of shy girls. She brings them forward, and places them in a position in which they can enjoy society; for there is a great deal of tact required in a large city to make a retiring girl enjoy herself. Society demands a certain amount of handling, which only the social expert understands. To this the chaperon should be equal. There are some women who have a social talent which is simply Napoleonic. They manage it as a great general does his corps de bataille.

Again, there are bad chaperons. A flirtatious married woman who is thinking of herself only, and who takes young girls about merely to enable herself to lead a gay life (and the world is full of such women), is worse than no chaperon at all. She is not a protection to the young lady, and she disgusts the honorable men who would like to approach her charge. A very young chaperon, bent on pleasure, who undertakes to make respectable the coaching party, but who has no dignity of character to impress upon it, is a very poor one. Many of the most flagrant violations of propriety, in what is called the fashionable set, have arisen from this choice of young chaperons, which is a mere begging of the question, and no chaperonage at all.

Too much champagne is drunk, too late hours are kept, silly stories are circulated, and appearances are disregarded by these gay girls and their young chaperons; and yet they dislike very much to see themselves afterwards held up to ridicule in the pages of a magazine by an Englishman, whose every sentiment of propriety, both educated and innate, has been shocked by their conduct.

A young Frenchman who visited America a few years ago formed the worst judgment of American women because he met one alone at an artist's studio. He misinterpreted the profoundly sacred and corrective influences of art. It had not occurred to the lady that if she went to see a picture she would be suspected of wishing to see the artist. Still, the fact that such a mistake could be made should render ladies careful of even the appearance of evil.

A chaperon should in her turn remember that she must not open a letter, She must not exercise an unwise surveillance. She must not suspect her charge. All that sort of Spanish espionage is always outwitted. The most successful chaperons are those who love their young charges, respect them, try to be in every way what the mother would have been. Of course, all relations of this sort are open to many drawbacks on both sides, but it is not impossible that it may be an agreeable relation, if both parties exercise a little tact.

In selecting a chaperon for a young charge, let parents or guardians be very particular as to the past history of the lady. If she has ever been talked about, ever suffered the bad reputation of flirt or coquette, do not think of placing her in that position. Clubs have long memories, and the fate of more than one young heiress has been imperilled by an injudicious choice of a chaperon. If any woman should have a spotless record and admirable character it should be the chaperon. It will tell against her charge if she have not. Certain needy women who have been ladies, and who precariously attach to society through their families, are always seeking for some young heiress. These women are very poor chaperons, and should be avoided.

This business of chaperonage is a point which demands attention on the part of careless American mothers. No mother should be oblivious of her duty in this respect. It does not imply that she doubts her daughter's honor or truth, or that she thinks she needs watching, but it is proper and respectable and necessary that she should appear by her daughter's side in society. The world is full of traps. It is impossible to be too careful of the reputation of a young lady, and it improves the tone of society vastly if an elegant and respectable woman of middle age accompanies every young party. It goes far to silence the ceaseless clatter of gossip; it is the antidote to scandal; it makes the air clearer; and, above all, it improves the character, the manners, and elevates the minds of the young people who are so happy as to enjoy the society and to feel the authority of a cultivated, wise, and good chaperon.

CHAPTER XXV

ETIQUETTE FOR ELDERLY GIRLS.

A brisk correspondent writes to us that she finds our restrictions as to the etiquette which single women should follow somewhat embarrassing. Being now thirty-five, and at the head of her father's house, with no intention of ever marrying, she asks if she requires a chaperon; if it is necessary that she should observe the severe self-denial of not entering an artist's studio without a guardian angel; if she must never allow a gentleman to pay for her theatre tickets; if she must, in short, assume a matron's place in the world, and never enjoy a matron's freedom.

From her letter we can but believe that this young lady of thirty-five is a very attractive person, and that she does "not look her age." Still, as she is at the head of her father's house, etiquette does yield a point and allows her to judge for herself as to the proprieties which must bend to her. Of course with every year of a woman's life after twenty-five she becomes less and less the subject of chaperonage. For one thing, she is better able to judge of the world and its temptations; in the second place, a certain air which may not be less winning, but which is certainly more mature, has replaced the wild grace of a giddy girlhood. She has, with the assumption of years, taken on a dignity which, in its way, is fully the compensation for some lost bloom. Many people prefer it.

But we must say here that she is not yet, in European opinion, emancipated from that guardianship which society dispenses with for the youngest widow. She must have a "companion" if she is a rich woman; and if she is a poor one she must join some party of friends when she travels. She can travel abroad with her maid, but in Paris and other Continental cities a woman still young-looking had better not do this. She is not safe from insult nor from injurious suspicion if she signs herself "Miss" Smith, and is without her mother, an elderly friend, a companion, or party.

In America a woman can go anywhere and do almost anything without fear of insult. But in Europe, where the custom of chaperonage is so universal, she must be more circumspect.

As to visiting an artist's studio alone, there is in art itself an ennobling and purifying influence which should be a protection. But we must not forget that saucy book by Maurice Sand, in which its author says that the first thing he observed in America was that women (even respectable ones) went alone to artists' studios. It would seem wiser, therefore, that a lady, though thirty-five, should be attended in her visits to studios by a friend or companion. This simple expedient "silences envious tongues," and avoids even the remotest appearance of evil.

In the matter of paying for tickets, if a lady of thirty-five wishes to allow a gentleman to pay for her admission to picture-galleries and theatres she has an indisputable right to do so. But we are not fighting for a right, only defining a law of etiquette, when we say that it is not generally allowed in the best society, abroad or here. In the case of young girls it is quite unallowable, but in the case of a lady of thirty-five it may be permitted as a sort of _camaraderie_, as one college friend may pay for another. The point is, however, a delicate one. Men, in the freedom of their clubs, recount to each other the clever expedients which many women of society use to extort from them boxes for the opera and suppers at Delmonico's. A woman should remember that it may sometimes be very inconvenient to young men who are invited by her to go to concerts and theatres to pay for these pleasures. Many a poor fellow who has become a defaulter has to thank for it the lady who first asked him to take her to Delmonico's to supper. He was ashamed to tell her that he was poor, and he stole that he might not seem a churl.

Another phase of the subject is that a lady in permitting a gentleman to expend money for her pleasures assumes an obligation to him which time and chance may render oppressive.

With an old friend, however, one whose claim to friendship is well established, the conditions are changed. In his case there can be no question of obligation, and a woman may accept unhesitatingly any of those small attentions and kindnesses which friendly feeling may prompt him to offer to her.

Travelling alone with a gentleman escort was at one time allowed in the West. A Kentucky woman of that historic period, "before the war," would not have questioned the propriety of it, and a Western man of to-day still has the desire to pay everything, everywhere, "for a lady."

The increase in the population of the Western States and the growth of a wealthy and fashionable society in the large towns have greatly modified this spirit of unwise chivalry, and such customs are passing away even on the frontier. Mr. Howells's novel, "The Lady of the Aroostook," has acquainted American readers with the unkind criticism to which a young lady who travels in Europe without a chaperon is subjected, and we believe that there are few mammas who would desire to see their daughters in the position of Miss Lydia Blood.

"An old maid," as our correspondent playfully calls herself, may do almost anything without violating etiquette, if she consents to become a chaperon, and takes with her a younger person. Thus an aunt and niece can travel far and wide; the position of an elder sister is always dignified; the youthful head of a house has a right to assert herself--she must do it--therefore etiquette bows to her (as "nice customs courtesy to great kings").

There is very much in the appearance of a woman. It is a part of the injustice of nature that some people look coquettish who are not so. Bad taste in dress, a high color, a natural flow of spirits, or a loud laugh have often caused a very good woman to be misinterpreted. Such a woman should be able to sit in judgment upon herself; and remembering that in a great city, at a crowded theatre, or at a watering-place, judgments must be hasty and superficial, she should tone down her natural exuberance, and take with her a female companion who is of a different type from herself. Calm and cold Puritanical people may not be more respectable than the fresh-colored and laughing "old maids" of thirty-five, but they look more so, and in this world women must consult appearances. An elderly girl must ever think how she looks. A woman who at a watering-place dresses conspicuously, wears a peignoir to breakfast, dyes her hair, or looks as if she did, ties a white blond veil over her locks and sits on a hotel piazza, showing her feet, may be the best, the most cultivated woman in the house, but a superficial observer will not think so. In the mind of every passer-by will lurk the feeling that she lacks the first grace of womanhood, modesty--and in the criticism of a crowd there is strength. A man passing such a person, and contrasting her with modestly dressed and unobtrusive ladies, would naturally form an unfavorable opinion of her; and were she alone, and her name entered on the books of the house as "Miss" Smith, he would not be too severe if he thought her decidedly eccentric, and certainly "bad style." If, however, "Miss" Smith were very plain and quiet, and dressed simply and in good taste, or if she sat on the sands looking at the sea, or attended an invalid or a younger friend, then Miss Smith might be as independent as she pleased: she would suffer from no injurious comments. Even the foreigner, who does not believe in the eccentricities of the English _mees_, would have no word to say against her. A good-looking elderly girl might say, "There is, then, a premium on ugliness;" but that we do not mean. Handsome women can conduct themselves so well that the breath of reproach need not and does not touch them, and ugly women may and do sometimes gain an undeserved reproach.

There are some people who are born with what we call, for want of a better name, a pinchbeck air. Their jewellery never looks like real gold; their manner is always bad; they have the faux air of fashion, not the real one. Such people, especially if single, receive many a snub which they do not deserve, and to a woman of this style a companion is almost necessary. Fortunately there are almost always two women who can join forces in travelling or in living together, and the independence of such a couple is delightful. We have repeated testimony in English literature of the pleasant lives of the Ladies of Llangollen, of the lives of Miss Jewsbury and Lady Morgan, and of the model sisters Berry. In our own country we have almost abolished the idea that a companion is necessary for women of talent who are physicians or artists or musicians; but to those who are still in the trammels of private life we can say that the presence of a companion need not destroy their liberty, and it may add very much to their respectability and happiness. There is, no doubt, a great pleasure in the added freedom of life which comes to an elderly girl. "I can wear a velvet dress now," said an exceedingly handsome woman on her thirtieth birthday. In England an unmarried woman of fifty is called "_Mrs._," if she prefers that title. So many delightful women are late in loving, so many are true to some buried love, so many are "elderly girls" from choice, and from no neglect of the stronger sex, that to them should be accorded all the respect which is supposed to accrue naturally to the married. "It takes a very superior woman to be an old maid," said Miss Sedgwick.

CHAPTER XXVI

NEW-YEAR'S CALLS.

"Le jour de l'an," as the French call the first day of January, is indeed the principal day of the year to those who still keep up the custom of calling and receiving calls. But in New York it is a custom which is in danger of falling into desuetude, owing to the size of the city and the growth of its population. There are, however, other towns and "much country" (as the Indians say) outside of New York, and there are still hospitable boards at which the happy and the light-hearted, the gay and the thoughtful, may meet and exchange wishes for a happy New-Year.

To those who receive calls we would say that it is well, if possible, to have every arrangement made two or three days before New-Year's, as the visiting begins early--sometimes at eleven o'clock--if the caller means to make a goodly day. A lady should have her hair dressed for the day when she rises, and if her dress be not too elaborate she should put it on then, so that she may be in the drawing-room when the first visitor arrives. In regard to the question of dress, we should say that for elderly ladies black satin or velvet, or any of the combination dresses so fashionable now, with handsome lace, and Swedish gloves of pearl or tan color (not white kids; these are decidedly rococo, and not in fashion), would be appropriate. A black satin, well made, and trimmed with beaded _passementerie_, is perhaps the handsomest dress that could be worn by any one. Brocaded silk, plain gros grain, anything that a lady would wear at the wedding reception of her daughter is suitable, although a plain dress is in better taste.

For young ladies nothing is so pretty as a dress of light cashmere and silk, cut high at the throat. These dresses, in the very pretty tints worn now, are extremely becoming, warm-looking, and appropriate for a reception, when the door is being often opened. White dresses of thick silk or cashmere, trimmed around the neck with lace, are also very elegant. In all countries young married women are allowed to be as magnificent as a picture of Marie de Medici, and can wear on New-Year's day rose-colored and white brocaded silks, with pearl trimmings, or plain ciel blue, or prawn-colored silk over white, or embossed velvet, or what they please, so that the dress is cut high, and has sleeves to the elbow. Each lady should have near her an ermine cloak, or a small camel's-hair shawl in case of draughts. It is not good taste to wear low-necked or sleeveless dresses during the day-time. They are worn by brides on their wedding-day sometimes, but at receptions or on New-Year's day scarcely ever.

While much magnificence is permissible, still a plain black or dark silk dress, if well made, with fresh ruffles at neck and wrists, is quite as proper as anything else, and men generally admire it more. But where a lady has several daughters to receive with her, she should study the effect of her rooms, and dress the young ladies in prettily contrasting colors. This may be cheaply done by using the soft, fine merinoes, which are to be had in all the delicate and fashionable shades. Short dresses of this material are much used; but now that imported dresses are so easily obtained, a mother with many daughters to dress cannot do better than buy costumes similar to those worn by economical French ladies on their _jour de l'an_. One article of dress is de rigeur. With whatever style of costume, gloves must be worn.

A lady who expects to have many calls, and who wishes to offer refreshments, should have hot tea and coffee and a bowl of punch on a convenient table; or, better still, a silver kettle filled with bouillon standing in the hall, so that a gentleman coming in or going out can take a cup of it unsolicited. If she lives in an English basement house, this table can be in the lower dining-room. In a house three rooms deep the table and all the refreshments can be in the usual dining-room or in the upper back-parlor. Of course, her "grand spread" can be as gorgeous as she pleases. Hot oysters, salads, boned turkey, quail, and hot terrapin, with wines _ad libitum_, are offered by the wealthy; but this is a difficult table to keep in order when ten men call at one o'clock, and forty at four, and none between. The best table is one which is furnished with boned turkey, jellied tongues, and sandwiches, and similar dishes, with cake and fruit as decorative additions. The modern and admirable adjunct of a spirit-lamp under a teakettle keeps the bouillon, tea, and coffee always hot, and these, with the teacups necessary to serve them, should be on a small table at one side. A maid-servant, neatly dressed, should be in constant attendance on this table, and a man-servant or two will be needed to attend the door and to wait at table.

The man at the door should have a silver tray or card-basket in which to receive the cards of visitors. If a gentleman is not known to the lady of the house, he sends in his card; otherwise he leaves it with the waiter, who deposits it in some receptacle where it should be kept until the lady has leisure to examine the cards of all her guests. If a gentleman is calling on a young lady, and is not known to the hostess, he sends in his card to the former, who presents him to the hostess and to all the ladies present. If the room is full, an introduction to the hostess only is necessary. If the room is comparatively empty, it is much kinder to present a gentleman to each lady, as it tends to make conversation general. As a guest is about to depart, he should be invited to take some refreshment, and be conducted towards the dining-room for that purpose. This hospitality should never be urged, as man is a creature who dines, and is seldom willing to allow a luncheon to spoil a dinner. In a country neighborhood, however, or after a long walk, a visitor is almost always glad to break his fast and enjoy a pickled oyster, a sandwich, or a cup of bouillon.

The etiquette of New-Year's day commands, peremptorily, that a gentleman shall not be asked to take off his overcoat nor to be relieved of his hat. He will probably prefer to wear his overcoat, and to carry his hat in his hand during his brief visit. If he wishes to dispose of either, he will do so in the hall; but on that point he is a free moral agent, and it is not a part of the duty of a hostess to suggest what he shall do with his clothes.

Many letters come to us asking "What subjects should be talked about during a New-Year's call." Alas! we can only suggest the weather and the good wishes appropriate to the season. The conversation is apt to be fragmentary. One good mot was evolved a few years ago, when roads were snowy and ways were foul. A gentleman complained of the mud and the dirty streets. "Yes," said the lady, "but it is very bright overhead." "I am not going that way," replied the gentleman.

A gentleman should not be urged to stay when he calls. He has generally but five minutes in which to express a desire that old and pleasant memories shall be continued, that new and cordial friendships shall be formed, and after that compliment, which every wall-bred man pays a lady, "How remarkably well you are looking to-day!" he wishes to be off.

In France it is the custom for a gentleman to wear a dress-coat when calling on a great public functionary on New-Year's day, but it is not so in America. Here he should, wear the dress in which he would make an ordinary morning visit. When he enters a room he should not remove his gloves, nor should he say, as he greets his hostess, "Excuse my glove." He should take her gloved hand in his and give it a cordial pressure, according to our pleasant American fashion. When leaving, the ceremony is very brief--simply, "Good-morning," or "Good-evening," as the case may be.

It is proper for gentlemen to call late in the evening of New-Year's day, and calls are made during the ensuing evenings by people who are otherwise occupied in the daytime. If the family are at dinner, or the lady is fatigued with the day's duties, the servant must say at the door that Mrs._____ desires to be excused. He must not present the card to her, and thus oblige her to send to her visitor a message which might be taken as a personal affront. But she must have the servant instructed to refuse all at certain hours; then none can be offended.

Many ladies in New York are no longer "at home" on New-Year's day; and when this is the case a basket is tied at the door to receive cards. They do this because so many gentlemen have given up the custom of calling that it seems to be dying out, and all their preparations for a reception become a hollow mockery. How many weary women have sat with novel in hand and luncheon-table spread, waiting for the callers who did not come! The practice of sending cards to gentlemen, stating that a lady would be at home on New-Year's day, has also very much gone out of fashion, owing to the fact that gentlemen frequently did not respond to them.

It is, however, proper that a married lady returning to her home after a long absence in Europe, or one who has changed her residence, or who is living at a hotel or boarding-house (or who is visiting friends), should send her card to those gentlemen whom she wishes to receive. It must be remembered that many gentlemen, generally those no longer young, still like very much the fashion of visiting on New-Year's day, and go to see as many people as they can in a brief winter's sunshine. These gentlemen deplore the basket at the door, and the decadence of the old custom in New York. Family friends and old friends, those whom they never see at any other time, are to be seen--or they should be seen, so these old friends think--on New-Year's day.

A personal call is more agreeable than a card. Let a gentleman call, and in person, or take no notice of the day. So say the most trustworthy authorities, and their opinion has an excellent foundation of common-sense.

Could we only go back to the old Dutch town where the custom started, where all animosities were healed, all offences forgotten, on New-Year's day, when the good Dutch housewives made their own cakes and spiced the loving-cup, when all the women stayed at home to receive and all the men called, what a different New-Year's day we should enjoy in New York. Nowadays, two or three visitors arrive before the hostess is ready to receive them; then one comes after she has appeared, vanishes, and she remains alone for two hours; then forty come. She remembers none of their names, and has no rational or profitable conversation with any of them.

But for the abusers of New-Year's day, the pretenders who, with no right to call, come in under cover of the general hospitality of the season--the bores, who on this day, as on all days, are only tiresome--we have no salve, no patent cure. A hostess must receive them with the utmost suavity, and be as amiable and agreeable as possible.

New-Year's day is a very brilliant one at Washington. All the world calls on the President at twelve o'clock; the diplomats in full dress, officers of the army and navy in full uniform, and the other people grandly attired. Later, the heads of departments, cabinet ministers, judges, etc., receive the lesser lights of society.

In Paris the same etiquette is observed, and every clerk calls on his chief.

In a small city or village etiquette manages itself, and ladies have only to let it be known that they will be at home, with hot coffee and oysters, to receive the most agreeable kind of callers--those who come because they really wish to pay a visit, to express goodwill, and to ask for that expression of friendship which our reserved Anglo-Saxon natures are so prone to withhold.

In New York a few years ago the temperance people made a great onslaught on ladies who invited young men to drink on New-Year's day. It was said to lead to much disorder and intemperance; and so, from fear of causing one's brother to sin, many have banished the familiar punch-bowl. In a number of well-known houses in New York no luncheon is offered, and a cup of bouillon or coffee and a sandwich is the usual refreshment in the richest and most stylish houses. It will be seen, therefore, that it is a day of largest liberty. There are no longer any sumptuary laws; but it is impossible to say why ladies of the highest fashion in New York do not still make it a gala-day. The multiplicity of other entertainments, the unseen yet all-powerful influence of fashion, these things mould the world insensibly. Yet in a thousand homes, thousands of cordial hands will be extended on the great First of January, and to all of them we wish a Happy New Year.

CHAPTER XXVII

MATINES AND SOIRES.

A matin‚e in America means an afternoon performance at the theatre of a play or opera. In Europe it has a wider significance, any social gathering before dinner in France being called a _matin‚e_, as any party after dinner is called a _soir‚e_.

The improper application of another foreign word was strikingly manifested in the old fashion of calling the President's evening receptions levees. The term "levee," as originally used, meant literally a king's getting up. When he arose, and while he was dressing, such of his courtiers as were privileged to approach him at this hour gathered in an anteroom-waiting to assist at his toilet, to wish him good morning, or perhaps prefer a request. In time this morning gathering grew to be an important court ceremonial, and some one ignorant of the meaning of the word named President Jackson's evening receptions "the President's levees." So with the word _matin‚e_. First used to indicate a day reception at court, it has now grown to mean a day performance at a theatre. Sometimes a lady, bolder than her neighbors, issues an invitation for "a _matin‚e dansante_," or "a _matin‚e musicale_," but this descriptive style is not common.

There are many advantages in a morning party. It affords to ladies who do not go to evening receptions the pleasure of meeting informally, and is also a well-chosen occasion for introducing a new pianist or singer.

For a busy woman of fashion nothing can be more conveniently timed than a _matin‚e_, which begins at two and ends at four or half past. It does not interfere with a five-o'clock tea or a drive in the park, nor unfit her for a dinner or an evening entertainment. Two o'clock is also a very good hour for a large and informal general lunch, if a lady wishes to avoid the expense, formality, and trouble of a "sit-down" lunch.

While the busy ladies can go to a _matin‚e_, the busy gentleman cannot; and as men of leisure in America are few, a morning entertainment at a theatre or in society is almost always an assemblage of women. To avoid this inequality of sex, many ladies have their _matin‚e_s on some one of the national holidays--Washington's Birthday, Thanksgiving, or Decoration-day. On these occasions a _matin‚e_, even in busy New York, is well attended by gentlemen.

When, as sometimes happens, a prince, a duke, an archbishop, an author of celebrity, a Tom Hughes, a Lord Houghton, a Dean Stanley, or some descendant of our French allies at Yorktown, comes on a visit to our country, one of the most satisfactory forms of entertainment that we can offer to him is a morning reception. At an informal _matin‚e_ we may bring to meet him such authors, artists, clergymen, lawyers, editors, statesmen, rich and public-spirited citizens, and beautiful and cultivated women of society, as we may be fortunate enough to know.

The primary business of society is to bring together the various elements of which it is made up--its strongest motive should be to lighten up the momentous business of life by an easy and friendly intercourse and interchange of ideas.

But if we hope to bring about us men of mind and distinction, our object must be not only to be amused but to amuse.

To persuade those elderly men who are maintaining the great American name at its present high place in the Pantheon of nations to spend a couple of hours at a _matin‚e_, we must offer some tempting bait as an equivalent. A lady who entertained Dean Stanley said that she particularly enjoyed her own _matin‚e_ given for him, because through his name she for the first time induced the distinguished clergy of New York to come to her house.

Such men are not tempted by the frivolities of a fashionable social life that lives by its vanity, its excitement, its rivalry and flirtation. Not that all fashionable society is open to such reproach, but its tendency is to lightness and emptiness; and we rarely find really valuable men who seek it. Therefore a lady who would make her house attractive to the best society must offer it something higher than that to which we may give the generic title fashion. Dress, music, dancing, supper, are delightful accessories-they are ornaments and stimulants, not requisites. For a good society we need men and women who are "good company," as they say in England--men and women who can talk. Nor is the advantage all on one side. The free play of brain, taste, and feeling is a most important refreshment to a man who works hard, whether in the pulpit or in Wall Street, in the editorial chair or at the dull grind of authorship. The painter should wash his brushes and strive for some intercourse of abiding value with those whose lives differ from his own. The woman who works should also look upon the divertissements of society as needed recreation, fruitful, may be, of the best culture.

On the other hand, no society is perfect without the elements of beauty, grace, taste, refinement, and luxury. We must bring all these varied potentialities together if we would have a real and living social life. For that brilliant thing that we call society is a finely-woven fabric of threads of different sizes and colors of contrasting shades. It is not intrigue, or the display of wealth, or morbid excitement that must bind together this social fabric, but sympathy, that pleasant thing which refines and refreshes, and "knits up the ravelled sleeve of care," and leaves us strong for the battle of life.

And in no modern form of entertainment can we better produce this finer atmosphere, this desirable sympathy between the world of fashion and that of thought, than by _matin‚es_, when given under favorable circumstances. To be sure, if we gave one every day it would be necessary, as we have said, to dispense with a large number of gentlemen; but the occasional matinee is apt to catch some very good specimens of the _genus homo_, and sometimes the best specimens. It is proper to offer a very substantial _buffet, as people rarely lunch before two o'clock, and will be glad of a bit of bird, a cup of bouillon, or a leaf of salad. It is much better to offer such an entertainment earlier than the five-o'clock tea; at which hour people are saving their appetites for dinner.

A _soir‚e_ is a far more difficult affair, and calls for more subtle treatment. It should be, not a ball, but what was formerly called an "evening party." It need not exclude dancing, but dancing is not its excuse for being. It means a very bright _conversazione_, or a reading, or a _musicale_, with pretty evening dress (not necessarily ball dress), a supper, and early hours. Such, at least, was its early significance abroad.

It has this advantage in New York, that it does attract gentlemen. They like very much the easy-going, early-houred _soir‚e_. We mean, of course, those gentlemen who no longer care for balls, and if aristocracy is to be desired, "the rule of the best," at American entertainments, all aspirants for social distinction should try to propitiate those men who are being driven from the ballroom by the insolence and pretension of the lower elements of fashionable society. In Europe, the very qualities which make a man great in the senate, the field, or the chamber of commerce, give him a corresponding eminence in the social world. Many a gray-mustached veteran in Paris leads the german. A senator of France aspires to appear well in the boudoir. With these men social dexterity is a requisite to success, and is cultivated as a duty. It is not so here, for the two great factors of success in America, wealth and learning, do not always fit a man for society, and still less does society adapt itself to them.

The _soir‚e_, if properly conducted, is an entertainment to which can be brought the best elements of our society: elderly, thoughtful, and educated men. A lady should not, however, in the matter of dress, confound a _soir‚e_ with a concert or reception. It is the height of impropriety to wear a bonnet to the former, as has been done in New York, to the everlasting disgust of the hostess.

When a hostess takes the pains to issue an invitation to a _soir‚e_ a week or a fortnight before it is to occur, she should be repaid by the careful dressing and early arrival of her guests. It may be proper to go to an evening reception in a bonnet, but never to a _soir‚e_ or an evening party.

There is no doubt that wealth has become a power in American society, and that we are in danger of feeling that, if we have not wealth, we can give neither _matin‚es_ nor _soir‚es_; but this is a mistake. Of course the possession of wealth is most desirable. Money is power, and when it is well earned it is a noble power; but it does not command all those advantages which are the very essence of social intercourse. It may pamper the appetite, but it does not always feed the mind. There is still a corner left for those that have but little money. A lady can give a matinee or a soiree in a small house with very little expenditure of money; and if she has the inspiration of the model entertainer, every one whom she honors with an invitation will flock to her small and unpretending menage. There are numbers of people in our large cities who can give great balls, dazzle the eye, confuse and delight the senses, drown us in a sensuous luxury; but how few there are who, in a back street and in a humble house, light that lamp by which the Misses Berry summoned to their little parlor the cleverest and best people!

The elegant, the unpretentious, the quiet _soir‚e_ to which the woman of fashion shall welcome the _litt‚rateur_ and the artist, the aristocrat who is at the top of the social tree and the millionaire who reached his culmination yesterday, would seem to be that Ultima Thule for which all people have been sighing ever since society was first thought of. There are some Americans who are so foolish as to affect the pride of the hereditary aristocracies, and who have some fancied traditional standard by which they think to keep their blue blood pure. A good old grandfather who had talent, or patriotism, or broad views of statesmanship, "who did the state some service," is a relation to be proud of, but his descendants should take care to show, by some more personal excellence than that of a social exclusiveness, their appreciation of his honesty and ability. What our grandfathers were, a thousand new-comers now are. They made their way--the early American men--untrammelled by class restraints; they arrived at wealth and distinction and social eminence by their own merits; they toiled for the money which buys for their grandsons purple and fine linen. And could they see the pure and perfect snob who now sometimes bears the name which they left so unsullied, they would be exasperated and ashamed, Of course, a certain exclusiveness must mark all our _matin‚es_ and _soir‚es_; they would fail of the chief element of diversion if we invited everybody. Let us, therefore, make sure of the aesthetic and intellectual, the sympathetic and the genial, and sift out the pretentious and the impure. The rogues, the pretenders, the adventurers who push into the penetralia of our social circles are many, and it is to the exclusion of such that a hostess should devote herself.

It is said that all women are born aristocrats, and it is sometimes said in the same tone with which the speaker afterwards adds that all women are born fools. A woman, from her finer sense, enjoys luxury, fine clothing, gorgeous houses, and all the refinements that money can buy; but even the most idle and luxurious and foolish woman desires that higher luxury which art and intelligence and delicate appreciation can alone bring; the two are necessary to each other. To a hostess the difficulty of entertaining in such a manner as to unite in a perfect whole the financiers, the philosophers, the cultivated foreigners, the people of fashion, the sympathetic and the artistic is very great; but a hostess may bring about the most genial democracy at the modern _matin‚e_ or _soir‚e_ if she manages properly.

CHAPTER XXVIII

AFTERNOON TEA.

The five-o'clock tea began in England, and is continued there, as a needed refreshment after a day's hunting, driving, or out-of-door exercise, before dressing for dinner--that very late dinner of English fashion. It is believed that the Princess of Wales set the fashion by receiving in her boudoir at some countryhouse in a very becoming "tea gown," which every lady knows to be the most luxurious change from the tight riding-habit or carriage-dress. Her friends came in, by her gracious invitation, to her sanctum, between five and seven, to take a cup of tea with her. The London belles were glad to have an excuse for a new entertainment, and gradually it grew to be a fashion, at which people talked so fast and so loud as to suggest the noise of a drum--a kettledrum, the most rattling of all drums. Then it was remembered that an old-fashioned entertainment was called a drum, and the tea suggested kettle, and the name fitted the circumstances. In England, where economy is so much the fashion, it was finally pronounced an excellent excuse for the suppression of expense, and it came over to New York during a calamitous period, just after "Black Friday." Ladies were glad to assemble their friends at an hour convenient for their servants, and with an entertainment inexpensive to their husbands. So a kettledrum became the most fashionable of entertainments. People after a while forgot its origin, and gave a splendid ball by daylight, with every luxury of the season, and called it tea at five o'clock, or else paid off all their social obligations by one sweeping "tea," which cost them nothing but the lighting of the gas and the hiring of an additional waiter. They became so popular that they defeated themselves, and ladies had to encompass five, six, sometimes nine teas of an afternoon, and the whole of a cold Saturday--the favorite day for teas--was spent in a carriage trying to accomplish the impossible.

The only "afternoon tea" that should prevail in a large city like New York is that given by one or two ladies who are usually "at home" at five o'clock every afternoon. If there is a well-known house where the hostess has the firmness and the hospitality to be always seated in front of her blazing urn at that hour, she is sure of a crowd of gentlemen visitors, who come from down-town glad of a cup of tea and a chat and rest between work and dinner. The sight of a pretty girl making tea is always dear to the masculine heart. Many of our young lawyers, brokers, and gay men of the hunt like a cup of hot tea at five o'clock. The mistake was in the perversion of the idea, the making it the occasion for the official presentation of a daughter, or the excuse for other and more elaborate entertainments. So, although many a house is opened this winter at the same convenient hour, and with perhaps only the bouillon and tea-kettle and bit of cake or sandwich (for really no one wants more refreshment than this before dinner and after luncheon), the name of these afternoon entertainments has been by mutual consent dropped, and we no longer see the word "kettledrum" or "afternoon tea" on a card, but simply the date and the hour.

There is a great deal to be said in this matter on both sides. The primal idea was a good one. To have a gathering of people without the universal oyster was at first a great relief. The people who had not money for grand "spreads" were enabled to show to their more opulent neighbors that they too had the spirit of hospitality. All who have spent a winter in Rome remember the frugal entertainment offered, so that an artist with no plentiful purse could still ask a prince to visit him. It became the reproach of Americans that they alone were ashamed to be poor, and that, unless they could offer an expensive supper, dinner, or luncheon, they could not ask their friends to come to see them. Then, again, the doctors, it was urged, had discovered that tea was the best stimulant for the athlete and for the brain-worker. English "breakfast tea" kept nobody awake, and was the most delightful of appetizers. The cup of tea and a sandwich taken at five o'clock spoiled no one's dinner. The ladies of the house began these entertainments, modestly receiving in plain but pretty dresses; their guests were asked to come in walking-dress. But soon the other side of the story began to tell. A lady going in velvet and furs into a heated room, where gas added its discomfort to the subterranean fires of a furnace, drank her hot cup of tea, and came out to take a dreadful cold. Her walking dress was manifestly a dress inappropriate to a kettledrum. Then the hostess and the guests both became more dressy, the afternoon tea lost its primitive character and became a gay reception. Then, again, the nerves! The doctors condemn even the afternoon cup of tea, and declare that it is the foundation of much of the nervous prostration, the sleeplessness, and the nameless misery of our overexcited and careworn oxygen driven people. We are overworked, no doubt. We are an overcivilized set, particularly in the large cities, and every one must decide for himself or herself if "tea" is not an insidious enemy. That the introduction of an informal and healthful and inexpensive way of entertaining is a grand desideratum no one can fail to observe and allow. But with the growth of an idea the tea blossomed into a supper, and the little knot into a crowd, and of course the name became a misnomer.

The ideal entertainment would seem to be a gathering between four and seven, which is thoroughly understood to be a large gas-lighted party, which a lady enters properly dressed for a hot room, having a cloak which she can throw off in the hall, and where she can make her call long or short, as she pleases, and can find a cup of hot bouillon if she is cold, or tea if she prefers it, or a more elaborate lunch if her hostess pleases; and this ideal entertainment is not afternoon tea; it is a reception. It is well enough indicated by the date on the card, and does not need a name.

The abuse of the "afternoon tea" was that it took the place of other entertainments. It has almost ruined the early evening party, which was so pleasant a feature of the past. People who could well afford to give breakfasts, lunches, dinners, and balls, where men and women could meet each other, and talk, and know each other well, did not give them; they gave an afternoon tea.

It may be because we have no "leisure class" that we do not give breakfasts. In all our Anglomania it is strange that we have not copied that plain, informal thing, an English breakfast, such as Sydney Smith was wont to give. Mr. Webster writes home in 1839: "In England the rule of politeness is to be quiet, act naturally, take no airs, and make no bustle. This perfect politeness has cost a great deal of drill." He delighted in the English breakfasts, where he met "Boz," Tom Moore, Wordsworth, Rogers (who never gave any entertainment but breakfasts). We are all workers in America, yet we might have an occasional breakfast-party. Dinners and ladies' lunches we know very well how to give, and there are plenty of them. Perhaps the only objection to them is their oversumptuousness. The ideal dinners of the past at Washington, with the old Virginia hospitality, the oysters, terrapin, wild turkeys, venison, served by negro cooks and waiters, the hostess keeping the idea of agreeability before her, instead of caring principally for her china, her glass, and her table-cloth. These gave way long ago in New York to the greater luxury of the prosperous city, and if there was any loss, it was in the conversation. New York women have been forced into a life of overdressing, dancing, visiting, shopping, gaining the accomplishments, and showing them off, and leading the life of society at its height; the men have been overwhelmingly engaged in commerce, and later in Wall Street. No wonder that four o'clock was an hour at which both paused, and called for a "cup of tea."

Nor because the name has passed away-temporarily, perhaps--will the fashion pass. People will still gather around the steaming urn. Young ladies find it a very pretty recreation to make the tea-table attractive with the floral arrangements, the basket of cake, the sandwiches, the silver tea-caddy, the alcohol lamp burning under the silver or copper kettle, the padded "cozy" to keep the tea warm, the long table around which young gentlemen and young ladies can sit, while mamma, patient American mamma--receives the elder people in the parlor.

It is no longer the elderly lady who presides at the tea-kettle; the tabbies do not make or drink the teas; the younger pussies are the queens of four-o'clock tea. It is whispered that it is a convenient alias for flirtation, or something even sweeter--that many engagements have been made at "four-o'clock teas."

Certainly it is a very good opportunity for showing one's tea-cups. The handsome china can be displayed at a four-o'clock tea, if it is not too large, to the best advantage. The very early assumption of a grand social entertainment under the name of "four-o'clock tea" rather blotted out one of the prettiest features of the English tea, that of the graceful garment the tea gown.

Tea gowns in France, under the _r‚gime_ of Worth, have become most luxurious garments. They are made of silk, satin, velvet, and lined with delicate surah. They are trimmed with real and imitation lace, and are of the most delicate shades of pink, blue, lavender, and pearl-color; cascades of lace extend down the front. In these, made loose to the figure, but still very elegant and most becoming, do the English princess, the duchess, and the Continental coroneted or royal dame, or the queen of fashion, receive their guests at afternoon tea. No wonder that in each bridal trousseau do we read of the wonderful "tea gowns." In America ladies have been in the habit of always receiving in the tight-fitting and elegant combinations of silk, surah, brocade, velvet, and cashmere which fill the wardrobe of modern fashion. The dresses of delicate cashmere, so becoming to young girls, are always very much patronized for afternoon tea. Indeed, the young lady dressed for afternoon tea was dressed for dinner. In this, as our American afternoon teas have been managed, the American young lady was right, for it is not _convenable_, according to European ideas, to wear a loose flowing robe of the tea-gown pattern out of one's bedroom or boudoir. It has been done by ignorant people at a watering-place, but it never looks well. It is really an undress, although lace and satin may be used in its composition. A plain, high, and tight-fitting g‚arment is much the more elegant dress for the afternoon teas as we give them.

Call it what you will--reception, kettledrum, afternoon tea, or something without a name--we have unconsciously, imitating a very different sort of informal gathering, gained an easy and a sensible entertainment in society, from four to seven; which seems to address itself to all kinds of needs. We are prone in America (so foreigners say) to overdo a thing--perhaps, also, to underdo it. Be that as it may, all agree with Lord Houghton, who laughed at the phrase, that we know how "to have a good time."

CHAPTER XXIX

CAUDLE AND CHRISTENING CUPS AND CEREMONIES.

We are asked by many young mammas as to the meaning of the phrase "caudle parties."

Formerly the persons who called to congratulate the happy possessor of a new boy or girl were offered mulled wine and plum-cake. Some early chronicler thinks that the two got mixed, and that caudle was the result.

Certain it is that a most delicious beverage, a kind of oatmeal gruel, boiled "two days," with raisins and spices, and fine old Madeira (some say rum) added, makes a dish fit to set before a king, and is offered now to the callers on a young mamma. The old English custom was to have this beverage served three days after the arrival of the little stranger. The caudle-cups, preserved in many an old family, are now eagerly sought after as curiosities; they have two handles, so they could be passed from one to another. They were handed down as heirlooms when these candle parties were more fashionable than they have been, until a recent date. Now there is a decided idea of reintroducing them. In those days the newly-made papa also entertained his friends with a stag party, when bachelors and also Benedicks were invited to eat buttered toast, which was sugared and spread in a mighty punch-bowl, over which boiling-hot beer was poured. After the punch-bowl was emptied, each guest placed a piece of money in the bowl for the nurse. Strong ale was brewed, and a pipe of wine laid by to be drunk on the majority of the child.

This greasy mess is fortunately now extinct, but the caudle, a really delicious dish or drink, is the fashion again. It is generally offered when master or miss is about six weeks old, and mamma receives her friends in a tea gown or some pretty convalescent wrap, very often made of velvet or plush cut in the form of a belted-in jacket and skirt, or in one long princesse robe, elaborately trimmed with cascades of lace down the front. The baby is, of course, shown, but not much handled. Some parents have the christening and the caudle party together, but of this, it is said, the Church does not approve.

The selection of god-parents is always a delicate task. It is a very great compliment, of course, to ask any one to stand in this relation, highly regarded in England, but not so much thought of here. Formerly there were always two godfathers and two godmothers, generally chosen from friends and relations, who were expected to watch over the religious education of the young child, and to see that he was, in due time, confirmed. In all old countries this relationship lasts through life; kindly help and counsel being given to the child by the godfather--even to adoption in many instances--should the parents die. But in our new country, with the absence of an established Church, and with our belief in the power of every man to take care of himself, this beautiful relationship has been neglected. We are glad to see by our letters that it is being renewed, and that people are thinking more of these time-honored connections.

After a birth, friends and acquaintances should call and send in their cards, or send them by their servants, with kind inquiries. When the mother is ready to see her friends, she should, if she wishes, signify that time by sending out cards for a "caudle party." But let her be rather deliberate about this unless she has a mother, or aunt, or sister to take all the trouble for her.

The godfather and godmother generally give some little present; a silver cup or porringer, knife, fork, and spoon, silver basin, coral tooth-cutter, or coral and bells, were the former gifts; but, nowadays, we hear of one wealthy godfather who left a check for $100,000 in the baby's cradle; and it is not unusual for those who can do so to make some very valuable investment for the child, particularly if he bears the name of the godfather.

Some people--indeed, most people--take their children to church to be baptized, and then give a luncheon at home afterwards to which all are invited, especially the officiating clergyman and his wife, as well as the sponsors. The presents should be given at this time. Old-fashioned people give the baby some salt and an egg for good luck, and are particular that he should be carried up-stairs before he is carried down, and that when he goes out first he shall be carried to the house of some near and dear relative.

Confirmation is in the Episcopal Church the sequel to baptism; and in France this is a beautiful and very important ceremony. In the month of May the streets are filled with white doves--young girls, all in muslin and lace veils, going with their mothers or chaperons to be confirmed. Here the duty of the godfather or the godmother comes in; and if a child is an orphan, or has careless or irreligious parents, the Church holds the godparent responsible that these children be brought to the bishop to be confirmed.

Notices of confirmation to be held are always given out in the various churches some weeks prior to the event; and persons desirous of being admitted to the rite are requested to make known their wish and to give their names to their clergyman. Classes are formed, and instruction and preparation given during the weeks preceding the day which the bishop has appointed. In England a noble English lady is as much concerned for her goddaughter through all this important period as she is for her daughter. In France the obligation is also considered sacred. We have known of a lady who made the journey from Montpellier to Paris--although she could scarcely afford the expense--to attend the confirmation of her goddaughter, although the young girl had a father and mother.

It is a ceremony well worth seeing, either in England or France. The girls walk in long processions through the streets; the dress uniformly of white with long veils. Youths follow in black suits, black ties, and gloves; they enter one aisle of the church, the girls the other. When the time arrives for the laying on of hands, the girls go first, two and two; they give their card or certificate into the hands of the bishop's chaplain, who stands near to receive them. The candidates kneel before the bishop, who lays his hands severally on their heads.

Of course persons not belonging to the Episcopal Church do not observe this rite. But as a belief in baptism is almost universal, there is no reason why the godfather and godmother should not be chosen and adhered to. We always name our children, or we are apt to, for some dear friend; and we would all gladly believe that such a friendship, begun at the altar when he is being consecrated to a Christian life, may go with him and be a help to the dear little man. In our belligerent independence and our freedom from creeds and cant we have thrown away too much, and can afford to reassert our belief in and respect for a few old customs.

Royalty has always been a respecter of these powers. King Edward VI. and his sisters were each baptized when only three days old, and the ceremony, which lasted between two and three days, took place at night, by torch-light. The child was carried under a canopy, preceded by gentlemen bearing in state the sponsors' gifts, and attended by a flourish of trumpets.

At a modern caudle party the invitations are sent out a week in advance, and read thus:

"Mr. and Mrs. Brown request the pleasure of your company on Tuesday afternoon, at three o'clock. 18 West Kent Street. Caudle. 'No presents are expected.'"

For the honor of being a godfather one receives a note in the first person, asking the friend to assume that kindly office, and also mentioning the fact that the name will be so and so. If the baby is named for the godfather, a very handsome present is usually made; if not, the godfather or godmother still sends some little token of regard. This, however, is entirely a matter of fancy. No one is obliged to give a present, of course.

The baby at his christening is shown off in a splendid robe, very much belaced and embroidered, and it is to be feared that it is a day of disturbance for him. Babies should not be too much excited; a quiet and humdrum existence, a not too showy nurse, and regular hours are conducive to a good constitution for these delicate visitors. The gay dresses and jingling ornaments of the Roman nurses are now denounced by the foreign doctors as being too exciting to the little eyes that are looking out on a new world. They are very pretty and picturesque, and many a travelling mamma goes into a large outlay for these bright colors and for the peasant jewelry. The practice of making a child ride backward in a push-wagon is also sternly denounced by modern physicians.

Fashionable mammas who give caudle parties should remember that in our harsh climate maternity is beset by much feebleness as to nerves in both mother and child; therefore a long seclusion in the nursery is advised before the dangerous period of entertaining one's friends begins. Let the caudle party wait, and the christening be done quietly in one's own bedroom, if the infant is feeble. Show off the young stranger at a later date: an ounce of prevention is worth a pound of cure.

CHAPTER XXX

THE MODERN DINNER-TABLE.

The appointments of the modern dinner-table strikingly indicate that growth of luxury of which the immediate past has been so fruitful. Up to twenty years ago a dinner, even in the house of a merchant prince, was a plain affair. There was a white tablecloth of double damask; there were large, handsome napkins; there was a rich service of solid silver, and perhaps some good china. Flowers, if used at all, were not in profusion; and as for glasses, only a few of plain white, or perhaps a green or a red one for claret or hock, were placed at the side of the plate.

Of course there were variations and exceptions to this rule, but they were few and far between. One man, or often one maid-servant, waited at the table; and, as a protection for the table-cloth, mats were used, implying the fear that the dish brought from the top of the kitchen-range, if set down, would leave a spot or stain. All was on a simple or economical plan. The grand dinners were served by caterers, who sent their men to wait at them, which led to the remark, often laughed at as showing English stupidity, made by the Marquis of Hartington when he visited New York at the time of our war. As he looked at old Peter Van Dyck and his colored assistants, whom he had seen at every house at which he had dined, he remarked, "How much all your servants resemble each other in America!" It was really an unintentional sarcasm, but it might well have suggested to our nouveaux riches the propriety of having their own trained servants to do the work of their houses instead of these outside men. A degree of elegance which we have not as a nation even yet attained is that of having a well-trained corps of domestic servants.

A mistress of a house should be capable of teaching her servants the method of laying a table and attending it, if she has to take, as we commonly must, the uneducated Irishman from his native bogs as a house-servant. If she employs the accomplished and well-recommended foreign servant, he is too apt to disarrange her establishment by disparaging the scale on which it is conducted, and to engender a spirit of discontent in her household. Servants of a very high class, who can assume the entire management of affairs, are only possible to people of great wealth, and they become tyrants, and wholly detestable to the master and mistress after a short slavery. One New York butler lately refused to wash dishes, telling his mistress that it would ruin his finger-nails. But this man was a consummate servant, who laid the table and attended it, with an ease and grace that gave his mistress that pleasant feeling of certainty that all would go well, which is the most comfortable of all feelings to a hostess, and without which dinner-giving is annoyance beyond all words.

The arrangement of a dinner-table and the waiting upon it are the most important of all the duties of a servant or servants, and any betrayal of ignorance, any nervousness or noise, any accident, are to be deplored, showing as they do want of experience and lack of training.

No one wishes to invite his friends to be uncomfortable. Those dreadful dinners which Thackeray describes, at which people with small incomes tried to rival those of large means, will forever remain in the minds of his readers as among the most painful of all revelations of sham. We should be real first, and ornamental afterwards.

In a wealthy family a butler and two footmen are employed, and it is their duty to work together in harmony, the butler having control. The two footmen lay the table, the butler looking on to see that it is properly done.

The butler takes care of the wine, and stands behind his mistress's chair. Where only one man is employed, the whole duty devolves upon him, and he has generally the assistance of the parlor-maid. Where there is only a maid-servant, the mistress of the house must see that all necessary arrangements are made.

The introduction of the extension-table into our long, narrow dining-rooms has led to the expulsion of the pretty round-table, which is of all others the most cheerful. The extension-table, however, is almost inevitable, and one of the ordinary size, with two leaves added, will seat twelve people. The public caterers say that every additional leaf gives room for four more people, but the hostess, in order to avoid crowding, would be wise if she tested this with her dining-room chairs. New York dinner-parties are often crowded, sixteen being sometimes asked when the table will only accommodate fourteen. This is a mistake, as heat and crowding should be avoided. In country houses, or in Philadelphia, Boston, Washington, and other cities where the dining-rooms are ordinarily larger than those in a New York house, the danger of crowding, of heat, and want of ventilation, is more easily avoided; but in a gas-lighted, furnace-heated room in New York the sufferings of the diners-out are sometimes terrible.

The arrangements for the dinner, whether the party be ten or twenty, should be the same. Much has been said about the number to be invited, and there is an old saw that one should not invite "fewer than the Graces nor more than the Muses." This partiality to uneven numbers refers to the difficulty of seating a party of eight, in which case, if the host and hostess take the head and foot of the table, two gentlemen and two ladies will come together. But the number of the Graces being three, no worse number than that could be selected for a dinner-party; and nine would be equally uncomfortable at an extension-table, as it would be necessary to seat three on one side and four on the other. Ten is a good number for a small dinner, and easy to manage. One servant can wait on ten people, and do it well, if well-trained. Twenty-four people often sit down at a modern dinner-table, and are well served by a butler and two men, though some luxurious dinner-givers have a man behind each chair. This, however, is ostentation.

A lady, if she issue invitations for a dinner of ten or twenty, should do so a fortnight in advance, and should have her cards engraved thus:

Mr. and Mrs. James Norman request the pleasure of Mr. and Mrs. John Brown's company at dinner on Thursday, February eighth, at seven o'clock.

These engraved forms, on note-paper, filled up with the necessary time and date, are very convenient and elegant, and should be answered by the fortunate recipient immediately, in the most formal manner, and the engagement should be scrupulously kept if accepted. If the subsequent illness or death of relatives, or any other cause, renders this impossible, the hostess should be immediately notified.

A gentleman is never invited without his wife, nor a lady without her husband, unless great intimacy exists between the parties, and the sudden need of another guest makes the request imperative.

The usual hour for dinner-parties in America is seven o'clock; but whatever the hour, the guests should take care to be punctual to the minute. In the hall the gentleman should find a card with his name, and that of the lady whom he is to take in, written on it, and also a small _boutonniere_, which he places in his button-hole. On entering the drawing-room the lady goes first, not taking her husband's arm. If the gentleman is not acquainted with the lady whom he is to take in to dinner, he asks his hostess to present him to her, and he endeavors to place himself on an agreeeble footing with her before they enter the dining-room.

When the last guest has arrived, dinner is ready, and the butler makes his announcement. The host leads the way, with the lady to whom the dinner is given, and the hostess follows last, with the gentleman whom she wishes to honor.

The people who enter a modern dining-room find a picture before them, which is the result of painstaking thought, taste, and experience, and, like all works of art, worthy of study.

The first thought of the observer is, "What a splendid bit of color!" The open-work, white tablecloth lies on a red ground, and above it rests a mat of red velvet, embroidered with peacock's feathers and gold lace. Above this stands a large silver salver or oblong tray, lined with reflecting glass, on which

Dresden swan and silver lilies seem floating in a veritable lake. In the middle of this long tray stands a lofty vase of silver or crystal, with flowers and fruit cunningly disposed in it, and around it are placed tropical vines. At each of the four corners of the table stand four ruby glass flagons set in gold, standards of beautiful and rare designs. Cups or silver-gilt vases, with centres of cut glass, hold the bonbons and smaller fruits. Four candelabra hold up red wax-candles with red shades, and flat, glass troughs, filled with flowers, stand opposite each place, grouped in a floral pattern.

At each place, as the servant draws back the chair, the guest sees a bewildering number of glass goblets, wine and champagne glasses, several forks, knives, and spoons, and a majolica plate holding oysters on the half shell, with a bit of lemon in the centre of the plate. The napkin, deftly folded, holds a dinner-roll, which the guest immediately removes. The servants then, seeing all the guests seated, pass red and black pepper, in silver pepper-pots, on a silver tray. A small, peculiarly-shaped fork is laid by each plate, at the right hand, for the oysters. Although some ladies now have all their forks laid on the left hand of the plate, this, however, is not usual. After the oysters are eaten, the plates are removed, and two kinds of soup are passed--a white and a brown soup.

During this part of the dinner the guest has time to look at the beautiful Queen Anne silver, the handsome lamps, if lamps are used (we may mention the fact that about twenty-six candles will well light a dinner of sixteen persons), and the various colors of lamp and candle shades. Then the beauty of the flowers, and, as the dinner goes on, the variety of the modern Dresden china, the Sevres, the Royal Worcester, and the old blue can be discussed and admired.

The service is _… la Russe_; that is, everything is handed by the servants. Nothing is seen on the table except the wines (and only a few of these), the bonbons, and the fruit. No greasy dishes are allowed. Each lady has a bouquet, possibly a painted reticule of silk filled with sugar-plums, and sometimes a pretty fan or ribbon with her name or monogram painted on it.

At his right hand each guest finds a goblet of elegantly-engraved glass for water, two of the broad, flat, flaring shape of the modern champagne glass (although some people are using the long vase-like glass of the past for champagne), a beautiful Bohemian green glass, apparently set with gems, for the hock, a ruby-red glass for the claret, two other large white claret or Burgundy glasses, and three wine-glasses of cut or engraved glass. Harlequin glasses, which give to the table the effect of a bed of tulips, are in fashion for those who delight in color and variety.

The hostess may prefer the modern napery, so exquisitely embroidered in gold thread, which affords an opportunity to show the family coat of arms, or the heraldic animals--the lion and the two-headed eagle and the griffin--intertwined in graceful shapes around the whole edge of the table and on the napkins.

As the dinner goes on the guest revels in unexpected surprises in the beauty of the plates, some of which look as if made of solid gold; and when the Roman punch is served it comes in the heart of a red, red rose, or in the bosom of a swan, or the cup of a lily, or the "right little, tight little" life-saying boat. Faience, china, glass, and ice are all pressed into the service of the Roman punch, and sometimes the prettiest dish of all is hewn out of ice.

We will try to see how all this picture is made, beginning at the laying of the table, the process of which we will explain in detail in the next chapter.

CHAPTER XXXI

LAYING THE DINNER-TABLE.

The table, after being drawn out to its proper length, should be covered with a cotton-flannel tablecloth--white, if the table-cover is the ordinary damask; red, if the open work table-cover is to be used. This broad cotton flannel can be bought for eighty cents a yard. The table-cloth, if of white damask, should be perfectly ironed, with one long fold down the middle, which must serve the butler for his mathematical centre. No one can be astray in using fine white damask. If a lady wishes to have the more rare Russian embroidery, the gold embroidered on the open-work table-cloth, she can do so, but let her not put any cloth on her table that will not wash. The mixed-up things trimmed with velvet or satin or ribbon, which are occasionally seen on vulgar tables, are detestable.

The butler then lays the red velvet carpet, or mat, or ornamental cover--whatever it may be called--down the centre of the table, to afford a relief of color to the _‚pergne_.

This is a mere fanciful adjunct, and may be used or not; but it has a very pretty effect over an openwork, white table-cloth, with the silver tray of the _‚pergne_ resting upon it. In many families there are silver _‚pergnes_ which are heirlooms. These are now valued for old association's sake; as are the silver candlesticks and silver compotiers. But where a family does not possess these table ornaments, a centre piece of glass is used. The flat basket of flowers, over which the guests could talk, has been discarded, and the ornaments of a dinner-table are apt to be high, including the lamps and candelabra which at present replace gas.

The table-cloth being laid, the centre and side ornaments placed, the butler sees that each footman has a clean towel on his arm, and then proceeds to unlock the plate chest and the glass closet. Measuring with his hand, from the edge of the table to the end of his middle finger, he places the first glass. This measurement is continued around the table, and secures a uniform line for the water goblet, and the claret, wine, hock, and champagne glasses, which are grouped about it. He then causes a plate to be put at each place, large enough to hold the majolica plate with the oysters, which will come later. One footman is detailed to fold the napkins, which should be large, thick, fine, and serviceable for this stage of the dinner. The napkins are not folded in any hotel device, but simply in a three-cornered pyramid that will stand holding the roll or bread. The knives, forks, and spoons, each of which is wiped by the footman with his clean towel, so that no dampness of his own hand shall mar their sparkling cleanliness, are then distributed. These should be all of silver; two knives, three forks, and a soup-spoon being the usual number laid at each plate.

Before each plate is placed a little salt-cellar, either of silver or china, in some fanciful shape. Tiny wheelbarrows are much used. A carafe holding water should be put on very late, and be fresh from the ice-chest.

Very thin glasses are now used for choice sherry and Madeira, and are not put on until the latter part of the dinner, as they may be broken.

Menu-holders or card-holders of china or silver are often placed before each plate, to hold the card on which the name of the guest is printed and the bill of fare from which he is to choose. These may be dispensed with, however, and the menu and name laid on each plate.

The butler now turns his attention to his sideboards and tables, from whence he is to draw his supplies. Many people make a most ostentatious display of plate and china on their sideboards, and if one has pretty things why not show them? The poorer and more modest have, on their sideboards, simply the things which will be needed. But there should be a row of large forks, a row of large knives, a row of small ones, a row of table-spoons, sauce-ladles, dessert- spoons, fish-slice and fork, a few tumblers, rows of claret, sherry, and Madeira glasses, and the reserve of dinner-plates.

On another table or sideboard should be placed the finger-bowls and glass dessert-plates, the smaller spoons and coffee cups and saucers. On the table nearest the door should be the carving-knives and the first dinner-plates to be used. Here the head footman or the butler divides the fish and carves the _piece de resistance_, the fillet of beef, the haunch of venison, the turkey, or the saddle of mutton. It is from this side-table that all the dinner should be served; if the dining-room is small, the table can be placed in the hall or adjacent pantry. As the fish is being served, the first footman should offer Chablis, or some kind of white wine; with the soup, sherry; with the roast, claret and champagne, each guest being asked if he will have dry or sweet champagne.

As the plates are removed they should not be kept in the dining- room, but sent to the kitchen immediately, a maid standing outside to receive them, so that no disorder of the dinner may reach the senses of the guests, nor even an unpleasant odor. As each plate is removed a fresh plate must be put in its place--generally a very beautiful piece of Sevres, decorated with a landscape, flowers, or faces.

Sparkling wines, hock and champagne, are not decanted, but are kept in ice-pails, and opened as required. On the sideboard is placed the wine decanted for Use, and poured out as needed; after the game has been handed, decanters of choice Madeira and port are placed before the host, who sends them round to his guests.

In England a very useful little piece of furniture, called a dinner- wagon, is in order. This is a series of open shelves, on which are placed the extra napkins or serviettes to be used; for in England the first heavy napkin is taken away, and a more delicate one brought with the Roman punch, with the game another, and with the ices still another. On this dinner-wagon are placed all the dessert- plates and the finger-glasses. On the plate which is to serve for the ice is a gold ice-spoon, and a silver dessert-knife and fork accompany the finger-bowl and glass plate. This dinner-wagon also holds the salad-bowl and spoon, of silver, the salad-plates, and the silver bread-basket, in which should be thin slices of brown bread- and-butter. A china dish in three compartments, with cheese and butter and biscuits to be passed with the salad, the extra sauces, the jellies for the meats, the relishes, the radishes and celery, the olives and the sifted sugar-all things needed as accessaries of the dinner-table-can be put on this dinner-wagon, or _‚tagere_, as it is called in France.

No table-spoons should be laid on the table, except those to be used for soup, as the style of serving _… la Russe_ precludes their being needed; and the extra spoons, cruets, and casters are put on the sideboard.

To wait on a large dinner-party the attendants average one to every three people, and when only a butler and one footman are kept, it is necessary to hire additional servants.

Previous to the announcement of the dinner, the footman places the soup-tureens and the soup-plates on the side-table. As soon as the oysters are eaten, and the plates removed, the butler begins with the soup, and sends it round by two footmen, one on each side, each carrying two plates. Each footman should approach the guests on the left, so that the right hand may be used for taking the plate. Half a ladleful of soup is quite enough to serve.

Some ladies never allow their butler to do anything but hand the wine, which he does at the right hand (not the left), asking each person if he will have Sauterne, dry or sweet champagne, claret, Burgundy, and so on. But really clever butlers serve the soup, carve, and pour out the wine as well. An inexperienced servant should never serve the wine; it must be done briskly and neatly, not explosively or carelessly. The overfilling of the glass should be avoided, and servants should be watched, to see that they give champagne only to those who wish it, and that they do not overfill glasses for ladies, who rarely drink anything.

A large plate-basket or two, for removing dishes and silver that have been used, are necessary, and should not be forgotten. The butler rings a bell which communicates with the kitchen when he requires anything, and after each _entr‚e_ or course he thus gives the signal to the cook to send up another.

Hot dinner-plates are prepared when the fish is removed, and on these hot plates the butler serves all the meats; the guests are also served with hot plates before the _entr‚es_, except   de foie gras_, for which a cold plate is necessary.

Some discretion should be shown by the servant who passes the _entr‚es_. A large table-spoon and fork should be placed on the dish, and the dish then held low, so that the guest may help himself easily, the servant standing at his left hand. He should always have a small napkin over his hand as he passes a dish. A napkin should also be wrapped around the champagne bottle, as it is often dripping with moisture from the ice-chest. It is the butler's duty to make the salad, which he should do about half an hour before dinner. There are now so many provocatives of appetite that it would seem as if we were all, after the manner of Heliogabalus, determined to eat and die. The best of these is the Roman punch, which, coming after the heavy roasts, prepares the palate and stomach for the canvas- back ducks or other game. Then comes the salad and cheese, then the ices and sweets, and then cheese savourie or cheese fondu. This is only toasted cheese, in a very elegant form, and is served in little silver shells, sometimes as early in the dinner as just after the oysters, but the favorite time is after the sweets.

The dessert is followed by the _liqueurs_, which should be poured into very small glasses, and handed by the butler on a small silver waiter. When the ices are removed, a dessert-plate of glass, with a finger-bowl, is placed before each person, with two glasses, one for sherry, the other for claret or Burgundy, and the grapes, peaches, pears, and other fruits are then passed. After the fruits go round, the sugar-plums and a little dried ginger--a very pleasant conserve --are passed before the coffee.

The hostess makes the sign for retiring, and the dinner breaks up. The gentlemen are left to wine and cigars, liqueurs and cognac, and the ladies retire to the drawing-room to chat and take their coffee.

In the selection of the floral decoration for the table the lady of the house has the final voice. Flowers which have a very heavy fragrance should not be used. That roses and pinks, violets and lilacs, are suitable, goes without saying, for they are always delightful; but the heavy tropical odors of jasmine, orange-blossom, hyacinth, and tuberose should be avoided. A very pretty decoration is obtained by using flowers of one color, such as Jacqueminot roses, or scarlet carnations, which, if placed in the gleaming crystal glass, produce a very brilliant and beautiful effect.

Flowers should not be put on the table until just before dinner is served, as they are apt to be wilted by the heat and the lights.

We have used the English term footman to indicate what is usually called a waiter in this country. A waiter in England is a hired hotel-hand, not a private servant.

Much taste and ingenuity are expended on the selection of favors for ladies, and these pretty fancies--_bonbonnieres_, painted ribbons and reticules, and fans covered with flowers--add greatly to the elegance and luxury of our modern dinner-table.

A less reasonable conceit is that of having toys--such as imitation musical instruments, crackers which make an unpleasant detonation, imitations of negro minstrels, balloons, flags, and pasteboard lobsters, toads, and insects-- presented to each lady. These articles are neither tasteful nor amusing, and have "no excuse for being" except that they afford an opportunity for the expenditure of more money.

CHAPTER XXXII

FAVORS AND BONBONNIERES.

Truly "the world is very young for its age." We are never too old to admire a pretty favor or a tasteful _bonbonniere_; and, looking back over the season, we remember, as among the most charming of the favors, those with flowers painted upon silken banners, with the owner's name intertwined. The technical difficulties of painting upon silk are somewhat conquered, one would think, in looking at the endless devices composed of satin and painted flowers on the lunch- tables. Little boxes covered with silk, in eight and six sided forms, with panels let in, on which are painted acorns and oak leaves, rosebuds or lilies, and always the name or the cipher of the recipient, are very pretty. The Easter-egg has long been a favorite offering in silk, satin, plush, and velvet, in covered, egg-shaped boxes containing bonbons; these, laid in a nest of gold and silver threads in a _cloisonn‚_ basket, afford a very pretty souvenir to carry home from a luncheon.

Menu-holders of delicate gilt-work are also added to the other favors. These pretty little things sometimes uphold a photograph, or a porcelain plate on which is painted the lady's name, and also a few flowers. The little porcelain cards are not larger than a visiting-card, and are often very artistic. The famous and familiar horseshoe, in silver or silver-gilt, holding up the menu-card, is another pretty favor, and a very nice one to carry home, as it becomes a penholder when it is put on the writing-table. Wire rests, shaped like those used for muskets in barracks yards, are also used for the name and menu-cards. Plateaus, shells, baskets, figurettes, vases holding flowers, dolphins, Tritons, swan, sea animals (in crockery), roses which open and disclose the sugarplums, sprays of coral, and gilt conch-shells, are all pretty, especially when filled with flowers.

Baskets in various styles are often seen. One tied with a broad ribbon at the side is very useful as a work-basket afterwards. Open-work baskets, lined with crimson or scarlet or pink or blue plush, with another lining of silver paper to protect the plums, are very tasteful. A very pretty basket is one hung between three gilt handles or poles, and filled with flowers or candies. Silvered and gilded beetles, or butterflies, fastened on the outside, have a fanciful effect.

Moss-covered trays holding dried grasses and straw, and piles of chocolates that suggest ammunition, are decorative and effective.

Wheelbarrows of tiny size for flowers are a favorite conceit. They are made of straw-work, entirely gilded, or painted black or brown, and picked out with gold; or perhaps pale green, with a bordering of brown. A very pretty one may be made of old cigarbox wood; on one side a monogram painted in red and gold, on the other a spray of autumn leaves. Carved-wood barrows fitted with tin inside may hold a growing plant--stephanotis, hyacinths, ferns, ivy, or any other hardy plant--and are very pleasing souvenirs.

The designs for reticules and _chƒtelaines_ are endless. At a very expensive luncheon, to which twenty-four ladies sat down, a silk reticule a foot square, filled with Maillard's confections and decorated with an exquisitely painted landscape effect, was presented to each guest. These lovely reticules may be any shape, and composed of almost any material. A very handsome style is an eight-sided, melon-shaped bag of black satin, with a decoration of bunches of scarlet flowers painted or embroidered. Silk braided with gold, brocade, and plush combined, and Turkish towelling with an _applique‚_ of brilliant color, are all suitable and effective.

In the winter a shaded satin muff, in which was hidden a _bonbonniere_, was the present that made glad the hearts of twenty- eight ladies. These are easily made in the house, and a plush muff with a bird's head is a favorite "favor."

A pair of bellows is a pretty and inexpensive bonbonniere. They can be bought at the confectioner's, and are more satisfactory than when made at home; but if one is ingenious, it is possible, with a little pasteboard, gilt paper, silk, and glue, to turn out a very pretty little knickknack of this kind. However, the French do these things so much better than we do that a lady giving a lunch-party had better buy all her favors at some wholesale place. There is a real economy in buying such articles at the wholesale stores, for the retail dealers double the price.

Bronze, iron, and glass are all pressed into the service, and occasionally we have at a lunch a whole military armament of cannon, muskets, swords, bronze helmets, whole suits of armor, tazza for jewellery, miniature cases, inkstands, and powder-boxes, all to hold a few sugar-plums.

At a christening party all the favors savor of the nursery--splendid cradles of flowers, a bassinet of brilliante trimmed with ribbons for a _bonbonniere_, powder-boxes, puffs, little socks filled with sugar instead of little feet, an infant's cloak standing on end (really over pasteboard), an infant's hood, and even the flannel shirt has been copied. Of course the baptismal dish and silver cup are easily imitated.

Perfumery is introduced in little cut-glass bottles, in leaden tubes like paint tubes, in perfumed artificial flowers, in sachets of powder, and in the handles of fans.

Boxes of satinwood, small wood covers for music and blotting cases, painted by hand, are rather pretty favors. The plain boxes and book covers can be bought and ornamented by the young artists of the family. Nothing is prettier than an owl sitting on an ivy vine for one of these. The owl, indeed, plays a very conspicuous part at the modern dinner-table and luncheon. His power of looking wise and being foolish at the same time fits him for modern society. He enters it as a pepper-caster, a feathered _bonbonniere_, a pickle- holder (in china), and is drawn, painted, and photographed in every style. A pun is made on his name: "Should owled acquaintance be forgot?" etc. He is a favorite in jewellery, and is often carved in jade. Indeed, the owl is having his day, having had the night always to himself.

The squirrel, the dog, "the frog that would a-wooing go," the white duck, the pig, and the mouse, are all represented in china, and in the various silks and gauzes of French taste, or in their native skins, or in any of the disguises that people may fancy. Bears with ragged staffs stand guard over a plate of modern faience, as they do over the gates of Warwick Castle. Cats mewing, catching mice, playing on the Jews-harp, elephants full of choicest confectionery, lions and tigers with chocolate insides, and even the marked face and long hair of Oscar Wilde, the last holding within its ample cranium caraway-seeds instead of brains, played their part as favors.

The green enamelled dragon-fly, grasshoppers and beetles, flies and wasps, moths and butterflies, bright-tinted mandarin ducks, peacocks, and ostriches, tortoises cut in pebbles or made of pasteboard, shrimps and crabs, do all coldly furnish forth the lunch-table as favors and bonbonnieres. Then come plaster or pasteboard gondolas, skiffs, wherries, steamships, and ferry-boats, all made with wondrous skill and freighted with caramels. Imitation rackets, battledoor and shuttlecock, hoops and sticks, castanets, cup and ball, tambourines, guitars, violins, hand-organs, banjos, and drums, all have their little day as fashionable favors.

Little statuettes of Kate Greenaway's quaint children now appear as favors, and are very charming. Nor is that "flexible curtain," the fan, left out. Those of paper, pretty but not expensive, are very common favors. But the opulent offer pretty satin fans painted with the recipient's monogram, or else a fan which will match flowers and dress. Fans of lace, and of tortoise-shell and carved ivory and sandal-wood, are sometimes presented, but they are too ostentatious. Let us say to the givers of feasts, be not too magnificent, but if you give a fan, give one that is good for something, not a thing which breaks with the "first fall."

A very pretty set of favors, called "fairies," are little groups of children painted on muslin, with a background of ribbon. The muslin is so thin that the children seem floating on air. The lady's name is also painted on the ribbon.

We find that favors for gentlemen, such as sunflowers, pin-cushions, small purses, scarf-pins, and sleeve-buttons, are more useful than those bestowed upon ladies, but not so ornamental.

Very pretty baskets, called huits (the baskets used by the vine- growers to carry earth for the roots of the vines), are made of straw ornamented with artificial flowers and grasses, and filled with bonbons.

Little Leghorn hats trimmed with pompons of muslin, blue, pink, or white, are filled with natural flowers and hung on the arm. These are a lovely variation.

Fruits--the apple, pear, orange, and plum, delightfully realistic-- are made of composition, and open to disclose most unexpected seeds.

At trowel, a knife, fork, and spoon, of artistically painted wood, and a pair of oars, all claim a passing notice as artistic novelties.

Bags of plush, and silk embroidered with daisies, are very handsome and expensive favors; heavily trimmed with lace, they cost four dollars apiece, but are sold a little cheaper by the dozen. Blue sashes, with flowers painted on paper (and attached to the sash a paper on which may be written the menu), cost eighteen dollars a dozen. A dish of snails, fearfully realistic, can be bought for one dollar a plate, fruits for eighteen dollars a dozen, and fans anywhere from twelve up to a hundred dollars a dozen.

A thousand dollars is not an unusual price for a luncheon, including flowers and favors, for eighteen to twenty-four guests. Indeed, a luncheon was given last winter for which the hostess offered a prize for copies in miniature of the musical instruments used in "Patience." They were furnished to her for three hundred dollars. The names of these now almost obsolete instruments were rappaka, tibia, archlute, tambour, kiffar, quinteme, rebel, tuckin, archviola, lyre, serpentine, chluy, viola da gamba, balalaika, gong, ravanastron, monochord, shopkar. The "archlute" is the mandolin. They represented all countries, and were delicate specimens of toy handiwork.

We have not entered into the vast field of glass, china, porcelain, _cloisonn‚_, Dresden, faience jugs, boxes, plates, bottles, and vases, which are all used as favors. Indeed, it would be impossible to describe half of the fancies which minister to modern extravagance. The bonbonniere can cost anything, from five to five hundred dollars; fifty dollars for a satin box filled with candy is not an uncommon price. Sometimes, when the box is of oxidized silver--a quaint copy of the antique from Benvenuto Cellini--this price is not too much; but when it is a thing which tarnishes in a month, it seems ridiculously extravagant.

We have seen very pretty and artistic cheap favors. Reticules made of bright cotton, or silk handkerchiefs with borders; cards painted by the artists of the family; palm-leaf fans covered with real flowers, or painted with imitation ones; sunflowers made of pasteboard, with portfolios behind them; pretty little parasols of flowers; Little Red Riding-hood, officiating as a receptacle for stray pennies; Japanese teapots, with the "cozy" made at home; little doyleys wrought with delightful designs from "Pretty Peggy," and numberless other graceful and charming trifles.

CHAPTER XXXIII

DINNER-TABLE NOVELTIES.

One would think that modern luxury had reached its ultimatum in the delicate refinements of dinner-giving, but each dinner-table reveals the fact that this is an inexhaustible subject. The floral world is capable of an infinity of surprises, and the last one is a cameo of flowers on a door, shaped like a four-leaved clover. The guests are thus assured of good-luck. The horseshoe having been so much used that it is now almost obsolete, except in jewelry, the clover-leaf has come in. A very beautiful dinner far up Fifth Avenue had this winter an entirely new idea, inasmuch as the flowers were put overhead. The delicate vine, resembling green asparagus in its fragility, was suspended from the chandelier to the four corners of the room, and on it were hung delicate roses, lilies-of-the-valley, pinks, and fragrant jasmine, which sent down their odors, and occasionally dropped themselves into a lady's lap. This is an exquisite bit of luxury.

Then the arrival, two months before Easter, of the fragrant, beautiful Easter lilies has added a magnificent and stately effect to the central bouquets. It has been found that the island of Bermuda is a great reservoir of these bulbs, which are sent up, like their unfragrant rivals the onions, by the barrelful. Even a piece of a bulb will produce from three to five lilies, so that these fine flowers are more cheap and plenty in January than usually in April. A dining-room, square in shape, hung with richly-embroidered, old- gold tapestry, with a round table set for twenty, with silver and glass and a great bunch of lilies and green ferns in the middle, and a "crazy quilt" of flowers over one's head, may well reproduce the sense of dreamland which modern luxury is trying to follow.

Truly we live in the days of Aladdin. Six weeks after the ground was broken in Secretary Whitney's garden in Washington for his ballroom, the company assembled in a magnificent apartment with fluted gold- ceiling and crimson brocade hangings, bronzes, statues, and Dresden candlesticks, and a large wood fire at one end, in which logs six feet long were burning--all looking as if it were part of an old baronial castle of the Middle Ages.

The florists will furnish you red clovers in January if you give your order in October. Great bunches of flowers, of a pure scarlet unmixed with any other color, are very fashionable, and the effect in a softly-lighted room is most startling and beautiful.

The lighting of rooms by means of lamps and candles is giving hostesses great annoyance. There is scarcely a dinner-party but the candles set fire to their fringed shades, and a conflagration ensues. Then the new lamps, which give such a resplendent light, have been known to melt the metal about the wick, and the consequences have been disastrous. The next move will probably be the dipping of the paper in some asbestos or other anti-inflammable substance, so that there will be no danger of fire at the dinner-table. The screens put over the candles should not have this paper- fringe; it is very dangerous. But if a candle screen takes fire, have the coolness to let it burn itself up without touching it, as thus it will be entirely innocuous, although rather appalling to look at. Move a plate under it to catch the flying fragments, and no harm will be done; but a well-intentioned effort to blow it out or to remove it generally results in a very much more wide-spread conflagration.

China and glass go on improving; and there are jewelled goblets and centre-pieces of yellow glass covered with gold and what looks like jewels. Knives and forks are now to be had with crystal handles set in silver, very ornamental and clean-looking; these come from Bohemia. The endless succession of beautiful plates are more and more Japanese in tone.

Satsuma vases and jugs are often sent to a lady, full of beautiful roses, thus making a lasting souvenir of what would be a perishable gift. These Satsuma jugs are excellent things in which to plant hyacinths, and they look well in the centre of the dinner-table with these flowers growing in them.

Faded flowers can be entirely restored to freshness by clipping the stems and putting them in very hot water; then set them away from the gas and furnace heat, and they come on the dinner-table fresh for several days after their disappearance in disgrace as faded or jaded bouquets. Flowers thus restored have been put in a cold library, where the water, once hot, has frozen stiff, and yet have borne these two extremes of temperature without loss of beauty--in fact, have lasted presentably from Monday morning to Saturday night. What flowers cannot stand is the air we all live in--at what cost to our freshness we find out in the spring--the overheated furnace and gas-laden air of the modern dining-room. The secret of the hot-water treatment is said to be this: the sap is sent up into the flower instead of lingering in the stems. Roses respond to this treatment wonderfully.

The fashion of wearing low-necked dresses at dinner has become so pronounced that the moralists begin to issue weekly essays against this revival as if it had never been done before. Our virtuous grandmothers would be astonished to hear that their ball-dresses (never cut high) were so immoral and indecent. The fact remains that a sleeveless gown, cut in a Pompadour form, is far more of a revelation of figure than a low-necked dinner-dress properly made. There is no line of the figure so dear to the artist as that one revealed from the nape of the neck to the shoulder. A beautiful back is the delight of the sculptor. No lady who understands the fine-art of dress would ever have her gown cut too low: it is ugly, besides being immodest. The persons who bring discredit on fashion are those who misinterpret it. The truly artistic modiste cuts a low-necked dress to reveal the fine lines of the back, but it is never in France cut too low in front. The excessive heat of an American dining-room makes this dress very much more comfortable than the high dresses which were brought in several years ago, because a princess had a goitre which she wished to disguise:

No fulminations against fashion have ever effected reforms. We must take fashion as we find it, and strive to mould dress to our own style, not slavishly adhering to, but respectfully following, the reigning mode, remembering that all writings and edicts against this sub-ruler of the world are like sunbeams falling on a stone wall. The sunbeams vanish, but the stone wall remains.

The modern married belle at a dinner is apt to be dressed in white, with much crystal trimming, with feathers in her hair, and with diamonds on her neck and arms, and a pair of long, brown Swedish gloves drawn up to her shoulders; a feather fan of ostrich feathers hangs at her side by a ribbon or a chain of diamonds and pearls. The long, brown Swedish gloves are an anomaly; they do not suit the rest of this exquisite dress, but fashion decrees that they shall be worn, and therefore they are worn.

The fine, stately fashion of wearing feathers in the hair has returned, and it is becoming to middle-aged women. It gives them a queenly air. Young girls look better for the simplest head-gear; they wear their hair high or low as they consider becoming.

Monstrous and inconvenient bouquets are again the fashion, and a very ugly fashion it is. A lady does not know what to do with her two or three bouquets at a musicale or a dinner, so they are laid away on a table. The only thing that can be done is to sit after dinner with them in her lap, and the prima donna at a musicale lays hers on the grand piano.

More and more is it becoming the fashion to have music at the end of a dinner in the drawing-room, instead of having it played during dinner. Elocutionists are asked in to amuse the guests, who, having been fed on terrapin and canvas-back ducks, are not supposed to be in a talking mood. This may be overdone. Many people like to talk after dinner with the people who are thus accidentally brought together; for in our large cities the company assembled about a dinner-table are very often fresh acquaintances who like to improve that opportunity to know each other better.

We have spoken of the dress of ladies, which, if we were to pursue, would lead us into all the details of velvet, satin, and brocade, and would be a departure from our subject; let us therefore glance at the gentlemen at a modern, most modern, dinner. The vests are cut very low, and exhibit a piqu‚ embroidered shirt front held by one stud, generally a cat's-eye; however, three studs are permissible. White plain-pleated linen, with enamel studs resembling linen, is also very fashionable. A few young men, sometimes called dudes--no one knows why--wear pink coral studs or pearls, generally black pearls. Elderly gentlemen content themselves with plain-pleated shirt-fronts and white ties, indulging even in wearing their watches in the old way, as fashion has reintroduced the short vest-chain so long banished.

It is pleasant to see the old-fashioned gold chain for the neck reappearing. It always had a pretty effect, and is now much worn to support the locket, cross, or medallion portrait which ladies wear after the Louis Quinze fashion. Gold is more becoming to dark complexions than pearls, and many ladies hail this return to gold necklaces with much delight.

Gentlemen now wear pearl-colored gloves embroidered in black to dinners, and do not remove them until they sit down to table. Seal rings for the third finger are replacing the sunken jewels in dead gold which have been so fashionable for several years for gentlemen.

All the ornamentation of the dinner-table is high this winter--high candlesticks, high vases, high glasses for the flowers, and tall glass compotiers. Salt-cellars are looking up; and a favorite device is a silver vase, about two inches high, with a shell for salt.

Silver and silver-gilt dishes, having been banished for five years, are now reasserting their pre-eminent fitness for the modern dinner- table. People grew tired of silver, and banished it to the plate- chest. Now all the old pieces are being burnished up and reappearing; and happy the hostess who has some real old Queen Anne. As the silver dollar loses caste, the silver soup tureen, or, as the French say, the soupiere (and it is a good word), rises in fashion, and the teapot of our grandmothers resumes its honored place.

CHAPTER XXXIV

SUMMER DINNERS.

There is a season when the lingerers in town accept with pleasure an invitation to the neighboring country house, where the lucky suburban cit likes to entertain his friends. It is to be doubted, however, whether hospitality is an unmixed pleasure to those who extend it. With each blessing of prosperity comes an attendant evil, and a lady who has a country house has always to face the fact that her servants are apt to decamp in a body on Saturday night, and leave her to take care of her guests as best she may. The nearer to town the greater the necessity for running a servant's omnibus, which shall take the departing offender to the train, and speed the arrival of her successor.

No lady should attempt to entertain in the country who has not a good cook and a very competent waiter or waitress. The latter, if well trained, is in every respect as good as a man, and in some respects more desirable; women-servants are usually quiet, neater than men-servants, as a rule, and require less waiting upon. Both men and women should be required to wear shoes that do not creak, and to be immaculately neat in their attire. Maid-servants should always wear caps and white aprons, and men dress-coats, white cravats, and perfectly fresh linen.

As the dinners of the opulent, who have butler, waiters, French cook, etc., are quite able to take care of themselves, we prefer to answer the inquiries of those of our correspondents who live in a simple manner, with two or three servants, and who wish to entertain with hospitality and without great expense.

The dining-room of many country houses is small, and not cheerfully furnished. The houses built recently are improved in this respect, however, and now we will imagine a large room that has a pretty outlook on the Hudson, carpeted with fragrant matting, or with a hard-wood floor, on which lie India rugs. The table should be oval, as that shape brings guests near to each other. The table-cloth should be of white damask, and as fresh as sweet clover, for dinner: colored cloths are permissible only for breakfast and tea. The chairs should be easy, with high, slanting backs. For summer, cane chairs are much the most comfortable, although those covered with leather are very nice. Some people prefer arm-chairs at dinner, but the arms are inconvenient to many, and, besides, take a great deal of room. The armless dinner-chairs are the best.

Now, as a dinner in the country generally occurs after the gentlemen come from town, the matter of light has to be considered. If our late brilliant sunsets do not supply enough, how shall we light our summer dinners? Few country houses have gas. Even if they have, it would be very hot, and attract mosquitoes.

Candles are very pretty, but exceedingly troublesome. The wind blows the flame to and fro; the insects flutter into the light; an unhappy moth seats himself on the wick, and burning into an unsightly cadaver makes a gutter down one side; the little red-paper shades take fire, and there is a general conflagration. Yet light is positively necessary to digestion, and no party can be cheerful without it. Therefore, try carcel or moderator lamps with pretty transparent shades, or a hanging lamp with ground-glass shade. These lamps, filled with kerosene--and it must be done neatly, so that it will not smell--are the best lamps for the country dinner. If possible, however, have a country dinner by the light of day; it is much more cheerful.

Now for the ornamentation of the dinner. Let it be of flowers--wild ones, if possible, grasses, clovers, buttercups, and a few fragrant roses or garden flowers. There is no end to the cheap decorative china articles that are sold now for the use of flowers. A contemporary mentions orchids placed in baskets on the shoulders of Arcadian peasants; lilies-of-the-valley, with leaves as pale as their flowers, wheeled in barrows by Cupids or set in china slippers; crocuses grown in a china pot shaped like a thumbed copy of Victor Hugo's "Notre Dame de Paris;" or white tulips in a cluster of three gilt _sabots_, large enough to form a capital flower-stand, mounted on gilt, rustic branches. Stout pitchers, glass bowls, china bowls, and even old teapots, make pretty bouquet-holders. The Greek vase, the classic-shaped, old-fashioned champagne glass, are, however, unrivalled for the light grasses, field daisies, and fresh garden flowers.

Pretty, modern English china, the cheap "old blue," the white and gold, or the French, with a colored border, are all good enough for a country dinner; for if people have two houses, they do not like to take their fragile, expensive china to the country. Prettily-shaped tureens and vegetable dishes add very much to the comfort and happiness of the diners, and fortunately they are cheap and easily obtained. Glass should always be thin and fine, and tea and coffee cups delicate to the lip: avoid the thick crockery of a hotel.

For a country dinner the table should be set near a window, or windows, if possible; in fine weather, in the hall or on the wide veranda. If the veranda have long windows, the servant can pass in and out easily. There should be a side-board and a side, table, relays of knives, forks and spoons, dishes and glasses not in use, and a table from which the servant can help the soup and carve the joint, as on a hot day no one wishes to see these two dishes on the table. A maid-servant should be taught by her mistress how to carve, in order to save time and trouble. Soup for a country dinner should be clear bouillon, with macaroni and cheese, _creme d'asperge_, or Julienne, which has in it all the vegetables of the season. Heavy mock-turtle, bean soup, or ox-tail are not in order for a country dinner. If the lady of the house have a talent for cookery, she should have her soups made the day before, all the grease removed when the stock is cold, and season them herself.

It is better in a country house to have some cold dish that will serve as a resource if the cook should leave. Melton veal, which can be prepared on Monday and which will last until Saturday, is an excellent stand-by; and a cold boiled or roast ham should always be on the side-board. A hungry man can make a comfortable dinner of cold ham and a baked potato.

Every country householder should try to have a vegetable garden, for pease, beans, young turnips, and salads fresh gathered are very superior to those which even the best grocer furnishes. And of all the luxuries of a country dinner the fresh vegetables are the greatest. Especially does the tired citizen, fed on the esculents of the corner grocery, delight in the green pease, the crisp lettuce, the undefiled strawberries. One old epicure of New York asks of his country friends only a piece of boiled salt pork with vegetables, a potato salad, some cheese, five large strawberries, and a cup of coffee. The large family of salads help to make the country dinner delightful. Given a clear beef soup, a slice of fresh-boiled salmon, a bit of spring lamb with mint sauce, some green pease and fresh potatoes, a salad of lettuce, or sliced tomatoes, or potatoes with a bit of onion, and you have a dinner fit for a Brillat-Savarin; or vary it with a pair of boiled chickens, and a jardiniere made of all the pease, beans, potatoes, cauliflower, fresh beets, of the day before, simply treated to a bath of vinegar and oil and pepper and salt. The lady who has conquered the salad question may laugh at the caprices of cooks, and defy the hour at which the train leaves.

What so good as an egg salad for a hungry company? Boil the eggs hard and slice them, cover with a mayonnaise dressing, and put a few lettuce leaves about the plate, and you have a sustaining meal.

Many families have cold meats and warm vegetables for their midday dinner during the summer. This is not healthy. Let all the dinner be cold if the meats are; and a dinner of cold roast beef, of salad, and cold asparagus, dressed with pepper, oil, and vinegar, is not a bad meal.

It is better for almost everybody, however, to eat a hot dinner, even in hot weather, as the digestion is aided by the friendly power of the caloric. Indeed dyspepsia, almost universal with Americans, is attributed to the habit which prevails in this country above all others of drinking ice-water.

Carafes of ice-water, a silver dish for ice, and a pair of ice- tongs, should be put on the table for a summer dinner. For desserts there is an almost endless succession, and with cream in her dairy, and a patent ice-cream freezer in her _cuisine_, the house-keeper need not lack delicate and delicious dishes of berries and fruits. No hot puddings should be served, or heavy pies; but the fruit tart is an excellent sweet, and should be made _… ravir_; the pastry should melt in the mouth, and the fruit be stewed with a great deal of sugar. Cream should be put on the table in large glass pitchers, for it is a great luxury of the country and of the summer season.

The cold custards, Charlotte-Russe, and creams stiffened with gelatine and delicately flavored, are very nice for a summer dinner. So is home-made cake, when well made: this, indeed, is always its only "excuse for being."

Stewed fruit is a favorite dessert in England, and the gooseberry, which here is but little used, is much liked there. Americans prefer to eat fruit fresh, and therefore have not learned to stew it. Stewing is, however, a branch of cookery well worth the attention of a first-class house-keeper. It makes even the canned abominations better, and the California canned apricot stewed with sugar is one of the most delightful of sweets, and very wholesome; canned peaches stewed with sugar lose the taste of tin, which sets the teeth on edge, and stewed currants are delicious.

Every house-keeper should learn to cook macaroni well. It is worth while to spend an hour at Martinelli's, for this Italian staple is economical, and extremely palatable if properly prepared. Rice, too, should have a place in a summer bill of fare, as an occasional substitute for potatoes, which some people cannot eat.

For summer dinners there should never be anything on the table when the guests sit down but the flowers and the dessert, the ice- pitchers or _carafes_, and bowls of ice, the glass, china, and silver: the last three should all be simple, and not profuse.

Many families now, fearing burglars, use only plated spoons, knives, forks, and dishes at their country houses. Modern plate is so very good that there is less objection to this than formerly; but the genuine house-keeper loves the real silver spoons and forks, and prefers to use them.

The ostentatious display of silver, however, is bad taste at a country dinner. Glass dishes are much more elegant and appropriate, and quite expensive enough to bear the title of luxuries.

Avoid all greasy and heavy dishes. Good roast beef, mutton, lamb, veal, chickens, and fresh fish are always in order, for the system craves the support of these solids in summer as well as in winter; but do not offer pork, unless in the most delicate form, and then in small quantities. Fried salt pork, if not too fat, is always a pleasant addition to the broiled bird.

Broiled fish, broiled chicken, broiled ham, broiled steaks and chops, are always satisfactory. The grid-iron made St. Lawrence fit for Heaven, and its qualities have been elevating and refining ever since. Nothing can be less healthy or less agreeable to the taste at a summer dinner than fried food. The frying-pan should have been thrown into the fire long ago, and burned up.

The house-keeper living near the sea has an ample store to choose from in the toothsome crab, clam, lobster, and other crustacea. The fresh fish, the roast clams, etc., take the place of the devilled kidneys and broiled bones of the winter. But every housewife should study the markets of her neighborhood. In many rural districts the butchers give away, or throw to the dogs, sweetbreads and other morsels which are the very essence of luxury. Calf's head is rejected by the rural buyer, and a Frenchman who had the _physiologie du go–t_ at his finger-ends, declared that in a country place, not five miles from New York, he gave luxurious dinners on what the butcher threw away.

CHAPTER XXXV

LUNCHEONS, INFORMAL AND SOCIAL.

The informal lunch is perhaps less understood in this country than in any other, because it is rarely necessary. In the country it is called early dinner, children's dinner, or ladies' dinner; in the city, when the gentlemen are all down town, then blossoms out the elaborate ladies' lunch.

But in England, at a country house, and indeed in London, luncheon is a recognized and very delightful meal, at which the most distinguished men and women meet over a joint and a cherry tart, and talk and laugh for an hour without the restraint of the late and formal dinner.

It occupies a prominent place in the history of hospitality, and Lord Houghton, among others, was famous for his unceremonious lunches. As it is understood to be an informal meal, the invitations are generally sent only a short time before the day for which the recipient is invited, and are written in the first person. Lord Houghton's were apt to be simply, "Come and lunch with me to-morrow." At our prominent places of summer resort, ladies who have houses of their own generally give their male friends a carte blanche invitation to luncheon. They are expected to avail themselves of it without ceremony, and at Newport the table is always laid with the "extra knife and fork," or two or three, as may be thought necessary. Ladies, however, should be definitely asked to this meal as to others.

It is a very convenient meal, as it permits of an irregular number, of a superfluity of ladies or gentlemen; it is chatty and easy, and is neither troublesome nor expensive.

The hour of luncheon is stated, but severe punctuality is not insisted upon. A guest who is told that he may drop in at half-past one o'clock every day will be forgiven if he comes as late as two.

Ladies may come in their hats or bonnets; gentlemen in lawn-tennis suits, if they wish. It is incumbent upon the hostess but not upon the host to be present. It is quite immaterial where the guests sit, and they go in separately, not arm-in-arm.

Either white or colored table-cloths are equally proper, and some people use the bare mahogany, but this is unusual.

The most convenient and easy-going luncheons are served from the buffet or side-table, and the guests help themselves to cold ham, tongue, roast beef, etc. The fruit and wine and bread should stand on the table.

Each chair has in front of it two plates, a napkin with bread, two knives, two forks and spoons, a small salt-cellar, and three glasses--a tumbler for water, a claret glass, and a sherry glass.

Bouillon is sometimes offered in summer, but not often. If served well, it should be in cups. Dishes of dressed salad, a cold fowl, game, or hot chops, can be put before the hostess or passed by the servant. Soup and fish are never offered at these luncheons. Some people prefer a hot lunch, and chops, birds on toast, or a beefsteak, with mashed potatoes, asparagus, or green pease, are suitable dishes.

It is proper at a country place to offer a full luncheon, or to have a cold joint on the sideboard; and after the more serious part of the luncheon has been removed, the hostess can dismiss the servants, and serve the ice-cream or tart herself, with the assistance of her guests. Clean plates, knives, and forks should be in readiness.

In England a "hot joint" is always served from the sideboard. In fact, an English luncheon is exactly what a plain American dinner was formerly--a roast of mutton or beef, a few vegetables, a tart, some fruit, and a glass of sherry. But we have changed the practice considerably, and now our luxurious country offers nothing plain.

In this country one waiter generally remains during the whole meal, and serves the table as he would at dinner--only with less ceremony. It is perfectly proper at luncheon for any one to rise and help himself to what he wishes.

Tea and coffee are never served after luncheon in the drawing-room or dining-room. People are not expected to remain long after luncheon, as the lady of the house may have engagements for the afternoon.

In many houses the butler arranges the luncheon, table with flowers or fruit, plates of thin bread-and butter, jellies, creams, cakes, and preserves, a dish of cold salmon _mayonnaise_, and decanters of sherry and claret. He places a cold ham or chicken on the sideboard, and a pitcher of ice-water on a side-table, and then leaves the dining-room, and takes no heed of the baser wants of humanity until dinner-time. An underman or footman takes the place of this lofty being, and waits at table.

In more modest houses, where there is only a maid-servant or one man, all arrangements for the luncheon and for expected guests should be made immediately after breakfast.

If the children dine with the family at luncheon, it, of course, becomes an important meal, and should include one hot dish and a simple dessert.

It is well for people living in the country, and with a certain degree of style, to study up the methods of making salads and cold dishes, for these come in so admirably for luncheon that they often save a hostess great mortification. By attention to small details a very humble repast may be most elegant. A silver bread-basket for the thin slices of bread, a pretty cheese-dish, a napkin around the cheese, pats of butter in a pretty dish, flowers in vases, fruits neatly served--these things cost little, but they add a zest to the pleasures of the table.

If a hot luncheon is served, it is not etiquette to put the vegetables on the table as at dinner; they should be handed by the waiter. The luncheon-table is already full of the articles for dessert, and there is no place for the vegetables. The hot _entr‚es_ or cold _entr‚es_ are placed before the master or mistress, and each guest is asked what he prefers. The whole aspect of luncheon is thus made perfectly informal.

If a lady gives a more formal lunch, and has it served _… la Russe_, the first _entr‚e_--let us say chops and green pease--is handed by the waiter, commencing with the lady who sits on the right hand of the master of the house. This is followed by vegetables. Plates having been renewed, a salad and some cold ham can be offered. The waiter fills the glasses with sherry, or offers claret. When champagne is served at lunch, it is immediately after the first dish has been served, and claret and sherry are not then given unless asked for.

After the salad a fresh plate, with a dessert-spoon and small fork upon it, is placed before each person. The ice-cream, pie, or pudding is then placed in front of the hostess, who cuts it, and puts a portion on each plate. After these dainties have been discussed, a glass plate, _serviette_, and finger-bowl are placed before each guest for fruit. The servant takes the plate from his mistress after she has filled it, and hands it to the lady of first consideration, and so on. When only members of the family are present at luncheon, the mistress of the house is helped first.

Fruit tarts, pudding, sweet omelette, jellies, blancmange, and ice- cream are all proper dessert for luncheon; also luncheon cake, or the plainer sorts of loaf-cake.

It is well in all households, if possible, for the children to breakfast and lunch with their parents. The teaching of table manners cannot be begun too soon. But children should never be allowed to trouble guests. If not old enough to behave well at table, guests should not be invited to the meals at which they are present. It is very trying to parents, guests, and servants.

When luncheon is to be an agreeable social repast, which guests are expected to share, then the children should dine elsewhere. No mother succeeds better in the rearing of her children than she who has a nursery dining-room, where, under her own eye, her bantlings are properly fed. It is not so much trouble, either, as one would think.

Table mats are no longer used in stylish houses, either at luncheon or at dinner. The waiter should have a coarse towel in the butler's pantry, and wipe each dish before he puts it on the table.

Menu-cards are never used at luncheon. Salt-cellars and small water carafes may be placed up and down the luncheon-table.

In our country, where servants run away and leave their mistress when she is expecting guests, it is well to be able to improvise a dish from such materials as may be at hand. Nothing is better than a cod mayonnaise. A cod boiled in the morning is a friend in the afternoon. When it is cold remove the skin and bones. For sauce put some thick cream in a porcelain saucepan, and thicken it with corn- flour which has been mixed with cold water. When it begins to boil, stir in the beaten yolks of two eggs. As it cools, beat it well to prevent it from becoming lumpy, and when nearly cold, stir in the juice of two lemons, a little tarragon vinegar, a pinch of salt, and a _soup‡on_ of Cayenne pepper. Peel and slice some very ripe tomatoes or cold potatoes; steep them in vinegar, with Cayenne, powdered ginger, and plenty of salt; lay these around the fish, and cover with the cream sauce. This makes a very elegant cold dish for luncheon. The tomatoes or potatoes should be taken out of the vinegar and carefully drained before they are placed around the fish.

Some giblets carefully saved from the ducks, geese, or chickens of yesterday's dinner should be stewed in good beef stock, and then set away to cool. Put them in a stewpan with dried split pease, and boil them until they are reduced to pulp; serve this mixture hot on toast, and, if properly flavored with salt and pepper, you have a good luncheon dish.

Vegetable salads of beet-root, potatoes, and lettuce are always delicious, and the careful housewife who rises early in the morning and provides a round of cold corned beef, plenty of bread, and a luncheon cake, need not regret the ephemeral cook, or fear the coming city guest.

Every country housewife should learn to garnish dishes with capers, a border of water-cresses, plain parsley, or vegetables cut into fancy forms.

Potatoes, eggs, and cold hashed meats, in their unadorned simplicity, do not come under the head of luxuries. But if the hashed meat is carefully warmed and well flavored, and put on toast, if the potatoes are chopped and browned and put around the meat, if the eggs are boiled, sliced, and laid around as a garnish, and a few capers and a border of parsley added, you have a Delmonico ragout that Brillat-Savarin would have enjoyed.

CHAPTER XXXVI

SUPPER-PARTIES.

After a long retirement into the shades, the supper-party, the "sit-down Supper," once so dear to our ancestors, has been again revived. Leaders of society at Newport have found that, after the hearty lunch which everybody eats there at one or three o'clock the twelve or fourteen course dinner at seven o'clock, is too much; that people come home reluctantly from their ocean drive to dress; and last summer, in consequence, invitations were issued for suppers at nine or half-past nine. The suppers at private houses, which had previously fallen out of fashion by reason of the convenience and popularity of the great restaurants, were resumed. The very late dinners in large cities have, no doubt, also prevented the supper from being a favorite entertainment; but there is no reason (except the disapproval of doctors) why suppers should not be in fashion in the country, or where people dine early. In England, where digestions are better than here, and where people eat more heavily, "the supper-tray" is an institution, and suppers are generally spread in every English country house; and we may acknowledge the fact that the supper--the little supper so dear to the hearts of our friends of the last century--seems to be coming again into fashion here. Nothing can be more significant than that _Harper's Bazar_ receives many letters asking for directions for setting the table for supper, and for the proper service of the meats which are to gayly cover the cloth and enrich this always pleasant repast.

In a general way the same service is proper at a supper as at a dinner, with the single exception of the soup-plates. Oysters on the half-shell and bouillon served in cups are the first two courses. If a hot supper is served, the usual dishes are sweetbreads, with green pease, _c“telettes … la financiere_, and some sort of game in season, such as reed-birds in autumn, canvas-back ducks, venison, or woodcock; salads of every kind are in order, and are often served with the game. Then ices and fruit follow. Cheese is rarely offered, although some gourmets insist that a little is necessary with the salad.

After each course all the dishes and knives and forks that have been in use are replaced by fresh ones, and the order and neatness of the table preserved to the end of the supper. We would think it unnecessary to mention this most obvious detail of table decorum, had not several correspondents asked to be informed concerning it.

There is, of course, the informal supper, at which the dishes are all placed on a table together, as for a supper at a large ball. Meats, dressed salmon, chicken _croquettes_, salads, jellies, and ices are a part of the alarming _m‚lange_ of which a guest is expected to partake, with only such discrimination as may be dictated by prudence or inclination. But this is not the "sit down," elegant supper so worthy to be revived, with its courses and its etiquette and its brilliant conversation, which was the delight of our grandmothers.

A large centre-piece of flowers, with fruit and candies in glass _compotiers_, and high forms of _nougat_, and other sugar devices, are suitable standards for an elegant supper-table. Three sorts of wine may be placed on the table in handsome decanters--sherry, or Madeira, and Burgundy. The guests find oysters on the half-shell, with little fish forks, all ready for them. The napkin and bread are laid at the side or in front of each plate. These plates being removed, other plain plates are put in their place, and cups of bouillon are served, with gold teaspoons. This course passed, other plates are put before the guest, and some chicken croquettes or lobster farci is passed. Sherry or Madeira should already have been served with the Oysters. With the third course iced champagne is offered. Then follow game, or fried oysters, salads, and a slice of _pƒt‚ de foie gras_, with perhaps tomato salad; and subsequently ices, jellies, fruit, and coffee, and for the gentlemen a glass of brandy or cordial. Each course is taken away before the next is presented. Birds and salad are served together.

There is a much simpler supper possible, which is often offered by a hospitable hostess after the opera or theatre. It consists of a few Oysters, a pair of cold roast chickens, a dish of lobster or plain salad, with perhaps a glass of champagne, and one sort of ice-cream, and involves very little trouble or expense, and can be safely said to give as much pleasure as the more sumptuous feast. This informal refreshment is often placed on a red table-cloth, with a dish of oranges and apples in the centre of the table, and one servant is sufficient. There should be, however, the same etiquette as to the changing of plates, knives, and forks, etc., as in the more elaborate meal.

The good house-keeper who gives a supper every evening to her hungry family may learn many an appetizing device by reading English books of cookery on this subject. A hashed dish of the meat left from dinner, garnished with parsley, a potato salad, a few slices of cold corned beef or ham, some pickled tongues, bread, butter, and cheese, with ale or cider, is the supper offered at nearly every English house in the country.

The silver and glass, the china and the fruit, should be as carefully attended to as for a dinner, and everything as neat and as elegant as possible, even at an informal supper.

Oysters, that universal food of the American, are invaluable for a supper. Fried oysters diffuse a disagreeable odor through the house, therefore they are not as convenient in a private dwelling as scalloped oysters, which can be prepared in the afternoon, and which send forth no odor when cooking. Broiled oysters are very delicate, and are a favorite dish at an informal supper. Broiled birds and broiled bones are great delicacies, but they must be prepared by a very good cook. Chicken in various forms hashed, fried, cold, or in salad--is useful; veal may be utilized for all these things, if chicken is not forthcoming. The delicately treated chicken livers also make a very good dish, and mushrooms on toast are perfect in their season. Hot vegetables are never served, except green pease with some other dish.

Beef, except in the form of a fillet, is never seen at a "sit-down" supper, and even a fillet is rather too heavy. Lobster in every form is a favorite supper delicacy, and the grouse; snipe, woodcock, teal; canvasback, and squab on toast, are always in order.

In these days of Italian warehouses and imported delicacies, the pressed and jellied meats, _pƒt‚s_, sausages, and spiced tongues furnish a variety for a cold supper. No supper is perfect without a salad.

The Romans made much of this meal, and among their delicacies were the ass, the dog, and the snail, sea-hedgehogs, oysters, asparagus, venison, wild boar, sea-nettles, fish, fowl, game, and cakes. The Germans to-day eat wild boar, head-cheese, pickles, goose's flesh dried, sausages, cheese, and salads for supper, and wash down with beer. The French, under Louis XIV., began to make the supper their most finished meal. They used gold and silver dishes, crystal cups and goblets, exquisite grapes crowned the _‚pergne_, and choicest fruits were served in golden dishes. The cooks sent up piquant sauces for the delicately cooked meats, the wines were drunk hot and spiced. The latter are taken iced now. Many old house-keepers, however, serve a rich, hot-mulled port for a winter supper. It is a delicious and not unhealthy beverage, and can be easily prepared.

The doctors, as we have said, condemn a late supper, but the pros and cons of this subject admit of discussion. Every one, indeed, must decide for himself.

Few people can undergo excitement of an evening--an opera or play or concert, or even the pleasant conversation of an evening party-- without feeling hungry. With many, if such an appetite is not appeased it will cause sleeplessness. To eat lightly and to drink lightly at supper is a natural instinct with people if they expect to go to bed at once; but excitement is a great aid to digestion, and a heavy supper sometimes gives no inconvenience.

Keats seems to have had a vision of a modern supper-table when he wrote:

"soft he set A table, and ...threw thereon A cloth of woven crimson, gold, and jet; ...from forth the closet brought a heap Of candied apple, quince, and plum, and gourd, With jellies soother than the creamy curd, And lucent syrops, tinct with cinnamon, Manna and dates: ...spiced dainties every one."

The supper being a meal purely of luxury should be very dainty. Everything should be tasteful and appetizing; the wines should be excellent, the claret not too cool, the champagne _frapp‚_, or almost so, the Madeira and the port the temperature of the room, and the sherry cool. If punch is served, it should be at the end of the supper.

Many indulgent hostesses now allow young gentlemen to smoke a cigarette at the supper-table, after the eating and drinking is at an end, rather than break up the delicious flow of conversation which at the close of a supper seems to be at its best. This, however, should not be done unless every lady at the table acquiesces, as the smell of tobacco-smoke sometimes gives women an unpleasant sensation.

Suppers at balls and parties include now all sorts of cold and hot dishes, even a haunch of venison, and a fillet of beef, with truffles; a cold salmon dressed with a green sauce; oysters in every form except raw--they are not served at balls; salads of every description; boned and truffled turkey and chicken; _pƒt‚s_ of game; cold partridges and grouse; _pƒt‚ de foie gras_; our American specialty, hot canvas-back duck; and the Baltimore turtle, terrapin, oyster and game patties; bonbons, ices, biscuits, creams, jellies, and fruits, with champagne, and sometimes, of later years, claret and Moselle cup, and champagne-cup--beverages which were not until lately known in America, except at gentlemen's clubs and on board yachts, but which are very agreeable mixtures, and gaining in favor. Every lady should know how to mix cup, as it is convenient both for supper and lawn-tennis parties, and is preferable in its effects to the heavier article so common at parties--punch.

CHAPTER XXXVII

SIMPLE DINNERS.

To achieve a perfect little dinner with small means at command is said to be a great intellectual feat. Dinner means so much--a French cook, several accomplished servants, a very well-stocked china closet, plate chest, and linen chest, and flowers, wines, bonbons, and so on. But we have known many simple little dinners given by young couples with small means which were far more enjoyable than the gold and silver "diamond" dinners.

Given, first, a knowledge of _how to do it_; a good cook (not a _cordon bleu_); a neat maid-servant in cap and apron--if the lady can carve (which all ladies should know how to do); if the gentleman has a good bottle of claret, and another of champagne--or neither, if he disapproves of them; if the house is neatly and quietly furnished, with the late magazines on the table; if the welcome is cordial, and there is no noise, no fussy pretence--these little dinners are very enjoyable, and every one is anxious to be invited to them.

But people are frightened off from simple entertainments by the splendor of the great luxurious dinners given by the very rich. It is a foolish fear. The lady who wishes to give a simple but good dinner has first to consult what is seasonable. She must offer the dinner of the season, not seek for those strawberries in February which are always sour, nor peaches in June, nor pease at Christmas. Forced fruit is never good.

For an autumnal small dinner here is a very good _menu_:

Sherry./Oysters on the half-shell./Chablis, Soupe … la Reine. Blue-fish, broiled./Hock, Filet de Boeuf aux Champignons./Champagne

Or,

Roast Beef or Mutton./Claret. Roast Partridges./ Burgundy, or Sherry Salad of Tomatoes. Cheese./Liqueurs

Of course, in these days, claret and champagne are considered quite enough for a small dinner, and one need not offer the other wines. Or, as Mrs. Henderson says in her admirable cook-book, a very good dinner maybe given with claret alone. A table claret to add to the water is almost the only wine drunk in France or Italy at an every-day dinner. Of course no wine at all is expected at the tables of those whose principles forbid alcoholic beverages, and who nevertheless give excellent dinners without them.

A perfectly fresh white damask table-cloth, napkins of equally delicate fabric, spotless glass and silver, pretty china, perhaps one high glass dish crowned with fruit and flowers--sometimes only the fruit--chairs that are comfortable, a room not too warm, the dessert served in good taste, but not overloaded--this is all one needs. The essentials of a good dinner are but few.

The informal dinner invitations should be written by the lady herself in the first person. She may send for her friends only a few days before she wants them to come. She should be ready five minutes before her guests arrive, and in the parlor, serene and cool, "mistress of herself, though china fall." She should see herself that the dinner-table is properly laid, the champagne and sherry thoroughly cooled, the places marked out, and, above all, the guests properly seated.

"Ay, there's the rub." To invite the proper people to meet each other, to seat them so that they can have an agreeable conversation, that is the trying and crucial test. Little dinners are social; little dinners are informal; little dinners make people friends. And we do not mean little in regard to numbers or to the amount of good food; we mean simple dinners.

All the good management of a young hostess or an old one cannot prevent accident, however. The cook may get drunk; the waiter may fall and break a dozen of the best plates; the husband may be kept down town late, and be dressing in the very room where the ladies are to take off their cloaks (American houses are frightfully inconvenient in this respect). All that the hostess can do is to preserve an invincible calm, and try not to care--at least not to show that she cares. But after a few attempts the giving of a simple dinner becomes very easy, and it is the best compliment to a stranger. A gentleman travelling to see the customs of a country is much more pleased to be asked to a modest repast where he meets his hostess and her family than to a state dinner where he is ticketed off and made merely one at a banquet.

Then the limitations of a dinner can be considered. It is not kind to keep guests more than an hour, or two hours at the most, at table. French dinners rarely exceed an hour. English dinners are too long and too heavy, although the conversation is apt to be brilliant. At a simple dinner one can make it short.

It is better to serve coffee in the drawing-room, although if the host and hostess are agreed on this point, and the ladies can stand smoke, it is served at table, and the gentlemen light their cigarettes. In some houses smoking is forbidden in the dining-room.

The practice of the ladies retiring first is an English one, and the French consider it barbarous. Whether we are growing more French or not, we seem to be beginning to do away with the separation after dinner.

It is the custom at informal dinners for the lady to help the soup and for the gentleman to carve; therefore the important dishes are put on the table. But the servants who wait should be taught to have sidetables and sideboards so well placed that anything can be removed immediately after it is finished. A screen is a very useful adjunct in a dining-room.

Inefficient servants have a disagreeable habit of running in and out of the dining-room in search of something that should have been in readiness; therefore the lady of the house had better see beforehand that French rolls are placed under every napkin, and a silver basket full of them ready in reserve. Also large slices of fresh soft bread should be on the side table, as every one does not like hard bread, and should be offered a choice.

The powdered sugar, the butter, the caster, the olives, the relishes, should all be thought of and placed where each can be readily found. Servants should be taught to be noiseless, and to avoid a hurried manner. In placing anything on or taking anything off a table a servant should never reach across a person seated at table for that purpose. However hurried the servant may be, or however near at hand the article, she should be taught to walk quietly to the left hand of each guest to remove things, while she should pass everything in the same manner, giving the guest the option of using his right hand with which to help himself. Servants should have a silver or plated knife-tray to remove the gravy-spoon and carving knife and fork before removing the platter. All the silver should be thus removed; it makes a table much neater. Servants should be taught to put a plate and spoon and fork at every place before each course.

After the meats and before the pie, pudding, or ices, the table should be carefully cleared of everything but fruit and flowers--all plates, glasses, carafes, salt-cellars, knives and forks, and whatever pertains to the dinner should be removed, and the table- cloth well cleared with brush or crumb-scraper on a silver waiter, and then the plates, glasses, spoons, and forks laid at each plate for the dessert. If this is done every day, it adds to a common dinner, and trains the waitress to her work.

The dinner, the dishes, and the plates should all be hot. The ordinary plate-warmer is now superseded by something far better, in which a hot brick is introduced. The most _recherch‚_ dinner is spoiled if hot mutton is put on a cold plate. The silver dishes should be heated by hot water in the kitchen, the hot dinner plates must be forthcoming from the plate-warmer, nor must the roasts or _entr‚es_ be allowed to cool on their way from the kitchen to the dining-room. A servant should have a thumb napkin with which to hand the hot dishes, and a clean towel behind the screen with which to wipe the platters which have been sent up on the dumb-waiter. On these trifles depend the excellence of the simple dinner.

CHAPTER XXXVIII

THE SMALL-TALK OF SOCIETY.

One of the cleverest questions asked lately is, "What shall I talk about at a dinner-party?" Now if there is a woman in the world who does not know what to talk about, is it not a very difficult thing to tell her? One can almost as well answer such a question as, "What shall I see out of my eyes?"

Yet our young lady is not the first person who has dilated of late years upon the "decay of conversation," nor the only one who has sometimes felt the heaviness of silence descend upon her at a modern dinner. No doubt this same great and unanswerable question has been asked by many a traveller who, for the first time, has sat next an Englishman of good family (perhaps even with a handle to his name), who has answered all remarks by the proverbial but unsympathetic "Oh!" Indeed, it is to be feared that it is a fashion for young men nowadays to appear listless, to conceal what ideas they may happen to have, to try to appear stupid, if they are not so, throwing all the burden of the conversation on the lively, vivacious, good- humored girl, or the more accomplished married woman, who may be the next neighbor.

Women's wits are proverbially quick, they talk readily, they read and think more than the average young man of fashion is prone to do; the result is a quick and a ready tongue. Yet the art of keeping up a flow of agreeable and incessant small- talk, not too heavy, not pretentious or egotistical, not scandalous, and not commonplace, is an art that is rare, and hardly to be prized too highly.

It has been well said that there is a great difference between a brilliant conversationalist and a ready small-talker. The former is apt to be feared, and to produce a silence around him. We all remember Macaulay and "his brilliant flashes of silence." We all know that there are talkers so distinguished that you must not ask both of them to dinner on the same day lest they silence each other, while we know others who bring to us just an average amount of tact, facility of expression, geniality, and a pleasant gift at a quotation, a bit of repartee; such a person we call a ready small- talker, a "most agreeable person," one who frightens nobody and who has a great popularity. Such a one has plenty of small change, very useful, and more easy to handle than the very large cheek of the conversationalist, who is a millionaire as to his memory, learning, and power of rhetoric, but who cannot and will not indulge in small- talk. We respect the one; we like the other. The first point to be considered, if one has no inspiration in regard to small-talk, would seem to be this; try to consider what subject would most interest the person next to you. There are people who have no other talent, whom we never call clever, but who do possess this instinct, and who can talk most sympathetically, while knowing scarcely anything about the individual addressed. There are others who are deficient in this gift, who can only say "Really" and "Indeed." These "Really" and "Indeed" and "Oh" people are the despair of the dinner-giver. The gay, chatty, light-hearted people who can glide into a conversation easily, are the best of dinner-table companions, even if they do sometimes talk too much about the weather and such commonplaces.

It is a good plan for a shy young person, who has no confidence in her own powers of conversation, to fortify herself with several topics of general interest, such as the last new novel, the last opera, the best and newest gallery of pictures, or the flower in fashion; and to invent a formula, if words are wanting in her organization, as to how these subjects should be introduced and handled. Many ideas will occur to her, and she can silently arrange them. Then she may keep these as a reserve force, using them only when the conversation drops, or she is unexpectedly brought to the necessity of keeping up the ball alone. Some people use this power rather unfairly, leading the conversation up to the point where they wish to enter; but these are not the people who need help--they can take care of themselves. After talking awhile in a perfunctory manner, many a shy young person has been astonished by a sudden rush of brilliant ideas, and finds herself talking naturally and well without effort. It is like the launching of a ship; certain blocks of shyness and habits of mental reserve are knocked away, and the brave frigate _Small-Talk_ takes the water like a thing of life.

It demands much tact and cleverness to touch upon the ordinary events of the day at a mixed dinner, because, in the first place, nothing should be said which can hurt any one's feelings, politics, religion, and the stock market being generally ruled out; nor should one talk about that which everybody knows, for such small-talk is impertinent and irritating. No one wishes to be told that which he already understands better, perhaps, than we do. Nor are matters of too private a nature, such as one's health, or one's servants, or one's disappointments, still less one's good deeds, to be talked about.

Commonplace people also sometimes try society very much by their own inane and wholly useless criticisms. Supposing we take up music, it is far more agreeable to hear a person say, "How do you like Nilsson?" than to hear him say, "I like Nilsson, and I have these reasons for liking her." Let that come afterwards. When a person really qualified to discuss artists, or literary people, or artistic points, talks sensibly and in a chatty, easy way about them, it is the perfection of conversation; but when one wholly and utterly incompetent to do so lays down the law on such subjects he or she becomes a bore. But if the young person who does not know how to talk treats these questions interrogatively, ten chances to one, unless she is seated next an imbecile, she will get some very good and light small-talk out of her next neighbor. She may give a modest personal opinion, or narrate her own sensations at the opera, if she can do so without egotism, and she should always show a desire to be answered. If music and literature fail, let her try the subjects of dancing, polo-playing, and lawn-tennis. A very good story was told of a bright New York girl and a very haw-haw-stupid Englishman at a Newport dinner. The Englishman had said "Oh," and "Really," and "Quite so," to everything which this bright girl had asked him, when finally, very tired and very angry, she said, "Were you ever thrown in the hunting-field, and was your head hurt?" The man turned and gazed admiringly. "Now you've got me," was the reply. And he talked all the rest of the dinner of his croppers. Perhaps it may not be necessary or useful often to unlock so rich a _r‚pertoire_ as this; but it was a very welcome relief to this young lady not to do all the talking during three hours.

After a first introduction there is, no doubt, some difficulty in starting a conversation. The weather, the newspaper, the last accident, the little dog, the bric-…-brac, the love of horses, etc., are good and unfailing resources, except that very few people have the readiness to remember this wealth of subjects at once. To recollect a thing apropos of the moment is the gift of ready-witted people alone, and how many remember, hours after, a circumstance which would have told at that particular moment of embarrassment when one stood twiddling his hat, and another twisted her handkerchief. The French call "_l'esprit d'escalier_"--the "wit of the staircase"--the gift of remembering the good thing you might have said in the drawing-room, just too late, as you go up-stairs. However, two new people generally overcome this moment of embarrassment, and then some simple offer of service, such as, "Can I get you a chair?" "Is that window too cold?" "Can I bring you some tea?" occurs, and then the small-talk follows.

The only curious part of this subject is that so little skill is shown by the average talker in weaving facts and incidents into his treatment of subjects of everyday character, and that he brings so little intelligence to bear on his discussion of them. It is not given to every one to be brilliant and amusing, but, with a little thought, passing events may always give rise to pleasant conversation. We have lately been visited by a succession of brilliant sunsets, concerning which there have been various theories. This has been a charming subject for conversation, yet at the average dinner we have heard but few persons mention this interesting topic. Perhaps one is afraid to start a conversation upon celestial scenery at a modern dinner. The things may seem too remote, yet it would not be a bad idea.

Gossip may promote small-talk among those who are very intimate and who live in a narrow circle. But how profoundly uninteresting is it to an outsider!--how useless to the real man or woman of the world! That is, unless it is literary, musical, artistic gossip. Scandal ruins conversation, and should never be included even in a definition of small-talk. Polite, humorous, vivacious, speculative, dry, sarcastic, epigrammatic, intellectual, and practical people all meet around a dinner-table, and much agreeable small-talk should be the result. It is unfortunately true that there is sometimes a failure in this respect. Let a hostess remember one thing: there is no chance for vivacity of intellect if her room is too warm; her flowers and her guests will wilt together. There are those also who prefer her good dishes to talking, and the old gentleman in Punch who rebuked his lively neighbor for talking while there were "such _entr‚es_ coming in" has his counterparts among ourselves.

Some shy talkers have a sort of empirical way of starting a subject with a question like this: "Do you know the meaning and derivation of the term 'bric-…-brac?'" "Do you believe in ghosts?" "What do you think of a ladies' club?" "Do you believe in chance?" "Is there more talent displayed in learning the violin than in playing a first-rate game of chess?" etc.

These are intellectual conundrums, and may be repeated indefinitely where the person questioned is disposed to answer. With a flow of good spirits and the feeling of case which comes from a knowledge of society, such questions often bring out what Margaret Fuller called "good talk."

But if your neighbor says "Oh," "Really," "Indeed," "I don't know," then the best way is to be purely practical, and talk of the chairs and tables, and the existing order of things, the length of trains, or the shortness of the dresses of the young ladies at the last ball, the prevailing idea that "ice-water is unhealthy," and other such extremely easy ideas. The sound of one's own voice is generally very sweet in one's own ears; let every lady try to cultivate a pleasant voice for those of other people, and also an agreeable and accurate pronunciation. The veriest nothings sound well when thus spoken. The best way to learn how to talk is, of course, to learn how to think: from full wells one brings up buckets full of clear water, but there can be small-talk without much thought. The fact remains that brilliant thinkers and scholars are not always good talkers, and there is no harm in the cultivation of the art of conversation, no harm in a little "cramming," if a person is afraid that language is not his strong point. The merest trifle generally suffices to start the flow of small-talk, and the person who can use this agreeable weapon of society is always popular and very much courted.

CHAPTER XXXIX

GARDEN-PARTIES.

Many of our correspondents ask us, "What shall we order for a garden-party?" We must answer that the first thing to order is a fine day. In these fortunate days the morning revelations of Old Probabilities give us an almost exact knowledge of what of rain or sunshine the future has in store.

A rain or tornado which starts from Alaska, where the weather is made nowadays, will almost certainly be here on the third day; so the hostess who is willing to send a hasty bidding can perhaps avoid rain. It is the custom, however, to send invitations for these garden-parties a fortnight before they are to occur. At Newport they are arranged weeks beforehand, and if the weather is bad the entertainment takes place in-doors.

When invitations are given to a suburban place to which people are expected to go by rail or any public means of conveyance, a card should also be sent stating the hours at which trains leave, which train or boat to take, and any other information that may add to the comfort of the guest. These invitations are engraved, and printed on note-paper, which should be perfectly plain, or bear the family crest in water-mark only, and read somewhat as follows:

_Mr. and Mrs. Edwin Smith request the pleasure of Mr. and Mrs. Conway Brown's company on Tuesday, the thirtieth of July, at four o'clock.

Garden Party. Yonkers, New York._

Then, on the card enclosed, might be printed,

Carriages will meet the 3.30 train from Grand Central Depot.

If the invitation is to a country place not easy of access, still more explicit directions should be given.

The garden-party proper is always held entirely in the open air. In England the refreshments are served under a marquee in the grounds, and in that inclement clime no one seems to think it a hardship if a shower of rain comes down, and ruins fine silks and beautiful bonnets. But in our fine sunshiny land we are very much afraid of rain, and our malarious soil is not considered always safe, so that the thoughtful hostess often has her table in-doors, piazzas filled with chairs, Turkey rugs laid down on the grass, and every preparation made that the elderly and timid and rheumatic may enjoy the garden-party without endangering their health.

A hostess should see that her lawn-tennis ground is in order, the croquet laid out, and the archery tools all in place, so that her guests may amuse themselves with these different games. Sometimes balls and races are added to these amusements, and often a platform is laid for dancing, if the turf be not sufficiently dry. A band of musicians is essential to a very elegant and successful garden- party, and a varied selection of music, grave and gay, should be rendered. Although at a dinner-party there is reason to fear that an orchestra may be a nuisance, at a garden-party the open air and space are sufficient guarantees against this danger.

If the hostess wishes her entertainment to be served out-of-doors, of course all the dishes must be cold. Salads, cold birds, and ham, tongue, and _pƒt‚ de foie gras_, cold _pƒt‚s_, and salmon dressed with a green sauce, jellies, Charlottes, ices, cakes, punch, and champagne, are the proper things to offer. A cup of hot tea should be always ready in the house for those who desire it.

At a garden-party proper the hostess receives out on the lawn, wearing her hat or bonnet, and takes it for granted that the party will be entirely out-of-doors. The carriages, however, drive up to the door, and the ladies can go up-stairs and deposit their wraps and brush off the dust, if they wish. A servant should be in attendance to show the guests to that part of the grounds in which the lady is receiving.

At Newport these parties are generally conducted on the principle of an afternoon tea, and after the mistress of the house has received her guests, they wander through the grounds, and, when weary, return to the house for refreshment. _Pƒt‚ de foie gras_, sandwiches, cold birds, plates of delicious jellied tongue, lobster salad, and sometimes hot cakes and hot broiled chicken, are served at these high teas. Coffee and tea and wine are also offered, but these are at mixed entertainments which have grown out of the somewhat unusual hours observed at Newport in the season.

There is a sort of public garden-party in this country which prevails on semi-official occasions, such as the laying of a foundation-stone for a public building, the birthday of a prominent individual, a Sunday-school festival, or an entertainment given to a public functionary. These are banquets, and for them the invitations are somewhat general, and should be officially issued. For the private garden-party it is proper for a lady to ask for an invitation for a friend, as there is always plenty of room; but it should also be observed that where this request is not answered affirmatively, offence should not be taken. It is sometimes very difficult for a lady to understand why her request for an invitation to her friend is refused; but she should never take the refusal as a discourtesy to herself. There may be reasons which cannot be explained.

Ladies always wear bonnets at a garden-party, and the sensible fashion of short dresses has hitherto prevailed; but it is rumored that a recent edict of the Princess of Wales against short dresses at her garden-parties will find followers on this side of the water, notably at Newport, which out-Herods Herod in its respect to English fashions.

Indeed, a long dress is very pretty on the grass and under the trees. At Buckingham Palace a garden-party given to the Viceroy of Egypt several years ago presented a very Watteau-like picture. Worth's handsomest dresses were freely displayed, and the lovely grounds and old trees at the back of the palace were in fine full dress for the occasion.

In fact, England is the land for garden-parties, with its turf of velvet softness, its flowing lime-trees, its splendid old oaks, and its finished landscape gardening. There are but few places as yet in America which afford the clipped-box avenues, the arcades of blossoming rose-vines, the pleached alleys, the finely kept and perfect gravel-walks, or, Better than all, the quiet, old-fashioned gardens, down which the ladies may walk, rivals of the flowers.

But there are some such places; and a green lawn, a few trees, a good prospect, a fine day, and something to eat, are really all the absolute requirements for a garden-party. In the neighborhood of New York very charming garden-parties have been given: at the Brooklyn Navy-yard and the camp of the soldier, at the head-quarters of the officers of marines, and at the ever-lovely Governor's Island.

Up the Hudson, out at Orange (with its multitudinous pretty settlements), all along the coast of Long Island, the garden-party is almost imperatively necessary. The owner of a fine place is expected to allow the unfortunates who must stay in town at least one sniff of his roses and new-mown hay.

Lawn-tennis has had a great share in making the garden-party popular; and in remote country places ladies should learn how to give these parties, and, with very little trouble, make the most of our fine climate. There is no doubt that a little awkwardness is to be overcome in the beginning, for no one knows exactly what to do. Deprived of the friendly shelter of a house, guests wander forlornly about; but a graceful and ready hostess will soon suggest that a croquet or lawn-tennis party be formed, or that a contest at archery be entered upon, or that even a card-party is in order, or that a game of checkers can be played under the trees.

Servants should be taught to preserve the proprieties of the feast, if the meal be served under the trees. There should be no piles of dishes, knives, forks, or spoons, visible on the green grass; baskets should be in readiness to carry off everything as soon as used. There should be a sufficient quantity of glass and china in use, and plenty of napkins, so that there need be no delay. The lemonade and punch bowls should be replenished from the dining-room as soon as they show signs of depletion, and a set of neat maid- servants can be advantageously employed in watching the table, and seeing that the cups, spoons, plates, wine-glasses, and forks are in sufficient quantity and clean. If tea is served, maid-servants are better than men, as they are careful that the tea is hot, and the spoons, cream, and sugar forthcoming. Fruit is an agreeable addition to a garden-party entertainment, and pines, melons, peaches, grapes, strawberries, are all served in their season. Pains should be taken to have these fruits of the very best that can be obtained.

Claret-cup, champagne-cup, and soda-water, brandy and shandy-gaff, are provided on a separate table for the gentlemen; Apollinaris water, and the various aerated waters so fashionable now, are also provided. Although gentlemen help themselves, it is necessary to have a servant in attendance to remove the wine-glasses, tumblers, and goblets as they are used, and to replenish the decanters and pitchers as they are emptied, and to supply fresh glasses. Many hospitable hosts offer their guests old Madeira, sherry, and port.

The decanters are placed on the regular luncheon-table, and glasses of wine are carried by servants, on silver trays, to the ladies who are sitting on the piazzas and under the trees. Small thin tumblers are used for the claret and champagne cup, which should be held in silver or glass pitchers.

If strawberries and cream are served, a small napkin should be put between the saucer and plate, and a dessert spoon and fork handed with each plate.

The servants who carry about refreshments from the tent or the table where they are served should be warned to be very careful in this part of the service, as many a fine gown has been spoiled, by a dish of strawberries and cream or a glass of punch or lemonade being overturned, through a servant's want of care.

Ices are now served at garden-parties in small paper cups placed on ice-plates--a fashion which is very neat, and which saves much of the mussiness which has heretofore been a feature of these entertainments. Numbers of small tables should be brought with the camp-stools, and placed at convenient intervals, where the guests can deposit their plates.

A lady should not use her handsome glass or china at these al fresco entertainments. It is sure to be broken. It is better to hire all the necessary glass, silver, and china from the caterer, as it saves a world of counting and trouble.

No doubt the garden-party is a troublesome affair, particularly if the refreshments are out-of-doors, but it is very beautiful and very amusing, and worth all the trouble. It is just as pleasant, however, if the table is in-doors.

CHAPTER XL

SILVER WEDDINGS AND OTHER WEDDING ANNIVERSARIES.

A very sensible reform is now being attempted in the matter of silver weddings. It was once a demand on the purse of at least fifty dollars to receive an invitation to a silver wedding, because every one was expected to send a piece of silver. Some very rich houses in New York are stocked with silver with the elaborate inscription, "Silver Wedding." To the cards of to-day is appended, "No presents received," which is a relief to the impecunious.

These cards are on plain white or silver-gray paper, engraved in silver letters, with the name of the lady as she was known before marriage appended below that of her husband; the date of the marriage is also added below the names.

The entertainment for a silver wedding, to be perfect, should occur at exactly the hour at which the marriage took place; but as that has been found to be inconvenient, the marriage hour is ignored, and the party takes place in the evening generally, and with all the characteristics of a modern party. The "bridal pair" stand together, of course, to receive, and as many of the original party of the groomsmen and bridesmaids as can be got together should be induced to form a part of the group. There can be no objection to the sending of flowers, and particular friends who wish can, of course, send other gifts, but there should be no obligation. We may say here that the custom of giving bridal gifts has become an outrageous abuse of a good idea. From being a pretty custom which had its basis in the excellent system of our Dutch ancestors, who combined to help the young couple by presents of bed and table linen and necessary table furniture and silver, it has now sometimes degenerated into a form of ostentation, and is a great tax on the friends of the bride. People in certain relations to the family are even expected to send certain gifts. It has been known to be the case that the bride allowed some officious friend to suggest that she should have silver, or pearls, or diamonds; and a rich old bachelor uncle is sure to be told what is expected from him. But when a couple have reached their silver wedding, and are able and willing to celebrate it, it may be supposed that they are beyond the necessity of appealing to the generosity of their friends; therefore it is a good custom to have this phrase added to the silver-wedding invitation, "No presents received."

The question has been asked if the ceremony should be performed over again. We should say decidedly not, for great danger has accrued to thoughtless persons in thus tampering with the wedding ceremony. Any one who has read Mrs. Oliphant's beautiful story of "Madonna Mary" will be struck at once with this danger. It is not safe, even in the most playful manner, to imitate that legal form on which all society, property, legitimacy, and the safety of home hang.

Now as to the dress of the bride of twenty-five years, we should say, "Any color but black." There is an old superstition against connecting black with weddings. A silver gray, trimmed with steel and lace, has lately been used with much success as a second bridal dress. Still less should the dress be white; that has become so canonized as the wedding dress of a virgin bride that it is not even proper for a widow to wear it on her second marriage. The shades of rose-color, crimson, or those beautiful modern combinations of velvet and brocade which suit so many matronly women, are all appropriate silver-wedding dresses.

Ladies should not wear jewelry in the morning, particularly at their own houses; so if the wedding is celebrated in the morning, the hostess should take care not to be too splendid.

Evening weddings are, in these anniversaries, far more agreeable, and can be celebrated with more elaborate dressing. It is now so much the fashion to wear low-necked dresses (sleeveless dresses were worn by bridesmaids at an evening wedding recently) that the bride of twenty-five years can appear, if she chooses, in a low-cut short- sleeved dinner dress and diamonds in the evening. As for the groom, he should be in full evening dress, immaculate white tie, and pearl- colored kid gloves. He plays, as he does at the wedding, but a secondary part. Indeed, it has been jocosely said that he sometimes poses as a victim. In savage communities and among the birds it is the male who wears the fine clothes; in Christian society it is the male who dresses in black, putting the fine feathers on his wife. It is to her that all the honors are paid, he playing for the time but a secondary part. In savage communities she would dig the earth, wait upon her lord, and stand behind him while he eats; in the modern silver wedding he helps her to fried oysters and champagne, and stands while she sits.

Now as to who shall be invited. A correspondent writes asking if a silver wedding celebrated in a new home would not be a good opportunity for making the "first onset of hospitality," inviting those neighbors who were not known before, or at least who were not visiting acquaintances. We should think it a very happy idea. It is a compliment to ask one's friends and neighbors to any ceremony or anniversary in which our own deep feelings are concerned, such as a christening, a child's wedding, and the celebration of a birthday. Why not still more when a married pair have weathered the storms of twenty-five years? People fully aware of their own respectability should never be afraid to bow first, speak first, or call first. Courtesy is the most cosmopolitan of good qualities, and politeness is one of the seven capital virtues. No people giving such an invitation need be hurt if it is received coldly. They only thus find out which of their new neighbors are the most worth cultivating. This sort of courtesy is as far as possible from the dreadful word "pushing." As dress was made to dignify the human body, so a generous courtesy clothes the mind. Let no one be afraid of draping the spirit with this purple and gold.

And in all fresh neighborhoods the new-comers should try to cultivate society. There is something in its attrition which stimulates the mind. Society brightens up the wits, and causes the dullest mind to bring its treasures to the surface.

The wedding anniversaries seem to begin with the fifth one--the wooden wedding. Here unique and appropriate presents seem to be very cheap. Cedar tubs and bowls and pails, wooden baskets filled with flowers, Shaker rocking-chairs and seats for the veranda, carved tables, cabinets of oak, wall brackets, paintings on wood, water- colors framed in wood-carvings in bog oak, and even a load of kindling wood, have been acceptably offered. The bride can dress as gayly as she pleases at this early anniversary. Then comes the tin wedding, which now is very much welcomed for the pretty tin candlesticks that it brings, fresh from London furnishers.

We hear of gorgeous silver weddings in California, that land of gold and silver, where the display of toilettes each represented a large fortune. But, after all, the sentiment is the thing,

"As when, amid the rites divine, I took thy troth, and plighted mine To thee, sweet wife, my second ring A token and a pledge I bring. This ring shall wed, till death us part, Thy riper virtues to my heart--Those virtues which, before untried, The wife has added to the bride."

The golden wedding is a rare festivity--the great marriage bell made of wheat fully ripe; sheaves of corn; roses of the pure gold-color (the Marshal Niel is the golden-wedding flower _par excellence_). We can well imagine the parlors beautifully decorated with autumn leaves and evergreens, the children grouped about the aged pair, perhaps even a great-grandchild as a child bridesmaid, a bridal bouquet in the aged white hand. We can fancy nothing more poetical and pathetic than this festivity.

Whether or not a ring should be given by the husband to the wife on this occasion we must leave to the individual taste of the parties. No doubt it is a pleasant occasion for the gift,

"If she, by merit since disclosed, Proved twice the woman I supposed,"

there is no doubt that she deserves another ring. We have read somewhere of a crown-diamond wedding; it is the sixty-fifth anniversary. Iron weddings are, we believe, the fifteenth anniversary. With silver, golden, and diamond weddings we are tolerably familiar, but, so far as we know, a crown-diamond wedding such as was celebrated a short time ago at Maebuell, in the island of Alsen, is a ceremony altogether without precedent in matrimonial annals. Having completed their sixty-fifth year of conjugal bliss, Claus Jacobsen and his venerable spouse were solemnly blessed by the parson of their parish, and went, for the fifth time in their long wedded life, through the form of mutual troth-plighting before the altar at which they had for the first time been united before the battle of Waterloo was fought. The united age of this crown- diamantine couple amount to _one hundred and seventy-eight years_!

We doubt if this constant pair needed any ring to remind them of their wedded duty. It is strange that the origin of the wedding ring is lost in obscurity. The "fyancel," or wedding ring, is doubtless of Roman origin, and was originally given at the betrothal as a pledge of the engagement. Juvenal says that at the commencement of the Christian era a man placed a ring on the finger of the lady whom he betrothed. In olden times the delivery of a signet-ring was a sign of confidence. The ring is a symbol of eternity and constancy. That it was placed on the woman's left hand denotes her subjection, and on the ring finger because it pressed a vein which communicates directly with the heart. So universal is the custom of wearing the wedding ring among Jews and Christians that no married woman is ever seen without her plain gold circlet, and she regards the loss of it as a sinister omen; and many women never remove it. This is, however, foolish, and it should be taken off and put on several times at first, so that any subsequent removal or loss need not jar painfully on the feelings.

The bride-cake cut by the bride, with the wedding ring for some fortunate future spouse, seems to be still potent. The twenty-five- year-old bride should cut a few pieces, then leave others to pass it; it is a day on which she should be waited upon.

Some persons, in celebrating their twenty-fifth wedding day, also repeat their wedding journey, and we know a very pleasant little route in England called the "silver-wedding journey," but this is, of course, a matter so entirely personal that it cannot be universally recommended.

The most graceful silver-wedding custom is for the bride and bridegroom to receive the greetings of their friends at first formally, then to leave the marriage bell or canopy of flowers and to go about among the company, becoming again host and hostess. They should spare their children, friends, and themselves tears and sad recollections. Some opulent brides and bridegrooms make it a silver wedding indeed by sending substantial presents to those who started in life with them but have been less fortunate than themselves.

CHAPTER XLI

SPRING AND SUMMER ENTERTAINMENTS.

As the season advances and the country bursts into glorious sudden spring, the garden party, the country dinner, the horseback excursions, and the asparagus parties, the hunts and the yacht voyages, the lawn-tennis and archery, the visits to the polo ground, and the delights of a visit to the friends who live within an hour of the city, at Orange and at Morristown, on the seagirt shore of Long Island or up the Hudson, begin to loom up before the city-bound worthy, and to throw a "rose hue o'er his russet cares."

Now the first question with the neophyte who would go to the hunts (for they "break the ice" in more senses than one), as the first of the spring out-of-door entertainments, is, What does a young girl require who would "ride to hounds"? for "pale Diana," chaste and fair, no longer hunts on foot, as she did in the days of Acteon.

She must have two thorough-bred hunters. She must have a groom, an English habit, a carefully-considered outfit, and she must be a perfect and a fearless horsewoman, and not mind a "cropper." One of the young riders at the Meadow Brook Hunt was thrown over her horse's head into a ditch last spring, and got up declaring she was not even bruised. Yes, she must learn even how to fall off her horse without breaking her ribs or her nose. It is an expensive amusement to be Diana nowadays. The result, however, of long practice on horseback seems to be that a woman becomes almost a centaur, and more fearless than a man. Then the hunt includes as its adjuncts to the young ladies certain men in pink. They "form" on a roadside, and the master of the hunt says, "Ladies and gentlemen, will you hunt?" and he motions to the whipper-in--a gallant creature in pink also-- to "throw off the dogs."

Then the prettiest forty dogs, all spotted, start on their mad career. It is a beautiful sight, with the red-coated huntsmen following, and it looks as if the real fox would be attainable after a time, instead of the farce of an anise-seed bag which now serves to make the ghost of a scent. The low, soft hat is a favorite with our young riders, but there is this to say for the hard hat, it does break a fall. Many a fair forehead has been saved from a terrible scar by the resistant hard hat.

The habit of riding every day and of getting thoroughly accustomed to one's seat should precede the daring attempt at a break-neck "jump." No one should pretend to hunt who has not a good seat, a good horse, and plenty of nerve. Much less should an incompetent rider venture on a friend's horse. It has been said in England that "a man will forgive you for breaking his own neck, but not that of his favorite hunter."

As the day for driving has come, many correspondents write to ask what is the best style of equipage for a young man. We can only say that a tilbury and one horse is very showy, that a dog-cart is the most "knowing," that a high chariot is very stately, but that the two-seated Park wagon is the most appropriate in which to take out a lady. There should always be a servant behind. The art of driving is simple enough, but requires much practice. The good driver should understand his horse well, and turn his curves gently and slowly; he must know how to harness and unharness a horse, and be ready to mend any trifling disarrangement if there is a break.

Now as to driving in a carriage with ladies, a correspondent writes to ask the etiquette which should govern a gentleman's conduct. He takes his seat with his back to the horses, opposite the ladies, nor should he assume to sit beside a lady unless requested to do so. When the carriage stops, he should jump out and assist her to alight, walking with her up her own steps, and ringing the bell. In entering the carriage he should put his left foot on the step, and enter the carriage with his right foot. This is, however, supposing that he sits facing the horses; if he sits with his back to the horses, he reverses the process. A gentleman should avoid treading on ladies' dresses, or shutting them in the door. Ladies who have country-houses should learn to drive as well as to ride. Indeed, in these days when young women drive alone in the Park in their pony phaetons and little carts, we need hardly advise that they should learn to drive well.

As to boating, which is practised so largely by men, we hear of but few ladies who pull the oar about New York; but doubtless it will be done on inland streams and lakes. One gentleman should stay in the boat and help to steady it, unless the oarswomen are very expert. Short dresses and round hats should be worn, with no superincumbent drapery, As the seat of honor in a boat is that occupied by the stroke oar, it is etiquette for the owner of the boat to offer it to his friend if he be a rower.

The asparagus party is a sort of a long picnic, in which a party of friends join, and drive or ride out to some convenient inn where a good dinner can be served, with the advantage of the early vegetable cut directly from the ground. As Long Island is famous for its asparagus, these parties from New York generally select some convenient locality there, near enough to the city to be not too fatiguing a drive.

The new passion for driving a coach has now become so much of an American taste that we need not describe the pastime here. At least four coaches will start from New York for some neighboring town-New Rochelle, Yonkers, etc.--during the summer, and there is no better way of spending a

May day than on top of one. As for al fresco entertainments, game pie, patties, cold beef, pressed tongue, potted meats, sandwiches, _pƒt‚ de foie gras_, champagne, are all taken out in hampers, and served on top of the coach by the obedient valets at the races, for those parties who go out with four horses and a London coach to see the favorite run.

We are often asked what would be the appropriate costume for a lawn party, and we can only answer that the costumes for these parties should be of a useful character. If it is a lawn party at a very elegant house, at Newport or up the Hudson, it may be, however, of a delicacy and elegance not proper if one is asked out in the country merely to "have a good time," when a person would be exposed to the weather, the wear and tear of games, and of a long day in the sun, Thick boots are indispensable. But if one is invited to a wedding in the country, even if the "lawn" is to play a decided part in the entertainment, one must dress very handsomely. At the regular lawn party the lady of the house and her daughters should receive on the lawn in their bonnets.

Yachting is a favorite "summer entertainment," and for those who love the sea it is unparalleled for its excitement, Yachting dresses should be made of serge or tweed, and possess warmth and durability, and young women can trim them according to taste with the name and insignia of their favorite yacht.

For a lawn-tennis party the players dress in flannels made for the purpose, and for a lady the jersey is indispensable, as giving so much freedom to the arms. These parties begin in May at all the country-houses and country parks about our larger towns, and certainly furnish as much healthful amusement as anything can do.

Archery has not yet become acclimated in America, but there are clubs in certain circles which promise a future for this game.

Now for those who go to country-houses to stay "over Sunday," as is the fashion about New York, let us give one word of advice. Always hold yourself at the disposal of those at whose house you are staying. If they propose a plan of action for you, fall in with it. If your visit is prolonged for a week, endeavor to amuse yourself as much as possible. Do not let your hostess see that you are dependent on her for amusement. Remember, however welcome you may be, you are not always wanted. A good hostess also learns when to let her guests alone. A gentleman visitor who neither shoots, fishes, boats, reads, writes letters, nor does anything but hang about, letting himself be "amused," is an intolerable nuisance. He had better go to the billiard-room and practice caroms by himself, or retire to the stables and smoke.

A lady visitor should show a similar tact in retiring to her own room to read or write letters, allowing her hostess to have her mornings or her afternoons to herself, as she pleases. Some people are "born visitors." They have the genius of tact to perceive, the genius of finesse to execute, case and frankness of manner, a knowledge of the world that nothing can surprise, a calmness of temper that nothing can disturb, and a kindness of disposition that can never be exhausted. Such a visitor is greatly in demand everywhere.

A good-natured host and hostess place everything at the disposal of a visitor--their horses, carriages, books, and grounds. And here the utmost delicacy should be observed. Never ride a horse too fast or too far. Never take the coachman beyond his usual limits. Never pluck a flower in the ornamental grounds without asking permission, for in these days of ornamental and fanciful gardening it is necessary to be careful and remember that each flower is a tint in a well-considered picture. Never dog's-ear or disfigure the books, or leave them lying about; if you take them from their shelves, put them back. Be thoughtful in your treatment of the servants, and give those who immediately wait upon you some small gratuity. And if family prayers are read, always try to be present.

So much for the possibility of a "summer entertainment" at a country-house, one of the most agreeable of all, if the apple- blossoms are just out, and the charm of spring is over the whole scene.

We hear of a "rustic masquerade" as one of the spring entertainments at a country-house in Orange. This, it would seem, might be very suitable all over the country, if woods and water are near enough for the shepherds and shepherdesses. A copy of the garden parties which made Boucher the painter that he was, and in which we almost hear the wind rustling through the sedge, the refreshing murmur of the fountain, and see the gayly dressed marquise put her violet slipper on the turf, and the elegant and stately gentlemen as they light up the neighboring arbor with their fine silk coats in his pictures--a copy of such garden parties as those which made Watteau's fame (he has put them all on the fans, and the young people have only to copy them)--this would indeed be a "rustic masquerade," which might amuse and "draw" for a charity. Many of our country towns on the borders of lakes, many of the places near New York in their own fine grounds, would offer a terrestrial paradise for such a garden party.

To drive out to Jerome Park to breakfast, to get the early strawberry and the delicious cream--this is a spring entertainment which many of our business men indulge in, coming back to their work in New York refreshed and invigorated. The men of pleasure of this period have, as they have always had, an ample provision of amusement--not always the most useful, it is true--yet we are glad to see that the out-of-door excitements begin to distance the excitements of the gaming-table. Betting on the turf is not carried to the ruinous extent here that it is in England, while the polo, the base-ball, the boating, and the "riding to hounds "--open to ridicule as it is, in some ways of looking at it--are all healthful. The spring season has its little dinners, lunches, and weddings, but very few evening entertainments.

After a young girl has ransacked the fashionable world all winter, and been at all the fˆtes and balls, concerts, operas, and suppers, she does not care for parties in May. Such infatuated ardor for amusement would make sad havoc of her charms if she did. It is quite enough if she finishes her exciting winter with a fancy dance or private theatricals at some charitable entertainment.

A high tea is served in courses like a dinner, excepting with less formality. The lady sits at one end of the table with the silver tea-tray before her, while the gentleman has before him cold chicken, or even, perhaps, a hot dish like roast partridges, to carve. Frequently scalloped oysters are passed, and always salads, so that those who are in the habit of dining at that hour have a solid meal. There are hot cakes and biscuits and sweetmeats on the table, so that it is really the old-fashioned tea of our grandmothers re-enforced by some solid dishes. It is intended to save the servants trouble on Sunday evening, but it is really more trouble to them as now served, as it gives the waiter additional dishes to wash, and quite as much service. It saves the cook, however.

CHAPTER XLII

FLORAL TRIBUTES AND DECORATIONS.

When every steamer leaving these shores goes out laden with people who are weighed down with flowers, it cannot but be a severe tax on the ingenuity of the florist to devise novel and appropriate forms for the typical basket that shall say bon voyage in a thousand new ways. Floral ships, anchors, stars, crosses, mottoes, monograms, and even the national flag, have been used for these steamer decorations.

But the language of flowers, so thoroughly understood among the Persians that a single flower expresses a complete declaration of love, an offer of marriage, and, presumably, a hint at the settlement, is, with our more practical visionaries and enthusiasts of the nineteenth century, rather an echo of the stock market than a poetical fancy. We fear that no prima donna looks at her flowers without a thought of how much they have cost, and that the belle estimates her bouquet according to the commercial value of a lily-of-the-valley as compared with that of a Jacqueminot rose, rather than as flowers simply. It is a pity that the overwhelming luxury of an extravagant period involves in its all-powerful grasp even the flowers of the field, those generous gifts of sunshine and of rain.

But so it is. It is a well-known fact that the lady who will give her order three months in advance for the flowers needed for her daughter's wedding, or for any other grand ceremonial, can, by offering a sufficiently large amount of money, command any flower she wishes. Even daisies and buttercups, red clover and white, the delicate forget-me-not of the garden, nasturtiums and marigolds, the shy and tender anemone, the dandelion and lilacs and lilies-of-the- valley, may be forced into unnatural bloom in January. It is a favorite caprice to put the field-flowers of June on a lunch-table in January.

This particular table is the greatest of all the consumers of flowers, therefore we may begin by describing some of the new fancies developed by that extraordinarily luxurious meal. A lady's lunch must show not only baskets of magnificent flowers up and down the table; but it must also bear a basket or a bouquet for each lady.

One of the most regal lunches, given to twenty-eight ladies, set the fashion for using little gilt baskets, with covers opening on either side of the handle-- the kind of basket, of a larger size, in which, in New England and in Old England, Dame Trot carried her multifarious parcels home from market. These pretty and useful baskets had on each side a bunch of flowers peeping out through the open cover, and on the gilt handle was tied a ribbon corresponding in color to the flowers. One of them, having soft pink rosebuds of exceeding size and loveliness on one side and a bunch of lilies-of- the-valley on the other, with a bow of pink satin ribbon on the handle, was as pretty a picture as ever Kate Greenaway devised. Another, showing the strong contrast of purple pansies and yellow daffodils, and tied with a lovely purple satin ribbon, was a dream of rich color.

The stiff, formal, flat bouquets of yellow daffodils and bunches of violets, tied with purple ribbon, make a very fine effect laid in regular order at each plate. Repetition of a favorite idea in flowers is not ugly, although it seems at first very far from the primeval and delicious confusion in which nature throws her bouquets down upon upland and meadow.

In the arrangement of roses the most varied and whimsical fancies may be displayed, although the most gorgeous effect is produced, perhaps, by massing a single color or group. A basket of the pink Gloire de Paris, however, with its redundant green foliage, alternated with deep-red Jacqueminots, is a very splendid fancy, and will fill a room with fragrance. In February these roses cost two dollars apiece, and it was no rare sight to see four or six baskets, each containing forty roses, on one table during the winter of 1884.

We advise all ladies going into the country to purchase some of the little "Dame Trot" baskets, as they will be lovely when filled with wild-flowers during the summer. Indeed, the gilt basket, fitted with a tin pan to hold earth or water, is such a cheap and pretty receptacle for either growing or cut flowers that it ought to be a belonging of every dinner-table.

From the lunch-table, with its baskets and floral fancies, we come to the dinner-table. Here the space is so valuable that the floral bag, an ingenious plan by which roses may be hung at the side of the wearer, has been invented.

This is a novel and very pretty way of wearing flowers. The roses or other flowers are tied together with wires, in the shape of a reticule, and a ribbon and pin provided, so that the lady may fasten her floral trophy at her side. The baskets of flowers and the adornments of the _‚pergne_ for a dinner are very apt to be all of one flower. If mixed, they are of two sorts, as yellow roses and red ones, or white and pink, or, may be, half of lilacs and half of roses, or purple pansies and bright yellow flowers. Some tables are set with scarlet carnations alone, and the effect is very fine.

For wedding decorations, houses are now filled with palm-trees in pots and orange-trees in full bearing. An entire suite of rooms is made into a bower of large-leaved plants. Mirrors are covered with vines, wreaths, and climbing roses, trained across a trellis of wire. The bride stands under a floral umbrella, which juts out into the room. The monograms of bride and bridegroom are put in floral shields against the wall, like the cartouche on which the names and the titles of an Egyptian king are emblazoned in the solitude of the Pyramids. The bouquets carried by brides and bridesmaids are now extraordinarily large, measuring a foot or more across the top.

Tulips have always been favorite ornaments for the dinner-table. These flowers, so fine in drawing and so splendid in color, produce an extremely brilliant effect in large masses. As Easter approaches, lilies come in for especial notice, and the deep Japan cup-lily, grouped with the stately callas, and the garden-lily, with its long yellow stamens and rich perfume, worthily fill the _‚pergnes_.

Hyacinths are lovely harbingers of spring, and are beautiful in color; but there is a strong objection to this flower as a decoration, its heavy perfume being unpleasant to some people.

A fish-basket filled with bunches of lilies, mignonette, deep pink moss-roses shaded to the pale tints of the rose known as the Baroness de Rothschild, with a glowing centre of warm red Jacqueminots and a fringe of purple pansies and Mar‚chal Niels, was one of many beautiful floral ornaments on a magnificent dinner- table.

In spite of the attempt to prevent the extravagant use of flowers at funerals, we still see on those sad occasions some new and rather poetic ideas expressed by floral emblems. One of these, called the "Gates Ajar," was very beautiful: the "gates" panelled with lilies, and surmounted by doves holding sprays of passion-vines in their beaks.

Palms crossed, and clasped by roses and ribbons, an oblique cross of roses lying on a bed of ivy, a basket made of ivy and autumn leaves, holding a sheaf of grain and a sickle of violets, an ivy pillow with a cross of flowers on one side, a bunch of pansies held by a knot of ribbon at one corner, a cross made of ivy alone, a "harvest-field" made of ears of wheat, are some of the many new funereal designs which break the monotony of the dreadful white crosses, crowns, and anchors, hearts and wreaths, of the past.

It is no longer necessary to exclude color from these tributes to the dead. Indeed, some of the most beautiful designs noticed at recent funerals have been composed of colored flowers.

For a christening, a floral cradle or swinging hammock, a bowl, a silver cup full of the tiniest flowers, are all favorite designs. A large table of flowers, with the baby's initials in the centre, was sent to one happy young mother on a recent auspicious occasion; and far more lovely was a manger of flowers, with the "Star of the East" hanging above it, all made of that pretty white flower the Star of Bethlehem.

Strange contrasts of flowers have been made: purple lilacs and the blue forget-me-nots were a favorite combination--"stylish, not pretty," was the whispered criticism.

The yellow marigold, a sort of small sunflower, has been the favorite "caprice" for bouquets de corsage. This is as near to an actual sunflower as the aesthetes have ventured to approach. With us, perhaps, there is no more splendid yellow than this marigold, and it admirably sets off a black or sage green dress.

An extravagant lady, at a ball, wore around her white dress skirt a fringe of real violets. Although less effective than the artificial ones, they had a pretty appearance until they drooped and faded. This adornment cost one hundred and fifty dollars.

A rainbow has been attempted in flowers, but with poor success. It will look like a ribbon--a very handsome ribbon, no doubt; but the _arc-en-ciel_ evades reproduction, even in the transcendent prismatic colors of flowers.

Ribbons have been used with flowers, and add much to their effect; for, since the Arcadian days of Rosalind and Celia, a flower, a ribbon, and a pretty girl, have been associated with each other in prose, poetry, painting, and romance.

The hanging-baskets, filled with blooming plants, trailers, and ferns, have been much used at weddings to add to the bower-like appearance of the rooms; and altars and steps of churches have been richly adorned with flowering plants and palm-trees and other luxuriant foliage.

The prices paid for flowers have been enormous. One thousand dollars for the floral decorations for a single dinner has not been an uncommon price. But the expenditure of such large sums for flowers has not been unprofitable. The flowers grow finer every day, and, as an enterprising florist, who had given a "rose tea" to his patrons, remarked, "Every large order inspires us to produce a finer flower."

CHAPTER XLIII

THE FORK AND THE SPOON.

A correspondent writes, "How shall I carry my fork to my mouth?" The fork should be raised laterally to the mouth with the right hand; the elbow should never be crooked, so as to bring the hand round at a right angle, or the fork directly opposite the mouth. The mother cannot begin too early to inculcate good manners at the table, and among the first things that young children should learn is the proper use of the fork.

Again, the fork should not be overloaded. To take meat and vegetables and pack them on the poor fork, as if it were a beast of burden, is a common American vulgarity, born of our hurried way of eating at railway-stations and hotels. But it is an unhealthy and an ill-mannered habit. To take but little on the fork at a time, a moderate mouthful, shows good manners and refinement. The knife must never be put into the mouth at any time--that is a remnant of barbarism.

Another correspondent asks, "Should cheese be eaten with a fork?" We say, decidedly, "Yes," although good authorities declare that it may be put on a morsel of bread with a knife, and thus conveyed to the mouth. Of course we refer to the soft cheeses--like Gorgonzola, Brie, cream-cheese, Neufchatel, Limburger, and the like--which are hardly more manageable than butter. Of the hard cheeses, one may convey a morsel to the month with the thumb and forefinger; but, as a general rule, it is better to use the fork.

Now as to the spoon: it is to be used for soup, for strawberries and cream, for all stewed fruit and preserves, and for melons, which, from their juiciness, cannot be conveniently eaten with a fork. Peaches and cream, all the "wet dishes," as Mrs. Glasse was wont to call them, must be eaten with a spoon. Roman punch is always eaten with a spoon.

On elegant tables, each plate or "cover" is accompanied by two large silver knives, a small silver knife and fork for fish, a small fork for the oysters on the half-shell, a large table-spoon for soup, and three large forks. The napkin is folded in the centre, with a piece of bread in it. As the dinner progresses, the knife and fork and spoon which have been used are taken away with the plate. This saves confusion, and the servant has not to bring fresh knives and forks all the time. Fish should be eaten with silver knife and fork; for if it is full of bones, like shad, for instance, it is very difficult to manage it without the aid of a knife.

For sweetbreads, cutlets, roast beef, etc., the knife is also necessary; but for the _croquettes_, _rissoles_, _bouch‚es … la Reine_, _timbales_, and dishes of that class, the fork alone is needed. A majority of the made dishes in which the French excel are to be eaten with the fork.

After the dinner has been eaten, and the dessert reached, we must see to it that everything is cleared off but the table-cloth, which is now never removed. A dessert-plate is put before each guest, and a gold or silver spoon, a silver dessert spoon and fork, and often a queer little combination of fork and spoon, called an "ice-spoon."

In England, strawberries are always served with the green stems, and each one is taken up with the fingers, dipped in sugar, and thus eaten. Many foreigners pour wine over their strawberries, and then eat them with a fork, but this seems to be detrimental to the natural flavor of the king of berries.

Pears and apples should be peeled with a silver knife, cut into quarters, and then picked up with the fingers. Oranges should be peeled, and cut or separated, as the eater chooses. Grapes should be eaten from behind the half-closed hand, the stones and skin falling into the fingers unobserved, and thence to the plate. Never swallow the stones of small fruits; it is extremely dangerous. The pineapple is almost the only fruit which requires both knife and fork.

So much has the fork come into use of late that a wit observed that he took everything with it but afternoon tea. The thick chocolate, he observed, often served at afternoon entertainments, could be eaten comfortably with a fork, particularly the whipped cream on top of it.

A knife and fork are both used in eating salad, if it is not cut up before serving. A large lettuce leaf cannot be easily managed without a knife, and of course the fork must be used to carry it to the mouth. Thus, as bread, butter, and cheese are served with the salad, the salad knife and fork are really essential. Salt-cellars are now placed at each plate, and it is not improper to take salt with your knife.

Dessert-spoons and small forks do not form a part of the original "cover;" that is, they are not put on at the beginning of the dinner, but are placed before the guests according as they are needed; as, for instance, when the Roman punch arrives before the game, and afterwards when the plum-pudding or pastry is served before the ices.

The knives and forks are placed on each side of the plate, ready for the hand.

For the coffee after dinner a very small spoon is served, as a large one would be out of place in the small cups that are used. Indeed, the variety of forks and spoons now in use on a well-furnished table is astonishing.

One of our esteemed correspondents asks, "How much soup should be given to each person?" A half-ladleful is quite enough, unless it is a country dinner, where a full ladleful may be given without offence; but do not fill the soup-plate.

In carving a joint of fowl the host ought to make sure of the condition of both knife and fork. Of course a good carver sees to both before dinner. The knife should be of the best cutlery, well sharpened, and the fork long, strong, and furnished with a guard.

In using the spoon be very careful not to put it too far into the mouth. It is a fashion with children to polish their spoons in a somewhat savage fashion, but the guest at a dinner-party should remember, in the matter of the dessert-spoon especially (which is a rather large implement for the mouth), not to allow even the clogging influences of cabinet pudding to induce him to give his spoon too much leeway; as in all etiquette of the table, the spoon has its difficulties and dangers. Particularly has the soup-spoon its Scylla and Charybdis, and if a careless eater make a hissing sound as he eats his soup, the well-bred diner-out looks round with dismay.

There are always people happy in their fashion of eating, as in everything else. There is no such infallible proof of good-breeding and of early usage as the conduct of a man or woman at dinner. But, as every one has not had the advantage of early training, it is well to study these minute points of table etiquette, that one may learn how to eat without offending the sensibility of the well-bred. Especially study the fork and the spoon. There is, no doubt, a great diversity of opinion on the Continent with regard to the fork. It is a common German fashion, even with princes, to put the knife into the month. Italians are not always particular as to its use, and cultivated Russians, Swedes, Poles, and Danes often eat with their knives or forks indiscriminately.

But Austria, which follows French fashions, the Anglo-Saxon race in England, America, and the colonies, all French people, and those elegant Russians who emulate French manners, deem the fork the proper medium of communication between the plate and the mouth.

CHAPTER XLIV

NAPKINS AND TABLE-CLOTHS.

The elegance of a table depends essentially upon its napery. The plainest of meals is made a banquet if the linen be fresh, fine, and smooth, and the most sumptuous repast can be ruined by a soiled and crumpled table-cloth. The housewife who wishes to conduct her house in elegance must make up her mind to use five or six sets of napkins, and to have several dozens of each ready for possible demands.

A napkin should never be put on the table a second time until it has been rewashed; therefore, napkin-rings should be abandoned-- relegated to the nursery tea-table.

Breakfast napkins are of a smaller size than dinner napkins, and are very pretty if they bear the initial letter of the family in the centre. Those of fine, double damask, with a simple design, such as a snow-drop or a mathematical figure, to match the table-cloth, are also pretty. In the end, the economy in the wear pays a young house- keeper to invest well in the best of napery-- double damask, good Irish linen. Never buy poor or cheap napkins; they are worn out almost immediately by washing.

Coarse, heavy napkins are perhaps proper for the nursery and children's table. If children dine with their parents, they should have a special set of napkins for their use, and some very careful mammas make these with tapes to tie around the youthful necks. It is better in a large family, where there are children, to have heavy and coarse table-linen for every-day use. It is not an economy to buy colored cloths, for they must be washed as often as if they were white, and no color stands the hard usage of the laundry as well as pure white.

Colored napery is, therefore, the luxury of a well-appointed country house, and has its use in making the breakfast and luncheon table look a little unlike the dinner. Never use a parti-colored damask for the dinner-table.

Those breakfast cloths of pink, or yellow, or light-blue and white, or drab, are very pretty with napkins to match; but after having been washed a few times they become very dull in tint, and are not as agreeable to the eye as white, which grows whiter with every summer's bleaching. Ladies who live in the city should try to send all their napery to the country at least once a year, and let it lie on the grass for a good bleaching. It seems to keep cleaner afterwards.

For dinner, large and handsome napkins, carefully ironed and folded simply, with a piece of bread inside, should lie at each plate. These should be removed when the fruit course is brought, and with each finger-bowl should be a colored napkin, with which to dry the fingers.

Pretty little fanciful doyleys are now also put under the finger- bowl, merely to be looked at. Embroidered with quaint designs, these little three-inch things are very ornamental; but the real and serviceable doyley should not be forgotten, and may be laid either beside or over the top of the finger-bowl.

Many ladies are so extravagant that they have a second napkin of small size put on for that part of the dessert which precedes the fruit, but this involves so much trouble to both the guest and the waiter that it is not ordinarily done.

The napkins made at Berlin, with drawn thread and knotted fringe and lace effects, are very handsome. They are also made at the South Kensington schools, and in Paris, and by the Decorative Art Society in New York, and are beautifully wrought with monogram and crest in red, white, and blue thread. But no napkin is ever more thoroughly elegant than the very thick, fine, and substantial plain damask, which becomes more pure and smooth every time that it is cleansed.

However, as one of our great dinner-givers in New York has ordered twenty-four dozen of the handsome, drawn-thread napkins from one establishment at Berlin, we must conclude that they will become the fashion.

When breakfast is made a formal meal--that is, when company is invited to come at a stated hour-_-serviettes_, or large dinner- napkins, must be placed at each plate, as for a dinner. But they are never used at a "stand-up" breakfast, nor are doyleys or finger- bowls.

If any accident happens, such as the spilling of a glass of wine or the upsetting of a plate, the _d‚bris_ should be carefully cleared away, and the waiter should spread a clean napkin over the desecrated table-cloth. Large, white napkins are invariably used at luncheon, and the smaller ones kept for breakfast and tea. Some ladies like the little, fringed napkins for tea, but to look well these must be very carefully washed and ironed.

Never fasten your napkin around your neck; lay it across your knees, convenient to the hand, and lift one corner only to wipe the mouth. Men who wear a mustache are permitted to "saw" the mouth with the napkin, as if it were a bearing-rein, but for ladies this would look too masculine.

Napkins at hotels are now folded, in a half-wet condition, into all sorts of shapes: a goose, a swan, a ship, a high boot, are all favorite and fanciful designs; but this is a dirty fashion, requiring the manipulation of hands which are not always fresh, and as the napkin must be damp at the folding, it is not always dry when shaken out. Nothing is so unhealthy as a damp napkin; it causes agony to a delicate and nervous lady, a man with the rose-cold, a person with neuralgia or rheumatism, and is offensive to every one. Never allow a napkin to be placed on the table until it has been well aired. There is often a conspiracy between the waiter and the laundress in great houses, both wishing to shirk work, the result of which is that the napkins, not prepared at the proper time, are put on the table damp.

A house-keeper should have a large chest to contain napery which is not to be used every day. This reserved linen should be washed and aired once a year at least, to keep it from moulding and becoming yellow.

Our Dutch ancestors were very fond of enriching a chest of this kind, and many housewives in New York and Albany are to-day using linen brought from Holland three hundred years ago.

The napery made in Ireland has, however, in our day taken the place of that manufactured in other countries. It is good, cheap, and sometimes very handsome, and if it can be bought unadulterated with cotton it will last many years.

Very little starch should be put in napkins. No one wishes to wipe a delicate lip on a board, and a stiff napkin is very like that commodity.

At dinner-parties in England, in the days of William the Fourth, a napkin was handed with each plate. As the guest took his plate and new napkin, he allowed the one which he had used to fall to the floor, and when he went away from the table he left a snowy pile of napery behind him.

The use of linen for the table is one of the oldest of fashions, The early Italian tables were served with such beautiful lace-worked napkins that we cannot equal them to-day. Queen Elizabeth's napkins were edged with lace made in Flanders, and were an important item of expense in her day-book.

Fringed, embroidered, and colored napkins made of silk are used by Chinese and Japanese magnates. These articles may be washed, and are restored to their original purity by detergent agents that are unknown to us. The Chinese also use little napkins of paper, which are very convenient for luncheon baskets and picnics.

One of our correspondents asks us if she should fold her napkin before leaving the table. At a fashionable meal, no. At a social tea or breakfast, yes, if her hostess does so. There is no absolute law on this subject.

At a fashionable dinner no one folds his napkin. He lets it drop to the floor, or lays it by the side of his plate unfolded. When the fruit napkin is brought he takes it from the glass plate on which it is laid, and either places it at his right hand or across his knee, and the "illuminated rag," as some wit called the little embroidered doyley, which is not meant for use, is, after having been examined and admired, laid on the table, beside the finger-bowl. These pretty little trifles can serve several times the purpose of ornamenting the finger-bowl.

Napkins, when laid away in a chest or drawer, should have some pleasant, cleanly herb like lavender or sweet-grass, or the old- fashioned clover, or bags of Oriental orris-root, put between them, that they may come to the table smelling of these delicious scents.

Nothing is more certain to destroy the appetite of a nervous dyspeptic than a napkin that smells of greasy soap. There is a laundry soap now in use which leaves a very unpleasant odor in the linen, and napkins often smell so strongly of it as to take away the desire for food.

Perhaps the influence of Delmonico upon the public has been in nothing more strongly shown than in the effect produced by his always immaculate napery. It was not common in American eating- houses, when he began, to offer clean table-cloths and clean napkins. Now no decent diner will submit to any other than a clean napkin. Every lady, therefore, who aspires to elegant housekeeping, should remember that she must never allow the same napkin to be put on her table twice. Once used, it must be sent to the laundry before it is put on the table again.

CHAPTER XLV

SERVANTS, THEIR DRESS AND DUTIES.

As we read that a West Point hotel-keeper has recently dismissed all his waiters who would not shave off their mustaches, we must begin to believe that the heretofore heedless American is considering the appearance of his house and carriage-servants. In the early days of the republic, before Thomas Jefferson tied his horse's rein to the palings of the fence and sauntered into the Capitol to be inaugurated, the aristocrats of the various cities had a livery for their servants. But after such a dash of cold water in the face of established usage by the Chief Magistrate of the Country, many of the old forms and customs of Colonial times fell into disuse, and among others the wearing of a livery by serving-men. A constantly declining grade of shabbiness was the result of this, as the driver of the horses wore a coat and hat of the same style as his master, only less clean and new. Like many of our American ideas so good in theory, the outcome of this attempt at "Liberty, Equality, and Fraternity," was neither conducive to neatness nor elegance.

But so strongly was the prejudice against liveries instilled into the public mind that only seven years ago a gentleman of the most aristocratic circle of aristocratic Philadelphia declared that he refrained from having a liveried servant behind his carriage from fear of shocking public opinion. In New York the presence of a large, foreign, social element long ago brought about a revulsion of opinion in this matter, and now most persons who desire a neat, plain, and appropriate style of dress for their coachmen and footmen put them in a livery, for which the master pays. Those who are particular in such matters do not allow a waiter or a footman to wear a mustache, and require all men-servants to be clean-shaven, except the coachman, who is permitted to wear whiskers. Each must have his hair cut short, and the waiter must wear white gloves while waiting at table or when handing refreshments; even a glass of water on a silver salver must be brought with a gloved hand.

Many ladies have much trouble in impressing upon their men-servants the necessity for personal neatness. The ordinary attire of a butler is a black dress-coat, with white cravat and white cotton gloves. A waiter who attends the door in a large establishment, and who is one of many servants, is usually in a quiet livery--a frock-coat with brass buttons, and a striped waistcoat. Some families affect the scarlet waistcoat for their footman, which, indeed, may be used with very good effect for the negro servant.

Neatness is indispensable; a slovenly and inattentive servant betrays a slovenly household. Yet servants often do their employers great injustice. They are slow to respond to the bell, they give uncivil answers, they deny one person and admit another, they fail to deliver notes, they are insolent, they neglect the orders of the mistress when she is out. We cannot expect perfection in our domestic service, but it is possible, by painstaking and patient teaching, to create a respectable and helpful serving class. Servants are very apt to take their tone from their employers--to be civil if they are civil, and insolent if they are insolent. The head of the house is very apt to be copied by his flunkies. One primal law we must mention--a hostess should never reprove her servants in the presence of her guests; it is cruel both to guest and servant, and always shows the hostess in an unamiable light. Whatever may go wrong, the lady of the house should remain calm; if she is anguished, who can be happy?

We have not here, nominally, that helpful treasure known in England as the parlor-maid. We call her a waitress, and expect her to do all the work of one floor. Such a person can be trained by a good housekeeper to be a most admirable servant. She must be told to rise early, to attend to the sweeping of the door-steps, to open the blinds, to light the fires, and to lay the breakfast-table. She must appear in a neat calico dress, white apron and cap, and wait upon the family at breakfast. After breakfast, the gentlemen will expect her to brush their hats, to bring overcoats and overshoes, and to find the umbrellas. She must answer the door-bell as well, so should be nimble-footed and quick-witted. When breakfast is over, she must remove the dishes and wash them, clean the silver, and prepare for the next meal. In well-regulated households there is a day for sweeping, a day for silver cleaning, a clay for mirror-polishing, and another for making bright and neat the fireplaces; but each one of these duties requires a certain share of attention every day. The parlor must be dusted, and the fires attended to, of course, so the parlor-maid, or the waitress, in a large family has much to do. The best girls for this arduous situation are English, but they are very difficult to procure. The Germans are not apt to remain long with one family. The best available parlor-maids are Irishwomen who have lived some time in this country.

A servant often sins from ignorance, therefore time spent in teaching her is not wasted. She should be supplied with such utensils as facilitate work, and one very good house-keeper declares that the virtue of a waitress depends upon an infinity of crash. And there is no doubt that a large supply of towels is a constant suggestion of cleanliness that is a great moral support to a waitress.

In these days, when parlors are filled with bric-…-brac, a parlor- maid has no time to do laundry-work, except such part of it as may pertain to her personally. The best of all arrangements is to hire a laundress, who will do all the washing of the house. Even in a very economical household this has been found to be the best plan, otherwise there is always an unexplained delay when the bell rings. The appearance at the door of a dishevelled maid, with arms covered with soapsuds, is not ornamental. If a cook can be found who will also undertake to do the washing and ironing, it is a better and more satisfactory arrangement. But in our growing prosperity this functionary has assumed new and extraordinary importance, and will do nothing but cook.

A young house-keeper beginning her life in a great city finds herself frequently confronted with the necessity of having four servants--a cook, a laundress, a waiter or parlor-maid (sometimes both), and a chamber-maid. None of these excellent auxiliaries is willing to do the other's work: they generally quarrel. So the first experience of house-keeping is not agreeable. But it is possible to find two servants who, if properly trained, will do all the service of a small family, and do it well.

The mistress must carefully define the work of each, or else hire them with the understanding that neither shall ever say, "This is not my work." It is sometimes quite impossible to define what is the exact duty of each servant. Our house-keeping in this country is so chaotic, and our frequent changes of house and fortune cause it to partake so much of the nature of a provisional government, that every woman must be a Louis Napoleon, and ready for a _coup d'‚tat_ at any moment.

The one thing which every lady must firmly demand from her servants is respect. The harassed and troubled American woman who has to cope with the worst servants in the world--the ill-trained, incapable, and vicious peasantry of Europe, who come here to be "as good as anybody," and who see that it is easily possible to make a living in America whether they are respectful or not--that woman has a very arduous task to perform.

But she must gain at least outward respect by insisting upon having it, and by showing her servants that she regards it as even a greater desideratum than the efficient discharge of duties. The mistress must not lose her temper. She must be calm, imperturbable, and dignified, always. If she gives an order, she must insist, at whatever personal cost, that it shall be obeyed. Pertinacity and inflexibility on this point are well bestowed.

Where there are children, the nurse is, of course, a most important part of the household, and often gives more trouble than any of the other servants, for she is usually an elderly person, impatient of control, and "set in her ways." The mistress must make her obey at once. Nurses are only human, and can be made to conform to the rules by which humanity is governed.

Ladies have adopted for their nurses the French style of dress--dark stuff gowns, white aprons, and caps. French nurses are, indeed, very much the fashion, as it is deemed all-important that children should learn to speak French as soon as they can articulate. But it is so difficult to find a French nurse who will speak the truth that many mothers have renounced the accomplished Gaul and hired the Anglo- Saxon, who is often not more veracious.

No doubt there was better service when servants were fewer, and when the mistress looked well after the ways of her household, and performed certain domestic duties herself. In those early days it was she who made the best pastry and sweetmeats. It was she who wrought at the quilting-frame and netted the best bed-curtains. It was she who darned the table-cloth, with a neatness and exactness that made the very imperfection a beauty. It was she who made the currant wine and the blackberry cordial. She knew all the secrets of clear starching, and taught the ignorant how to do their work through her educated intelligence. She had, however, native Americans to teach, and not Irish, Germans, or Swedes. Now, few native-born Americans will become servants, and the difficulties of the mistress are thereby increased.

A servant cannot be too carefully taught her duty to visitors. Having first ascertained whether her mistress is at home or not, in order to save a lady the trouble of alighting from her carriage, she should answer the ring of the door-bell without loss of time. She should treat all callers with respect and civility, but at the same time she should be able to discriminate between friend and foe, and not unwarily admit those innumerable cheats, frauds, and beggars who, in a respectable garb, force an entrance to one's house for the purpose of theft, or perhaps to sell a cement for broken crockery, or the last thing in hair-dye.

Conscientious servants who comprehend their duties, and who try to perform them, should, after a certain course of discipline, be allowed to follow their own methods of working. Interference and fault-finding injure the temper of an inferior; while suspicion is bad for anybody, and especially operates against the making of a good servant.

To assure your servants that you believe them to be honest is to fix in them the habit of honesty. To respect their rights, their hours of recreation, their religion, their feelings, to wish them good- night and good-morning (after the pretty German fashion), to assist them in the writing of their letters and in the proper investment of their earnings, to teach them to read and write and to make their clothes, so that they may be useful to themselves when they leave servitude--all this is the pleasurable duty of a good mistress, and such a course makes good servants.

All ignorant natures seek a leader; all servants like to be commanded by a strong, honest, fair, judicious mistress. They seek her praise; they fear her censure, not as slaves dread the whip of the tyrant, but as soldiers respect their superior officer. Bad temper, injustice, and tyranny make eye-service, but not heart- service.

Irresolute persons who do not know their own minds, and cannot remember their own orders, make very poor masters and mistresses. It is better that they should give up the business of house-keeping, and betake themselves to the living in hotels or boarding-houses with which our English cousins taunt us, little knowing that the nomadic life they condemn is the outcome of their own failure to make good citizens of those offscourings of jail and poorhouse and Irish shanty which they send to us under the guise of domestic servants.

Familiarity with servants always arouses their contempt; a mistress can be kind without being familiar. She must remember that the servant looks up to her over the great gulf of a different condition of life and habit--over the great gulf of ignorance, and that, in the order of nature, she should respect not only the person in authority, but the being, as superior to herself. This salutary influence is thrown away if the mistress descend to familiarity and intimacy. Certain weak mistresses vary their attitude towards their servants, first assuming a familiarity of manner which is disgusting, and which the servant does not mistake for kindness, and then a tyrannical severity which is as unreasonable as the familiarity, and, like it, is only a spasm of an ill-regulated mind.

Servants should wear thin shoes in the house, and be told to step lightly, not to slam doors, or drop china, or to rattle forks and spoons. A quiet servant is the most certain of domestic blessings. Neatness, good manners, and faithfulness have often insured a stupid servant of no great efficiency a permanent home with a family. If to these qualities be added a clear head, an active body, and a respectful manner, we have that rare article--a perfect servant.

CHAPTER XLVI

THE HOUSE WITH ONE SERVANT.

Many large families in this country employ but one servant. Although when life was simpler it was somewhat easier than it is now to conduct a house with such assistance as may be offered by a maid-of- all-work, it was necessary even then for the ladies of the house to do some portion of the lighter domestic work.

It is a very good plan, when there are several daughters in the family, to take turns each to test her talent as a house-keeper and organizer. If, however, the mistress keep the reins in her own hands, she can detail one of these young ladies to sweep and dust the parlors, another to attend to the breakfast dishes, another to make sure that the maid has not neglected any necessary cleansing of the bedrooms.

A mother with young children must have a thoroughly defined and understood system for the daily work to render it possible for one servant to perform it all.

The maid must rise very early on Monday morning, and do some part of the laundry work before breakfast. Many old American servants (when there were such) put the clothes in water to soak, and sometimes to boil, on Sunday night, that night not having the religious significance in New England that Saturday night had.

Nowadays, however, Irish girls expect to have a holiday every other Sunday afternoon and evening, and it would probably be vain to expect this service of them. But at least they should rise by five o'clock, and do two hours' good work before it is time to prepare the breakfast and lay the table.

A neat-handed Phyllis will have a clean gown, cap, and apron hanging in the kitchen closet, and slip them on before she carries in the breakfast, which she has cooked and must serve. Some girls show great tact in this matter of appearing neat at the right time, but many of them have to be taught by the mistress to have a clean cap and apron in readiness. The mistress usually furnishes these items of her maid's attire, and they should be the property of the mistress, and remain in the family through all changes of servants. They can be bought at almost any repository conducted in the interest of charity for less than they can be made at home, and a dozen of them in a house greatly improves the appearance of the servants.

The cook, having prepared the breakfast and waited at table, places in front of her mistress a neat, wooden tub, with a little cotton- yarn mop and two clean towels, and then retreats to the kitchen with the heavy dishes and knives and forks. The lady proceeds to wash the glass, silver, and china, draining the things on a waiter, and wiping them on her dainty linen towels. It is not a disagreeable operation, and all gentlemen say they like to eat and drink from utensils which have been washed by a lady.

Having put away the glass and china, the lady shakes the table-cloth, folds it, and puts it away. She then takes a light brush broom and sweeps the dining-room, and dusts it carefully, opening a window to air the apartment. When this is done she sets the parlor in order. The maid-of-all-work should, in the mean time, make a visit to the bedrooms, and do the heavy work of turning mattresses and making beds. When this is accomplished she must return to the kitchen, and after carefully cleaning the pots and kettles that have been in use for the morning meal, devote an undivided attention to her arduous duties as laundress. A plain dinner for washing-day--a beefsteak and some boiled potatoes, a salad, and a pie or pudding made on the preceding Saturday--is all that should be required of a maid-of-all-work on Monday.

The afternoon must be spent in finishing the washing, hanging out the clothes, and preparing the tea--an easy and informal meal, which should consist of something easy to cook; for, after all that she has done during the day, this hard-worked girl must "tidy up" her kitchen before she can enjoy a well-earned repose. It is so annoying to a maid-of-all-work to be obliged to open the door for visitors that ladies often have a little girl or boy for this purpose. In the country it can be more easily managed.

Tuesday is ironing-day all over the world, and the maid must be assisted in this time of emergency by her mistress. Most ladies understand the process of clear starching and the best method of ironing fine clothing; if they do not, they should. In fact, a good house-keeper should know everything; and when a lady gives her attention to this class of household duties she is invariably more successful in performing them than a person of less education and intelligence.

On Wednesday the maid must bake a part of the bread, cake, and pies that will be required during the week. In this the mistress helps, making the light pastry, stoning the raisins, washing the currants, and beating the eggs. Very often a lady fond of cookery makes all her dainty dishes, her desserts, and her cakes and pies. She should help herself with all sorts of mechanical appliances. She should have the best of egg-beaters, sugar-sifters, bowls in plenty, and towels and aprons ad libitum. She has, if she be a systematic house-keeper, a store closet, which is her pride, with its neat, labelled spice-boxes, and its pots of pickles and preserves which she has made herself, and which, therefore, must be nice.

The cooking of meat is a thing which so affects the health of people that every lady should study it thoroughly. No roasts should be baked. The formulary sounds like a contradiction; but it is the custom in houses where the necessity of saving labor is an important consideration, to put the meat that should be roasted in the oven and bake it. This is very improper, as it dries up all the juice, which is the life-giving, life-sustaining property of the meat.

Let every young house-keeper buy a Dutch oven, and either roast the meat before the coals of a good wood fire, or before the grating of a range, in which coals take the place of wood. By this method she saves those properties of a piece of roast beef which are the most valuable. Otherwise her roast meat will be a chip, a tasteless and a dry morsel, unpalatable and indigestible.

The cooking of vegetables is also to be studied; potatoes should not be over-boiled or underdone, as they are exceedingly unhealthy if not properly cooked. Bread must be well kneaded and delicately baked; a woman who understands the uses of fire--and every householder should--has stolen the secret of Prometheus.

On Thursday the maid must sweep the house thoroughly, if there are heavy carpets, as this is work for the strong-armed and the strong- handed. The mistress can follow with the dusting-brush and the cloth, and, again, the maid may come in her footstep with step- ladder, and wipe off mirrors and windows.

Many ladies have a different calendar from this, and prefer to have their work done on different days; but whatever may be the system for the management of a house, it should be strictly carried out, and all the help that may accrue from punctuality and order rendered to a maid in the discharge of her arduous and multifarious duties.

Most families have a sort of general house-cleaning on Friday: floors are scrubbed and brasses cleaned, the silver given a better cleansing, and the closets examined, the knives are scoured more thoroughly, and the lady puts her linen-closet in order, throwing sweet lavender between the sheets. On Saturday more bread and cake are baked, the Sunday's dinner prepared, that the maid may have her Sunday afternoon out, and the busy week is ended with a clean kitchen, a well-swept and garnished house, and all the cooking done except the Sunday meat and vegetables.

To conduct the business of a house through the week, with three meals each day, and all the work well done; by one maid, is a very creditable thing to the mistress. The "order which is Heaven's first law" must be her chief help in this difficult matter; she must be willing to do much of the light work herself, and she must have a young, strong, willing maid.

CHAPTER XLVII

THE HOUSE WITH TWO SERVANTS.

The great problem of the young or middle-aged house-keeper in large cities is how to form a neat, happy, comfortable home, and so to order the house that two servants can accomplish all its work.

These two servants we call the cook and the waiter, and they must do all that there is to do, including the washing.

When life was simpler, this was done without murmuring; but now it is difficult to find good and trained servants, particularly in New York, who will fill such places. For to perform the work of a family--to black the boots, sweep and wash the sidewalk, attend the door and lay the table, help with the washing and ironing, and make the fires, as well as sweep and dust, and take care of the silver-- would seem to require the hands of Briareus.

It is better to hire a girl "for general house-work," and train her for her work as waitress, than to take one who has clone nothing else but wait at table. Be particular, when engaging a girl, to tell her what she has to do, as many of the lofty kind object particularly to blacking boots; and as it must be done, it is better to define it at once.

A girl filling this position should have, first, the advantage of system, and the family must keep regular hours. She must rise at six, or earlier, if necessary, open the front-door and parlor- blinds, and the dining-room windows, and then proceed to cleanse the front steps and sidewalk, polish the bell-pull, and make all tidy about the mats. She must next make the fires, if fires are used in the house, and carry down the ashes, carefully depositing them where they will not communicate fire. She must then gather the boots and shoes from the doors of the sleeping-rooms, and take them to the laundry, where she should brush them, having a closet there for her brushes and blacking. Having replaced the boots beside the respective doors to which they belong, she should make herself neat and clean, put on her cap and apron, and then prepare for laying the table for breakfast. This she does not do until she has brushed up the floor, caused the fire to burn brightly, and in all respects made the dining-room respectable.

The laying of the table must be a careful and neat operation; a clean cloth should be put on, with the fold regularly running down the middle of the table, the silver and glass and china placed neatly and in order, the urn-lamp lighted, and the water put to boil, the napkins fresh and well-folded, and the chairs drawn up in order on either side. It is well worth a mistress's while to preside at this work for two or three mornings, to see that her maid understands her wishes.

All being in order, the maid may ring a bell, or knock at the doors, or rouse the family as they may wish. When breakfast is over she removes the dishes, and washes the silver and china in the pantry. After putting everything away, and opening a window in the dining- room, she proceeds to the bedrooms.

Every one should, before leaving his bedroom, open a window and turn back the clothes, to air the room and the bed thoroughly. If this has been neglected, it is the servant's business to do it, and to make the beds, wash the basins, and leave everything very clean. She must also dust the bureaus and tables and chairs, hang up the dresses, put away the shoes, and set everything in order.

She then descends to the parlor floor, and makes it neat, and thence to the kitchen, where, if she has time, she does a little washing; but if there is to be luncheon or early dinner, she cannot do much until that is prepared, particularly if it is her duty to answer a bell. In a doctor's house, or in a house where there are many calls, some one to attend exclusively at the door is almost indispensable.

After the early dinner or lunch, the maid has a few hours' washing and ironing before getting ready for the late dinner or tea, which is the important meal of the day. If she is systematic, and the family are punctual, a girl can do a great deal of washing and ironing on Monday, Tuesday, and Wednesday, even if she has to answer the bell; but if she is not systematic, and the meals are not at regular hours, she cannot do much.

On Thursday, which we have already designated as sweeping day, she must sweep the whole house, all the carpets, shake the rugs in the back yard, shake and sweep down the heavy curtains, and dust the mirror-frames with a long feather-duster. The mistress can help her by insisting that her family shall leave their rooms early, and by herself refusing to see visitors on sweeping day.

On Friday, in addition to the usual daily work, the silver must be polished, the brass rubbed, and the closets (which, in the hurry of the week's work, may have been neglected), carefully cleaned and ventilated, On Friday afternoon the napkins and towels should be washed.

On Saturday these should be ironed, and everything, so far as possible, made ready for Sunday.

The cook, meantime, should rise even earlier than the waiter; should descend in time to receive the milkman, the iceman, and the breadman; should unlock the basement-door, sweep out the hall, and take in the barrels which have been left out with the ashes and other refuse.

A cook should be instructed never to give away the beef-dripping, as, if clarified in cold water, it is excellent for frying oysters, etc., and saves butter. The cook should air the kitchen and laundry, build the fire in the range, and sweep carefully before she begins to cook.

A careful house-keeper takes care that her cook shall make her toilet in her room, not in the kitchen. Particularly should she be made to arrange her hair upstairs, as some cooks have an exceedingly nasty habit of combing their hair in the kitchen. It will repay a house-keeper to make several visits to the kitchen at unexpected hours.

Cooks vary so decidedly in their way of preparing meals that no general directions can be given; but the best should be made to follow certain rules, and the worst should be watched and guarded. A great cleanliness as to pots and kettles, particularly the teakettle, should be insisted upon, and the closets, pails, barrels, etc., be carefully watched. Many a case of typhoid fever can be traced to the cook's slop-pail, or closets, or sink, and no lady should be careless of looking into all these places.

A cook, properly trained, can get up a good breakfast out of remains of the dinner of the preceding day, or some picked-up cod-fish, toast, potatoes sliced and fried, or mashed, boiled, stewed, or baked. The making of good clear coffee is not often understood by the green Irish cook. The mistress must teach her this useful art, and also how to make good tea, although the latter is generally made on the table.

With the sending up of the breakfast comes the first chance of a collision between cook and waiter; and disagreeable, bad-tempered servants make much of this opportunity. The cook in city houses puts the dinner on the dumb-waiter and sends it up to the waiter, who takes it off. All the heavy meat-dishes and the greasy plates are sent down to the cook to wash, and herein lies many a grievance which the mistress can anticipate and prevent by forbidding the use of the dumb-waiter if it leads to quarrelling, and by making the maids carry all the plates and dishes up and down. This course of treatment will soon cure them of their little tempers.

In plain households the cook has much less to do than the waiter; she should therefore undertake the greater part of the washing and ironing. Many very good cooks will do all the washing and ironing except the table linen and the towels used by the waiter; and if this arrangement is made at first, no trouble ensues. The great trouble in most households comes from the fact that the work is not definitely divided, and that one servant declares that the other is imposing upon her.

If a mistress is fair, honorable, strict, and attentive, she can thus carry on a large household (if there are no young children) with two energetic servants. She cannot, of course, have elegant house-keeping; it is a very arduous undertaking to conduct a city house with the assistance of only two people. Many young house- keepers become discouraged, and many old ones do so as well, and send the washing and ironing to a public laundry. But as small incomes are the rule, and as most people must economize, it has been done, and it can be done. The mistress will find it to her advantage to have a very great profusion of towels and dusters, and also to supply the kitchen with every requisite utensil for cooking a good dinner, or for the execution of the ordinary daily work--such tools as an ice-hammer, a can-opener, plenty of corkscrews, a knife- sharpener and several large, strong knives, a meat-chopper and bread-baskets, stone pots and jars. The modern refrigerator has simplified kitchen-work very much, and no one who has lived long enough to remember when it was not used can fail to bless its airy and cool closets and its orderly arrangements.

The "privileges" of these hard-worked servants should be respected. "An evening a week, and every other Sunday afternoon," is a formula not to be forgotten. Consider what it is to them! Perhaps a visit to a sick sister or mother, a recreation much needed, a simple pleasure, but one which is to them what a refreshing book, a visit to the opera, or a drive in the park, is to their employers. Only a very cruel mistress will ever fail to keep her promise to a faithful servant on these too infrequent holidays.

The early Sunday dinner is an inconvenience, but it is due to the girls who count on their "Sunday out" to have it always punctually given to them.

Many devout Catholics make their church-going somewhat inconvenient, but they should not be thwarted in it. It is to them something more than it is to Protestants, and a devout Catholic is to be respected and believed in. No doubt there are very bad-tempered and disagreeable girls who make a pretence of religion, but the mistress should be slow to condemn, lest she wrong one who is sincerely pious.

In sickness, Irish girls are generally kind and accommodating, being themselves unselfish, and are apt to show a better spirit in a time of trouble than the Swedes, the Germans, or the Scotch, although the latter are possessed of more intelligence, and are more readily trained to habits of order and system. The warm heart and the confused brain, the want of truth, of the average Irish servant will perplex and annoy while it touches the sympathies of a woman of generous spirit.

The women who would make the best house-servants are New England girls who have been brought up in poor but comfortable homes. But they will not be servants. They have imbibed the foolish idea that the position of a girl who does house-work is inferior in gentility to that of one who works in a factory, or a printing-office, or a milliner's shop. It is a great mistake, and one which fills the country with incapable wives for the working-man; for a woman who cannot make bread or cook a decent dinner is a fraud if she marry a poor man who expects her to do it.

That would be a good and a great woman who would preach a crusade against this false doctrine--who would say to the young women of her neighborhood, "I will give a marriage portion to any of you who will go into domestic service, become good cooks and waiters, and will bring me your certificates of efficiency at the end of five years."

And if those who employ could have these clear brains and thrifty hands, how much more would they be willing to give in dollars and cents a month!

CHAPTER XLVIII

THE HOUSE WITH MANY SERVANTS.

A lady who assumes the control of an elegant house without previous training had better, for a year at least, employ an English house-keeper, who will teach her the system necessary to make so many servants work properly together; for, unless she knows how to manage them, each servant will be a trouble instead of a help, and there will be no end to that exasperating complaint, "That is not my work."

The English house-keeper is given full power by her mistress to hire and discharge servants, to arrange their meals, their hours, and their duties, so as to make the domestic wheels run smoothly, and to achieve that perfection of service which all who have stayed in an English house can appreciate. She is a personage of much importance in the house. She generally dresses in _moire antique_, and is lofty in her manners. She alone, except the maid, approaches the mistress, and receives such general orders as that lady may choose to give. The house-keeper has her own room, where she takes her meals alone, or invites those whom she wishes to eat with her. Thus we see in English novels that the children sometimes take tea "in the house- keeper's room." It is generally a comfortable and snug place.

But in this country very few such house-keepers can be found. The best that can be done is to secure the services of an efficient person content to be a servant herself, who will be a care-taker, and will train the butler, the footmen, and the maid-servants in their respective duties.

Twelve servants are not infrequently employed in large houses in this country, and in New York and at Newport often a larger number. These, with the staff of assistants required to cook and wash for them, form a large force for a lady to control.

The house-keeper should hire the cook and scullery-maid, and be responsible for them; she orders the dinner (if the lady chooses); she gives out the stores; the house linen is under her charge, and she must attend to mending and replenishing it; she must watch over the china and silver, and every day visit all the bedrooms to see that the chamber-maids have done their duty, and that writing-paper and ink and pens are laid on the tables of invited guests, and that candles, matches, and soap and towels are in their respective places.

A house-keeper should be able to make fine desserts, and to attend to all the sewing of the family, with the assistance of a maid--that is, the mending, and the hemming of the towels, etc. She should be firm and methodical, with a natural habit of command, and impartial in her dealings, but strict and exacting; she should compel each servant to do his duty, as she represents the mistress, and should be invested with her authority.

It is she who must receive the dessert when it comes from the dining-room, watch the half-emptied bottles of wine, which men- servants nearly always appropriate for their own use, and be, in all respects, a watch-dog for her master, as in large families servants are prone to steal all that may fall in their way.

Unfortunately a bad house-keeper is worse than none, and can steal to her heart's content. Such a one, hired by a careless, pleasure- loving lady in New York, stole in a twelvemonth enough to live on for several years.

The house-keeper and the butler are seldom friends, and consequently many people consider it wise to hire a married couple competent to perform the duties of these two positions. If the two are honest, this is an excellent arrangement.

The butler is answerable for the property put in his charge, and for the proper performance of the duties of the footmen under his control. He must be the judge of what men can and should do. He is given the care of the wine, although every gentleman should keep the keys, only giving just so much to the butler as he intends shall be used each day. The plate is given to the butler, and he is made responsible for any articles missing; he also sees to the pantry, but has a maid or a footman to wash the dishes and cleanse the silver. All the arrangements for dinner devolve upon him, and when it is served he stands behind his mistress's chair. He looks after the footman who answers the bell, and takes care that he shall be properly dressed and at his post.

In houses where there are two or three footmen the butler serves breakfast, luncheon, tea, and dinner, assisted by such of his acolytes as he may choose. He should also wait upon his master, if required, see that the library and smoking-room are aired and in order, the newspaper brought in, the magazines cut, and the paper- knife in its place. Many gentlemen in this country send their butlers to market, and leave entirely to them the arrangement of the table.

If there is but one footman in a large house, the butler has a great deal to do, particularly if the family be a hospitable one. When the footman is out with the carriage the butler answers the front-door bell, but in very elegant houses there are generally two footmen, as this is not strictly the duty of a butler.

A lady's-maid is indispensable to ladies who visit much, but this class of servant is the most difficult to manage. Ladies'-maids must be told, when hired, that they can have no such position in America as they have in England: that they must make their own beds, wash their own clothing, and eat with the other servants. They must be first-rate hair-dressers, good packers of trunks, and understand dress-making and fine starching, and be amiable, willing, and pleasant. A woman who combines these qualifications commands very high wages, and expects, as her perquisite, her mistress's cast-off dresses.

French maids are in great demand, as they have a natural taste in all things pertaining to dress and the toilet, but they are apt to be untruthful and treacherous. If a lady can get a peasant girl from some rural district, she will find her a most useful and valuable maid after she has been taught.

Many ladies educate some clever girl who has been maid for the position of house-keeper, and such a person, who can be trusted to hire an assistant, becomes invaluable. She often accomplishes all the dress-making and sewing for the household, and her salary of thirty dollars a month is well earned.

As the duties of a lady's-maid, where there are young ladies, include attending them in the streets and to parties, she should be a person of unquestioned respectability. The maid should bring up the hot water for her ladies, and an early cup of tea, prepare their bath, assist at their toilet, put their clothes away, be ready to aid in every change of dress, put out their various dresses for riding, dining, walking, and for afternoon tea, dress their hair for dinner, and be ready to find for them their gloves, shoes, and other belongings.

A maid can be, and generally is, the most disagreeable of creatures; but some ladies have the tact to make good servants out of most unpromising materials.

The maid, if she does not accompany her mistress to a party and wait for her in the dressing-room, should await her arrival at home, assist her to undress, comb and brush her hair, and get ready the bath. She should also have a cup of hot tea or chocolate in readiness for her. She must keep her clothes in order, sew new ruffles in her dresses, and do all the millinery and dress-making required of her.

Very often the maid is required to attend to the bric-…-brac and pretty ornaments of the mantel, to keep fresh flowers in the drawing-room or bedroom, and, above all, to wash the pet dog. As almost all women are fond of dogs, this is not a disagreeable duty to a French maid, and she gives Fifine his bath without grumbling. But if she be expected to speak French to the children, she sometimes rebels, particularly if she and the nurse should not be good friends.

A lady, in hiring a maid, should specify the extra duties she will be required to perform, and thus give her the option of refusing the situation. If she accepts it, she must be made strictly to account for any neglect or omission of her work. A maid with an indulgent mistress is free in the evenings, after eight o'clock, and every Sunday afternoon.

In families where there are many children, two nurses are frequently required--a head nurse and an assistant.

The nursery governess is much oftener employed now in this country than in former years. This position is often filled by well-mannered and well-educated young women, who are the daughters of poor men, and obliged to earn their own living. These young women, if they are good and amiable, are invaluable to their mistresses. They perform the duties of a nurse, wash and dress the children, eat with them and teach them, the nursery-maid doing the coarse, rough work of the nursery. If a good nursery governess can be found, she is worth her weight in gold to her employer. She should not cat with the servants; there should be a separate table for her and her charges. This meal is prepared by the kitchen-maid, who is a very important functionary, almost an under-cook, as the chief cook in such an establishment as we are describing is absorbed in the composition of the grand dishes and dinners.

The kitchen-maid should be a good plain-cook, and clever in making the dishes suitable for children. Much of the elementary cooking for the dining-room, such as the foundation for sauces and soups, and the roasted and boiled joints, is required of her, and she also cooks the servants' dinner, which should be an entirely different meal from that served in the dining-room. Nine meals a day are usually cooked in a family living in this manner-- breakfast for servants, children, and the master and mistress, three; children's dinner, servants' dinner, and luncheon, another three; and the grand dinner at seven, the children's tea, and the servants' supper, the remaining three.

Where two footmen are in attendance, the head footman attends the door, waits on his mistress when she drives out, carries notes, assists the butler, lays the table and clears it, and washes glass, china, and silver. The under-footman rises at six, makes fires, cleans boots, trims and cleans the lamps, opens the shutters and the front-door, sweeps down the steps, and, indeed, does the rougher part of the work before the other servants begin their daily duties. Each should be without mustache, clean shaven, and clad in neat livery. His linen and white neck-tie should be, when he appears to wait on the family at table or in any capacity, immaculate.

The servants' meals should be punctual and plenteous, although not luxurious. It is a bad plan to feed servants on the luxuries of the master's table, but a good cook will be able to compound dishes for the kitchen that will be savory and palatable.

CHAPTER XLIX

MANNERS.--A STUDY FOR THE AWKWARD AND THE SHY.

It is a comfort to those of us who have felt the cold perspiration start on the brow, at the prospect of entering an unaccustomed sphere, to remember that the best men and women whom the world has known have been, in their day, afflicted with shyness. Indeed, it is to the past that we must refer when the terrible disease seizes us, when the tongue becomes dry in the mouth, the hands tremble, and the knees knock together.

Who does not pity the trembling boy when, on the evening of his first party, he succumbs to this dreadful malady? The color comes in spots on his face, and his hands are cold and clammy. He sits down on the stairs and wishes he were dead. A strange sensation is running down his back. "Come, Peter, cheer up," his mother says, not daring to tell him how she sympathizes with him. He is afraid to be afraid, he is ashamed to be ashamed. Nothing can equal this moment of agony. The whole room looks black before him as some chipper little girl, who knows not the meaning of the word "embarrassment," comes to greet him. He crawls off to the friendly shelter of a group of boys, and sees the "craven of the playground, the dunce of the school," with a wonderful self-possession, lead off in the german with the prettiest girl. As he grows older, and becomes the young man whose duty it is to go to dinners and afternoon parties, this terrible weakness will again overcome him. He has done well at college, can make a very good speech at the club suppers, but at the door of a parlor he feels himself a drivelling idiot. He assumes a courage, if he has it not, and dashes into a room (which is full of people) as he would attack a forlorn hope. There is safety in numbers, and he retires to a corner.

When he goes to a tea-party a battery of feminine eyes gazes at him with a critical perception of his youth and rawness. Knowing that he ought to be supremely graceful and serene, he stumbles over a footstool, and hears a suppressed giggle. He reaches his hostess, and wishes she were the "cannon's mouth," in order that his sufferings might be ended; but she is not. His agony is to last the whole evening. Tea-parties are eternal: they never end; they are like the old-fashioned ideas of a future state of torment--they grow hotter and more stifling. As the evening advances towards eternity he upsets the cream-jug. He summons all his will-power, or he would run away. No; retreat is impossible. One must die at the post of duty. He thinks of all the formulas of courage--"None but the brave deserve the fair," "He either fears his fate too much, or his deserts are small," "There is no such coward as self-consciousness," etc. But these maxima are of no avail. His feet are feet of clay, not good to stand on, only good to stumble with. His hands are cold, tremulous, and useless. There is a very disagreeable feeling in the back of his neck, and a spinning sensation about the brain. A queer rumbling seizes his ears. He has heard that "conscience makes cowards of us all." What mortal sin has he committed? His moral sense answers back, "None. You are only that poor creature, a bashful youth." And he bravely calls on all his nerves, muscles, and brains to help him through this ordeal. He sees the pitying eyes of the woman to whom he is talking turn away from his countenance (on which he knows that all his miserable shyness has written itself in legible characters). "And this humiliation, too?" he asks of himself, as she brings him the usual refuge of the awkward--a portfolio of photographs to look at. Women are seldom troubled, at the age at which men suffer, with bashfulness or awkwardness. It is as if Nature thus compensated the weaker vessel. Cruel are those women, however, and most to be reprobated, who laugh at a bashful man!

The sufferings of a shy man would fill a volume. It is a nervous seizure for which no part of his organization is to blame; he cannot reason it away, he can only crush it by enduring it: "To bear is to conquer our Fate." Some men, finding the play not worth the candle, give up society and the world; others go on, suffer, and come out cool veterans who fear no tea-party, however overwhelming it may be.

It is the proper province of parents to have their children taught all the accomplishments of the body, that they, like the ancient Greeks, may know that every muscle will obey the brain. A shy, awkward boy should be trained in dancing, fencing, boxing; he should be instructed in music, elocution, and public speaking; he should be sent into society, whatever it may cost him at first, as certainly as he should be sent to the dentist's. His present sufferings may save him from lifelong annoyance.

To the very best men--the most learned, the most graceful, the most eloquent, the most successful--has come at some one time or other the dreadful agony of bashfulness. Indeed, it is the higher order of man being that it most surely attacks; it is the precursor of many excellences, and, like the knight's vigil, if patiently and bravely borne, the knight is twice the hero. It is this recollection, which can alone assuage the sufferer, that he should always carry with him. He should remember that the compound which he calls himself is of all things most mixed.

"The web of our life is of a mingled yarn, good and ill together." Two antagonistic races--it may be his Grandfather Brown and his Grandmother Williams--are struggling in him for the mastery; and their exceedingly opposite natures are pulling his arms and legs asunder. He has to harmonize this antagonism before he becomes himself, and it adds much to his confusion to see that poor little pretender, Tom Titmouse, talking and laughing and making merry. There are, however, no ancestral diversities fighting for the possession of Tom Titmouse. The grandfathers and grandmothers of Tom Titmouse were not people of strong character; they were a decorous race on both sides, with no heavy intellectual burdens, good enough people who wore well. But does our bashful man know this? No. He simply remembers a passage in the "Odyssey" which Tom Titmouse could not construe, but which the bashful man read, to the delight of the tutor:

"O gods! How beloved he is, and how honored by all men to whatsoever land or city he comes! He brings much booty from Troy, but we, having

accomplished the same journey, are returning home having empty hands!"
And this messenger from Troy is Tom Titmouse!

Not that all poor scholars and inferior men have fine manners, nor do all good scholars and superior men fail in the drawing-room. No rule is without an exception. It is, however, a comfort to those who are awkward and shy to remember that many of the great and good and superior men who live in history have suffered, even as they suffer, from the pin-pricks of bashfulness. The first refuge of the inexperienced, bashful person is often to assume a manner of extreme hauteur. This is, perhaps, a natural fence--or defence; it is, indeed, a very convenient armor, and many a woman has fought her battle behind it through life. No doubt it is the armor of the many so-called frigid persons, male and female, who must either suffer the pangs of bashfulness, or affect a coldness which they do not feel. Some people are naturally encased in a column of ice which they cannot break, but within is a fountain which would burst out at the lips in words of kindliness if only the tongue could speak them. These limitations of nature are very strange; we cannot explain them. It is only by referring to Grandfather Brown and Grandmother Williams again that we understand them at all. One person will be furnished with very large feet and very small hands, with a head disproportionately large for the body, or one as remarkably small. Differences of race must account for these eccentricities of nature; we cannot otherwise explain them, nor the mental antagonisms, But the awkward and the shy do not always take refuge in a cold manner; Sometimes they study manner as they would the small-sword exercise, and exploit it-with equal fervor. Exaggeration of manner is quite as common a refuge for these unfortunates as the other extreme of calmness. They render themselves ridiculous by the lowness of their bows and the vivid picturesqueness of their speech. They, as it were, burst the bounds of the calyx, and the flower opens too wide. Symmetry is lost, graceful outline is destroyed. Many a bashful man, thinking of Tom Titmouse, has become an acrobat in his determination to be lively and easy. He should remember the _juste milieu_, recommended by Shakespeare when he says,

"They are as sick that surfeit with too much. As they that starve with nothing."

The happy people who are born unconscious of their bodies, who grow through life more and more graceful, easy, cordial, and agreeable; the happy few Who were never bashful, never nervous, never had clammy hands, they need not read these pages--they are not written for such blessed eyes. It is for the well-meaning, but shy and awkward, people that the manners of artificial society are most useful.

For the benefit of such persons we must "improve a ceremonial nicety into a substantial duty," else we shall see a cultivated scholar confused before a set of giggling girls, and a man who is all Wisdom, valor and learning, playing the donkey at an evening party. If he lack the inferior arts of polite behavior, who will take the trouble to discover a Sir Walter Raleigh behind his cravat?

A man who is constrained, uneasy, and ungraceful, can spoil the happiness of a dozen people. Therefore he is bound to create an artificial manner, if a natural one does not come to him, remembering always that "manners are shadows of virtues."

The manners of artificial society have this to commend them: they meditate the greatest good to the greatest number. We do not like the word "artificial," or to commend anything which is supposed to be the antipodes of the word "sincere," but it is a recipe, a doctor's prescription that we are recommending as a cure for a disease. "Good manners are to special societies what good morals are to society in general--their cement and their security. True politeness creates perfect ease and freedom; it and its essence is to treat others as you would have others treat you." Therefore, as you know how embarrassing embarrassment is to everybody else, strive not to be embarrassed.

CHAPTER L

HOW TO TREAT A GUEST.

No one possessed of his senses would invite a person to his country house for the purpose of making him unhappy. At least so we should say at first thought. But it is an obvious fact that very many guests are invited to the country houses of their friends, and are made extremely miserable while there. They have to rise at unusual hours, eat when they are not hungry, drive or walk or play tennis when they would prefer to do everything else, and they are obliged to give up those hours which are precious to them for other duties or pleasures; so that many people, after an experience of visiting, are apt to say, "No more of the slavery of visiting for me, if you please!"

Now the English in their vast country houses have reduced the custom of visiting and receiving their friends to a system. They are said to be in all respects the best hosts in the world, the masters of the letting-alone system. A man who owns a splendid place near London invites a guest for three days or more, and carefully suggests when he shall come and when he shall go--a very great point in hospitality. He is invited to come by the three o'clock train on Monday, and to leave by the four o'clock train on Thursday. That means that he shall arrive before dinner on Monday, and leave after luncheon on Thursday. If a guest cannot accede to these hours, he must write and say so. Once arrived, he rarely meets his host or hostess until dinner-time. He is conducted to his room, a cup of tea with some light refreshment is provided, and the well-bred servant in attendance says at what hour before dinner he will be received in the drawing-room. It is possible that some member of the family may be disengaged and may propose a drive before dinner, but this is not often done; the guest is left to himself or herself until dinner. General and Mrs. Grant were shown to their rooms at Windsor Castle, and locked up there, when they visited the Queen, until the steward came to tell them that dinner would be served in half an hour; they were then conducted to the grand salon, where the Queen presently entered. In less stately residences very much the same ceremony is observed. The hostess, after dinner and before the separation for the night, tells her guests that horses will be at their disposal the next morning, and also asks if they would like to play lawn-tennis, if they wish to explore the park, at what hour they will breakfast, or if they will breakfast in their rooms. "Luncheon is at one; and she will be happy to see them at that informal meal."

Thus the guest has before him the enviable privilege of spending the day as he pleases. He need not talk unless he choose; he may take a book and wander off under the trees; he may take a horse and explore the county, or he may drive in a victoria, phaeton, or any other sort of carriage. To a lady who has her letters to write, her novel to read, or her early headache to manage, this liberty is precious.

It must also be said that no one is allowed to feel neglected in an English house. If a lady guest says, "I am a stranger; I should like to see your fine house and your lovely park," some one is found to accompany her. Seldom the hostess, for she has much else to do; but there is often a single sister, a cousin, or a very intelligent governess, who is summoned. In our country we cannot offer our guests all these advantages; we can, however, offer them their freedom, and give them, with our limited hospitality, their choice of hours for breakfast and their freedom from our society.

But the questioner may ask, Why invite guests, unless we wish to see them? We do wish to see them--a part of the day, not the whole day. No one can sit and talk all day. The hostess should have her privilege of retiring after the mid-day meal, with her novel, for a nap, and so should the guest: Well-bred people understand all this, and are glad to give up the pleasure of social intercourse for an hour of solitude. There is nothing so sure to repay one in the long run as these quiet hours.

If a lady invites another to visit her at Newport or Saratoga, she should evince her thought for her guest's comfort by providing her with horses and carriage to pay her own visits, to take her own drives, or to do her shopping. Of course, the pleasure of two friends is generally to be together, and to do the same things; but sometimes it is quite the reverse.

The tastes and habits of two people staying in the same house may be very different, and each should respect the peculiarities of the other. It costs little time and no money for an opulent Newport hostess to find out what her guest wishes to do with her day, and she can easily, with a little tact, allow her to be happy in her own way.

Gentlemen understand this much better than ladies, and a gentleman guest is allowed to do very much as he pleases at Newport. No one asks anything about his plans for the day, except if he will dine at home. His hostess may ask him to drive or ride with her, or to go to the Casino, perhaps; but if she be a well-bred woman of the world she will not be angry if he refuses. A lady guest has not, however, such freedom; she is apt to be a slave, from the fact that as yet the American hostess has not learned that the truest hospitality is to let her guest alone, and to allow her to enjoy herself in her own way. A thoroughly well-bred guest makes no trouble in a house; she has the instinct of a lady, and is careful that no plan of her hostess shall be disarranged by her presence. She mentions all her, separate invitations, desires to know when her hostess wishes her presence, if the carriage can take her hither and yon, or if she may be allowed to hire a carriage.

There are hostesses, here and in England, who do not invite guests to their houses for the purpose of making them happy, but to add to their own importance. Such hostesses are not apt to consider the individual rights of any one, and they use a guest merely to add to the brilliancy of their parties, and to make the house more fashionable and attractive. Some ill-bred women, in order to show their power, even insult and ill treat the people who have accepted their proffered hospitality. This class of hostess is, fortunately, not common, but it is not unknown.

A hostess should remember that, when she asks people to visit her, she has two very important duties to perform--one, not to neglect her guests; the other, not to weary them by too much attention. Never give a guest the impression that he is "being entertained," that he is on your mind; follow the daily life of your household and of your duties as you desire, taking care that your guest is never in an unpleasant position or neglected. If you have a tiresome guest who insists upon following you around and weighing heavily on your hands, be firm, go to your own room, and lock the door. If you have a sulky guest who looks bored, throw open the library-door, order the carriage, and make your own escape. But if you have a very agreeable guest who shows every desire to please and be pleased, give that model guest the privilege of choosing her own hours and her own retirement.

The charm of an American country-house is, generally, that it is a home, and sacred to home duties. A model guest never infringes for one moment on the rights of the master of the house. She never spoils his dinner or his drive by being late; she never sends him back to bring her parasol; she never abuses his friends or the family dog; she is careful to abstain from disagreeable topics; she joins his whist-table if she knows how to play; but she ought never to be obliged to rise an hour earlier than her wont because he wishes to take an early train for town. These early-morning, perfunctory breakfasts are not times for conversation, and they ruin the day for many bad sleepers.

In a country neighborhood a hostess has sometimes to ask her guests to go to church to hear a stupid preacher, and to go to her country neighbors, to become acquainted with what may be the slavery of country parties. The guest should always be allowed to refuse these hospitalities; and, if he be a tired townsman, he will prefer the garden, the woodland, the retirement of the country, to any church or tea-party in the world. He cannot enter into his host's interests or his neighbor's. Leave him to his solitude if in that is his happiness.

At Newport guest and hostess have often different friends and different invitations. When this is understood, no trouble ensues if the host and hostess go out to dinner and leave the guest at home. It often happens that this is done, and no lady of good-breeding takes offence. Of course a nice dinner is prepared for her, and she is often asked to invite a friend to share it.

On the other hand, the guest often has invitations which do not include the hostess. These should be spoken of in good season, so that none of the hostess's plans may be disarranged, that the carriage may be ordered in time, and the guest sent for at the proper hour. Well-bred people always accept these contingencies as a matter of course, and are never disconcerted by them.

There is no office in the world which should be filled with such punctilious' devotion, propriety, and self-respect as that of hostess. If a lady ever allows her guest to feel that she is a cause of inconvenience, she violates the first rule of hospitality. If she fail in any way in her obligations as hostess to a guest whom she has invited, she shows herself to be ill-bred and ignorant of the first principles of politeness. She might better invite twelve people to dinner and then ask them to dine on the pavement than ignore or withdraw from a written and accepted invitation, unless sickness or death afford the excuse; and yet hostesses have been known to do this from mere caprice. But they were necessarily ill- bred people.

CHAPTER LI

LADY AND GENTLEMAN.

The number of questions asked by correspondents on the subject of the proper use of the familiar words lady and _woman_, and of the titles of married women, induces the reflection that the "woman" question is one which rivals in universal interest those of Nihilism, Irish rebellion, and the future presidency. It is not, however, of ultimate importance to a woman what she is called, as arose by any other name would smell as sweet, but it is of importance to those who speak of her, because by their speech "shall ye know them," whether fashionable or unfashionable, whether old or young, whether welt-bred or ill-bred, whether stylish or hopelessly _rococo_!

Nothing, for instance, Can be in worse taste than to say "she is a beautiful lady," or "a clever lady." One should always say "beautiful _woman_," "clever woman." The would-be genteel make this mistake constantly, and in the Rosa-Matilda style of novel the gentleman always kneels to the lady, and the fair ladies are scattered broadcast through the book, while the fine old Saxon word "woman" is left out, or not properly used.

Now it would be easy enough to correct this if we could only tell our correspondents always to use the word "woman." But unfortunately we are here constrained to say that would be equally "bad form." No gentleman would say, "I am travelling with women." He would say, "I am travelling with ladies." He would not say, "When I want to take my women to the theatre." He would say, "When I want to take my ladies." He would speak of his daughters as "young ladies," etc., etc. But if he were writing a novel about these same young ladies, he would avoid the word "lady" as feeble, and in speaking of emotions, looks, qualities, etc., he would use the word "woman."

Therefore, as a grand generic distinction, we can say that "woman" should be used when the realities of life and character are treated of. "Lady" should be used to express the outside characteristics, the conditions of cultivated society, and the respectful, distant, and chivalric etiquette which society claims for women when members thereof.

Then, our querist may ask, Why is the term, "she is a beautiful _lady_," so hopelessly out of style? Why does it betray that the speaker has not lived in a fashionable set? Why must we say "nice woman," "clever woman," "beautiful woman," etc.

The only answer to this is that the latter phraseology is a caprice of fashion into which plain-spoken people were driven by the affectations of the shabby-genteel and half-instructed persons who have ruined two good words for us by misapplication. One is "genteel," which means gentle, and the other is "lady," which means everything which is refined, cultivated, elegant, and aristocratic. Then as to the term "woman," this nomenclature has been much affected by the universal _sans-culottism_ of the French Revolution, when the queen was called citoyenne. Much, again, from a different cause, comes from our own absurd want of self-respect, which has accrued in this confusion of etiquette in a republic, as for instance, "I am a lady--as much a lady as anybody--and I want to be called a lady," remarked a nurse who came for a situation to the wife of one of our presidents. "I have just engaged a colored lady as a cook," remarked a nouveau riche. No wonder that when the word came to be thus misapplied the lover of good English undefiled began to associate the word "lady" with pretension, ignorance, and bad grammar.

Still, no "real lady" would say to her nurse, "A woman is coming to stay with me." To servants the term "lady," as applied to a coming guest, is indispensable. So of a gentleman she would say to her servant, "A gentleman is coming to stay here for a week;" but to her husband or son she would say, "He is a clever man," rather than, "He is a clever gentleman."

We might almost say that no women talk to men about "gentlemen," and no men talk to women about "ladies," in fashionable society. A woman in good society speaks of the hunting men, the dancing men, the talking men. She does not say "gentleman," unless in some such connection as this, "No gentleman would do such a thing," if some breach of etiquette had occurred. And yet no man would come into a lady's drawing-room saying, "Where are the girls?" or "Where are the women?" He would Say; "Where are the young ladies?"

It therefore requires a fine ear and a fine sense of modern fashion and of eternal propriety always to choose the right word in the delicate and almost unsettled estate of these two epithets. "Ladylike" can never go out of fashion. It is at once a compliment of the highest order and a suggestion of subtle perfection. The word "woman" does not reach up to this, because in its broad and strong etymology it may mean a washer-woman, a fighting woman, a coarse woman, alas! a drunken woman. If we hear of "a drunken lady," we see a downfall, a glimpse of better days; chloral, opium, even cologne, may have brought her to it. The word still saves her miserable reputation a little. But the words "a drunken woman" merely suggest whiskey, degradation, squalor, dirt, and the tenement-house.

It is evident, therefore, that we cannot do without the word "lady." It is the outgrowth of years of chivalric devotion, and of that progress in the history of woman which has ever been raising her from her low estate. To the Christian religion first does she owe her rise; to the institution of chivalry, to the growth of civilization since, has woman owed her continual elevation. She can never go back to the degradation of those days when, in Greece and Rome, she was not allowed to eat with her husband and sons. She waited on them as a servant. Now they in every country serve her, if they are gentlemen. But, owing to a curious twist in the way of looking at things, she is now undoubtedly the tyrant, and in fashionable society she is often imperiously ill-bred, and requires that her male slaves be in a state of servitude to which the Egyptian bondage would have been light frivolity.

American women are said to be faulty in manners, particularly in places of public amusement, in railway travelling, in omnibuses, and in shops. Men complain very much that the fairer sex are very brutal on these occasions. "I wish women would behave like _ladies_," said a man at a _matin‚e_. "Yes," said his friend, "I wish they would behave like men." Just then a sharp feminine elbow was thrust into his chest. "I wish gentlemen would not crowd so," was the remark which accompanied the "dig under the fifth rib" from a person whom no one could call a lady.

In speaking to a servant, either a lady or a gentleman will ever be patient, courteous, kind, not presuming on his or her power. But there should always be a certain ceremony observed, and a term of respect to the person spoken of. Therefore a mistress will not say "Have the girls come in?" "Is Lucy home?" She will say: "Have the young ladies come in?" "Is Miss Lucy at home?" This sort of dignified etiquette has the happiest and the most beneficial result on the relations of mistress and servant.

In modern literature the terms man and woman have nearly obliterated the words gentleman and lady, and we can hardly imagine a more absurd phrase than the following: "I asked Mary what she thought of Charles, and she said he was a beautiful gentleman, and Charles said that Mary was a lovely lady; so it was quite natural that I should try to bring them together," etc., etc.

Still, in poetry we like the word lady. "If my lady loves me true," is much better than "if my woman loves me true" would be; so there, again, we have the contradiction, for the Anglo-Saxon rule of using the word "woman" when anything real or sincere in emotion is in question is here honored in the breach. But this is one of the many shadowy conflicts which complicate this subject.

The term "lady" is like the word "gentry" in England--it is elastic. All persons coming within the category of "gentry" may attend the Queen's Drawing-room, yet it is well understood that birth, wealth, association, and position give the _raison d'ˆtre_ for the use of such a privilege, and in that carefully guarded English society the wife or daughters of an officer in the navy or in a line regiment whose means are slender and whose position is obscure would not be justified in presenting themselves at court. The same remark holds good of the wives and daughters of clergymen, barristers, doctors, authors, and artists, although the husband, if eminent, might attend a lev‚e if he wished. Yet these women are very tenacious of the title of lady, and no tradesman's wife would deny it to them, while she would not, if ever so rich, aspire to be called a lady herself.

"I ain't no lady myself, but I can afford to have 'em as governesses," remarked a Mrs. Kicklebury on the Rhine. She was not at all ashamed of the fact that she was no lady herself, yet her compeer and equal in America, if she kept a gin-shop, would insist upon the title of lady.

A lady is a person of refinement, of education, of fashion, of birth, of prestige, of a higher grade of some sort, if we apply the term rightly. She may be out of place through loss of fortune, or she may have sullied her title, but a something tells us that she is still a lady. We have a habit of saying, as some person, perhaps well decked out with fortune's favors, passes us, "She is not a lady," and every one will know what we mean. The phrase "vulgar lady," therefore, is an absurdity; there is no such thing; as well talk of a white blackbird; the term is self-contradictory. If she is vulgar, she is not a lady; but there is such a thing as a vulgar woman, and it is a very real thing.

In England they have many terms to express the word "woman" which we have not. A traveller in the rural districts speaks of a "kindly old wife who received me," or a "wretched old crone," or a "saucy lassie," or a "neat maid," etc. We should use the word "woman," or "old woman," or "girl," for all these.

Now as to the term "old woman" or "old lady." The latter has a pretty sound. We see the soft white curls, so like floss silk, the delicate white camel's-hair shawl, the soft lace and appropriate black satin gown, the pretty old-fashioned manner, and we see that this is a real lady. She may have her tricks of old-fashioned speech; they do not offend us. To be sure, she has no slang; she does not talk about "awfully jolly," or a "ghastly way off;" she does not talk of the boys as being a "bully lot," or the girls as being "beastly fine;" she does not say that she is "feeling rather seedy to-day," etc. No, "our old lady" is a "lady," and it would be in bad taste to call her an "old woman," which somehow sounds disrespectful.

Therefore we must, while begging of our correspondents to use the word "woman" whenever they can, tell them not entirely to drop the word "lady." The real lady or gentleman is very much known by the voice, the choice of words, the appropriate term. Nothing can be better than to err on the side of simplicity, which is always better than gush, or over-effort, or conceit of speech. One may be "ignorant of the shibboleth of a good set," yet speak most excellent English.

Thackeray said of George the Fourth that there was only one reason why he should not have been called the "first gentleman in Europe," and that was because he was not a gentleman. But of the young Duke of Albany, just deceased, no one could hesitate to speak as a gentleman. Therefore, while we see that birth does not always make a gentleman, we still get the idea that it may help to make one, as we do not readily connect the idea with Jeames, who was a "gentleman's gentleman." He might have been "fine," but not "noble."

As for titles for married women, we have only the one word, "Mrs.," not even the pretty French "Madame." But no woman should write herself "Mrs." on her checks or at the foot of her notes; nowhere but in a hotel register or on a card should she give herself this title, simple though it be. She is always, if she writes in the first person, "Mary Smith," even to a person she does not know. This seems to trouble some people, who ask, "How will such a person know I am married?" Why should they? If desirous of informing some distant servant or other person of that fact, add in a parenthesis beneath "Mary

Smith" the important addenda, "Mrs. John Smith."

When women are allowed to vote, perhaps further complications may arise. The truth is, women have no real names. They simply are called by the name of father or husband, and if they marry several times may well begin to doubt their own identity. Happy those who never have to sign but one new name to their letters!

CHAPTER LII

THE MANNERS OF THE PAST.

In these days, amid what has been strongly stated as "the prevailing mediocrity of manners," a study of the manners of the past would seem to reveal to us the fact that in those days of ceremony a man who was beset with shyness need then have suffered less than he would do now in these days of impertinence and brass.

A man was not then expected to enter a room and to dash at once into a lively conversation. The stately influence of the minuet de la cour was upon him; he deliberately entered a room, made a low bow, and sat down, waiting to be spoken to.

Indeed, we may go farther back and imagine ourselves at the court of Louis XIV., when the world was broadly separated into the two classes--the noble and the bourgeois. That world which Moliere divided in his dramatis personae into the courtier, the provincial noble, and the plain gentleman; and secondly, into the men of law and medicine, the merchant, and the shopkeeper. These divisions shall be for a moment considered. Now, all these men knew exactly, from the day when they reached ten years of age, how they were expected to behave in the sphere of life to which they were called. The marquis was instructed in every art of graceful behavior, the bel air was taught him as we teach our boys how to dance, even more thoroughly. The grand seigneur of those days, the man who would not arrange the folds of his own cravat with his own hands, and who exacted an observance as punctilious from his valets as if he were the king himself, that marquis of whom the great Moliere makes such fun, the courtier whom even the grand monarque liked to see ridiculed--this man had, nevertheless, good manners.

We see him reflected with marvellous fidelity in those wonderful comedies of the French Shakespeare; he is more than the fashion of an epoch--he is one of the eternal types of human nature. We learn what a man becomes whose business is "deportment." Even despicable as he is in "Le Bourgeois Gentilhomme"---flattering, borrowing money, cheating the poor citizen, and using his rank as a mask and excuse for his vices--we still read that it was such a one as he who took poor Moliere's cold hands in his and put them in his muff, when, on the last dreadful day of the actor's life (with a liberality which does his memory immortal honor), he strove to play, "that fifty poor workmen might receive their daily pay." It was such a one as this who was kind to poor Moliere. There was in these gens de cour a copy of fine feeling, even if they had it not, They were polite and elegant, making the people about them feel better for the moment, doing graceful acts courteously, and gilding vice with the polish of perfect manners. The _bourgeois_, according to Moliere, was as bad a man as the courtier, but he had, besides, brutal manners; and as for the magistrates and merchants, they were harsh and surly, and very sparing of civility. No wonder, when the French Revolution came, that one of the victims, regretting the not-yet-forgotten marquis, desired the return of the aristocracy; for, said he, "I would rather be trampled upon by a velvet slipper than a wooden shoe."

It is the best definition of manners--"a velvet slipper rather than a wooden shoe." We ask very little of the people whom we casually meet but that the salutation be pleasant; and as we remember how many crimes and misfortunes have arisen from sudden anger, caused sometimes by pure breaches of good manners, we almost agree with Burke that "manners are of more importance than laws. Upon them, in a great measure, the laws depend."

Some one calls politeness "benevolence in trifles, the preference of others to ourselves in little, daily, hourly occurrences in the business of life, a better place, a more commodious seat, priority in being helped at table," etc.

Now, in all these minor morals the marquis was a benevolent man; he was affable and both well and fair spoken, "and would use strange sweetness and blandishment of words when he desired to affect or persuade anything that he took to heart"--that is, with his equals. It is well to study this man, and to remember that he was not always vile. The Prince of Cond‚ had these manners and a generous, great heart as well. Gentleness really belongs to virtue, and a sycophant can hardly imitate it well. The perfect gentleman is he who has a strong heart under the silken doublet of a perfect manner.

We do not want all the decent drapery of life torn off; we do not want to be told that we are full of defects; we do not wish people to show us a latent antagonism; and if we have in ourselves the elements of roughness, severity of judgment, a critical eye which sees defects rather than virtues, we are bound to study how to tone down that native, disagreeable temper--just as we are bound to try to break the icy formality of a reserved manner, and to cultivate a cordiality which we do not feel. Such a command over the shortcomings of our own natures is not insincerity, as we often find that the effort to make ourselves agreeable towards some one whom we dislike ends in leading us to like the offending person. We find that we have really been the offender, going about with a moral tape-measure graduated by ourselves, and measuring the opposite party with a serene conceit which has called itself principle or honor, or some high-sounding name, while it was really nothing but prejudice.

We should try to carry entertainment with us, and to seem entertained with our company. A friendly behavior often conciliates and pleases more than wit or brilliancy; and here we come back to those polished manners of the past, which were a perfect drapery, and therefore should be studied, and perhaps in a degree copied, by the awkward and the shy, who cannot depend upon themselves for inspirations of agreeability. Emerson says that "fashion is good- sense entertaining company; it hates corners and sharp points of character, hates quarrelsome, egotistical, solitary, and gloomy people, hates whatever can interfere with total blending of parties, while it values all particularities as in the highest degree refreshing which can consist with good-fellowship."

It does the awkward and the shy good to contemplate these words. It may not immediately help them to become graceful and self-possessed, but it will certainly have a very good effect in inducing them to try.

We find that the successful man of the world has studied the temper of the finest sword. He can bend easily, he is flexible, he is pliant, and yet he has not lost the bravery and the power of his weapon. Men of the bar, for instance, have been at the trouble to construct a system of politeness, in which even an offensive self- estimation takes on the garb of humility. The harmony is preserved, a trial goes on with an appearance of deference and respect each to the other, highly, most highly, commendable, and producing law and order where otherwise we might find strife, hatred, and warfare. Although this may be a mimic humility, although the compliments may be judged insincere, they are still the shadows of the very highest virtues. The man who is guarding his speech is ruling his spirit; he is keeping his temper, that furnace of all affliction, and the lofty chambers of his brain are cool and full of fresh air.

A man who is by nature clownish, and who has what he calls a "noble sincerity," is very apt to do injustice to the polished man; he should, however, remember that "the manner of a vulgar man has freedom without ease, and that the manner of a gentleman has ease without freedom." A man with an obliging, agreeable address may be just as sincere as if he had the noble art of treading on everybody's toes. The "putter-down-upon-system" man is quite as often urged by love of display as by a love of truth; he is ungenerous, combative, and ungenial; he is the "bravo of society."

To some people a fine manner is the gift of nature. We see a young person enter a room, make himself charming, go through the transition period of boy to man, always graceful, and at man's estate aim to still possess that unconscious and flattering grace, that "most exquisite taste of politeness," which is a gift from the gods. He is exactly formed to please, this lucky creature, and all this is done for him by nature. We are disposed to abuse Mother Nature when we think of this boy's heritage of joy compared with her step-son, to whom she has given the burning blushes, the awkward step, the heavy self-consciousness, the uncourtly gait, the hesitating speech, and the bashful demeanor.

But nothing would be omitted by either parent or child to cure the boy if he had a twisted ankle, so nothing should be omitted that can, cure the twist of shyness, and therefore a shy young person should not be expected to confront such a trial.

And to those who have the bringing up of shy young persons we commend these excellent words of Whately: "There are many otherwise sensible people who seek to cure a young person of that very common complaint--

shyness--by exhorting him not to be shy, telling him what an awkward appearance it has, and that it prevents his doing himself justice, all of which is manifestly pouring oil on the fire to quench it; for the very cause of shyness is an over-anxiety as to what people are thinking of you, a morbid attention to your own appearance. The course, therefore, that ought to be pursued is exactly the reverse. The sufferer should be exhorted to think as little as possible about himself and the opinion formed of him, to be assured that most of the company do not trouble their heads about him, and to harden him against any impertinent criticisms that he supposed to be going on, taking care only to do what is right, leaving others to say and to think what they will."

All this philosophy is excellent, and is like the sensible archbishop. But the presence of a set of carefully cultivated, artificial manners, or a hat to hold in one's hand, will better help the shy person when he is first under fire, and when his senses are about deserting him, than any moral maxims can be expected to do.

Carlyle speaks of the fine manners of his peasant father (which he does not seem to have inherited), and he says: "I think-that they came from his having, early in life, worked for Maxwell, of Keir, a Scotch gentleman of great dignity and worth, who gave to all those under him a fine impression of the governing classes." Old Carlyle had no shame in standing with his hat off as his landlord passed; he had no truckling spirit either of paying court to those whose lot in life it was to be his superiors.

Those manners of the past were studied; they had, no doubt, much about them which we should now call stiff, formal, and affected, but they were a great help to the awkward and the shy.

In the past our ancestors had the help of costume, which we have not. Nothing is more defenceless than a being in a dress-coat, with no pockets allowable in which he can put his hands. If a man is in a costume he forgets the sufferings of the coat and pantaloon. He has a sense of being in a fortress. A military man once said that he always fought better in his uniform--that a fashionably cut coat and an every-day hat took all heroism out of him.

Women, particularly shy ones, feel the effect of handsome clothes as a reinforcement. "There is an appui in a good gown," said Madame de Sta‰l. Therefore, the awkward and the shy, in attempting to conquer the manners of artificial society, should dress as well as possible. Perhaps to their taste in dress do Frenchmen owe much of their easy civility and their success in social politics; and herein women are very much more fortunate than men, for they can always ask, "Is it becoming?" and can add the handkerchief, fan, muff, or mantle as a refuge for trembling hands. A man has only his pockets; he does not wish to always appear with his hands in them.

Taste is said to be the instantaneous, ready appreciation of the fitness of things. To most of us who may regret the want of it in ourselves, it seems to be the instinct of the fortunate few. Some women look as if they had simply blossomed out of their inner consciousness into a beautiful toilet; others are the creatures of chance, and look as if their clothes had been hurled at them by a tornado.

Some women, otherwise good and true, have a sort of moral want of taste, and wear too bright colors, too many glass beads, too much hair, and a combination of discordant materials which causes the heart of a good dresser to ache with anguish. This want of taste runs across the character like an intellectual bar-sinister, forcing us to believe that their conclusions are anything but legitimate. People who say innocently things which shock you, who put the listeners at a dinner-table upon tenter-hooks, are either wanting in taste or their minds are confused with shyness.

A person thus does great injustice to his own moral qualities when he permits himself to be misrepresented by that disease of which we speak. Shyness perverts the speech more than vice even. But if a man or a woman can look down on a well-fitting, becoming dress (even if it is the barren and forlorn dress which men wore to parties in 1882), it is still an appui. We know how it offends us to see a person in a dress which is inappropriate. A chief-justice in the war-paint and feathers of an Indian chief would scarcely be listened to, even if his utterances were those of a Marshall or a Jay.

It takes a great person, a courageous person, to bear the shame of unbecoming dress; and, no doubt, to a nature shy, passionate, proud, and poor, the necessity of wearing poor or unbecoming clothes has been an injury for life. He despised himself for his weakness, but the weakness remained.

When the French Revolution came in with its _sans-culotteism_, and republican simplicity found its perfect expression in Thomas Jefferson, still, the prejudices of powdered hair and stiff brocades remained. They gradually disappeared, and the man of the nineteenth century lost the advantages of becoming dress, and began anew the battle of life stripped of all his trappings. Manners went with these flowing accessaries, and the abrupt speech, curt bow, and rather exaggerated simplicity of the present day came in.

But it is a not unworthy study--these manners of the past. We are returning, at least on the feminine side, to a great and magnificent "princess," or queenly, style of dress. It is becoming the fashion to make a courtesy, to flourish a fan, to bear one's self with dignity when in this fine costume. Cannot the elegance, the repose, and the respectfulness of the past return also?

CHAPTER LIII

THE MANNERS OF THE OPTIMIST.

It is very easy to laugh at the optimist, and to accuse him of "poetizing the truth." No doubt, an optimist will see excellence, beauty, and truth where pessimists see only degradation, vice, and ugliness. The one hears the nightingale, the other the raven only. To one, the sunsetting forms a magic picture; to the other, it is but a presage of bad weather tomorrow. Some people seem to look at nature through a glass of red wine or in a Claude Lorraine mirror; to them the landscape has ever the bloom of summer or a spring-tide grace. To others, it is always cloudy, dreary, dull. The desolate ravine, the stony path, the blighted heath--that is all they can find in a book which should have a chapter for everybody. And the latter are apt to call the former dreamers, visionaries, fools. They are dubbed in society often flatterers, people whose "geese are all swans."

But are those, then, the fools who see only the pleasant side? Are they alone the visionaries who see the best rather than the worst? It is strange that the critics see only weakness in the "pleasant- spoken," and only truth and safety in those who croak.

The person who sees a bright light in an eye otherwise considered dull, who distrusts the last scandal, is supposed to be foolish, too easily pleased, and wanting in that wise scepticism which should be the handmaid of common-sense; and if such a person in telling a story poetizes the truth, if it is a principle or a tendency to believe the best of everybody, to take everybody at their highest note, is she any the less canny? Has she necessarily less insight? As there are always two sides to a shield, why not look at the golden one?

An excess of the organ of hope has created people like Colonel Sellers in the play, who deluded himself that there were "millions in it," who landed in poverty and wrecked his friends; but this excess is scarcely a common one. Far more often does discouragement paralyze than does hope exalt. Those who have sunshine for themselves and to spare are apt to be happy and useful people; they are in the aggregate the successful people.

But, although good-nature is temperamental, and although some men and women are, by their force of imagination and charity, forced to poetize the truth, the question remains an open one, Which is the nearest to truth, a pessimist or an optimist? Truth is a virtue more palpable and less shadowy than we think; It is not easy to speak the unvarnished, uncorrupted truth (so the lawyers tell us). The faculty of observation differs, and the faculty of language is variable. Some people have no intellectual apprehension of the truth, although they morally believe in it. People who abstractly revere the truth have never been able to tell anything but falsehoods. To such the power of making a statement either favorable or prejudicial depends upon the mood of the moment, not upon fact. Therefore a habit of poetizing the truth would seem to be of either excess the safest. Society becomes sometimes a hot-bed of evil passions--one person succeeds at the expense of another. How severe is the suffering proceeding from social neglect and social stabs! It might, much of it, be smoothed away by poetizing the truth ever so little. Instead of bearing an ill-natured message, suppose we carry an amiable one. Instead of believing that an insult was intended, suppose a compliment.

"Should he upbraid, I'll own that he prevail, And sing more sweetly than the nightingale! Say that he frown, I'll own his looks I view Like morning roses newly dipped in dew."

People who are thus calmly serene and amiable through the frowns and smiles, the ups and downs, of a social career are often called worldly.

Well, let us suppose that they are. Some author has wisely said: "That the world should be full of worldliness seems as right as that a stream should be full of water or a living body full of blood." To conquer this world, to get out of it a full, abounding, agreeable life, is what we are put here for. Else, why such gifts as beauty, talent, health, wit, and a power of enjoyment be given to us? To be worldly, or worldlings, is supposed to be incurring the righteous anger of the good. But is it not improperly using a term of implied reproach? For, although the world may be too much with us, and a worldling may be a being not filled to the brim with the deeper qualities or the highest aims, still he is a man necessary to the day, the hour, the sphere which must be supplied with people fitted to its needs. So with a woman in society. She must be a worldling in the best sense of the word. She must keep up her corner of the great mantle of the Field of the Cloth of Gold. She must fill the social arena with her influence; for in society she is a most important factor.

Then, as a "complex overgrowth of wants and fruitions" has covered our world as with a banyan-tree, we must have something else to keep alive our umbrageous growth of art, refinement, inventions, luxuries, and delicate sensibilities. We must have wealth.

"Wealth is the golden essence of the outer world,"

and therefore to be respected.

Of course the pessimist sees purse-pride, pompous and outrageous arrogance, a cringing of the pregnant hinges of the knee, false standards, and a thousand faults in this admission. And yet the optimist finds the "very rich," with but few exceptions, amiable, generous, and kindly, often regretting that poorer friends will allow their wealth to bar them off, wishing often that their opulence need not shut them off from the little dinners, the homely hospitality, the small gifts, the sincere courtesies of those whose means are moderate, The cheerful people who are not dismayed by the superior magnificence of a friend are very apt to find that friend quite as anxious for sympathy and for kindness as are the poor, especially if his wealth has caused him, almost necessarily, to live upon the superficial and the external in life.

We all know that there is a worldly life, poor in aim and narrow in radius, which is as false as possible. To live only for this world, with its changing fashions, its imperfect judgments, its toleration of snobs and of sinners, its forgiveness of ignorance under a high-sounding name, its exaggeration of the transient and the artificial, would be a poor life indeed. But, if we can lift ourselves up into the higher comprehension of what a noble thing this world really is, we may well aspire to be worldlings.

Julius Caesar was a worldling; so was Shakespeare. Erasmus was a worldling. We might increase the list indefinitely. These men brought the loftiest talents to the use of worldly things. They showed how great conquest, poetry, thought might become used for the world. They were full of this world.

To see everything through a poetic vision (the only genuine idealization) is and has been the gift of the benefactors of our race. B‚ranger was of the world, worldly; but can we give him up? So were the great artists who flooded the world with light--Titian, Tintoretto, Correggio, Raphael, Rubens, Watteau. These men poetized the truth. Life was a brilliant drama, a splendid picture, a garden ever fresh and fair;

The optimist carries a lamp through dark, social obstructions. "I would fain bind up many wounds, if I could be assured that neither by stupidity nor by malice I need make one!" is her motto, the true optimist.

It is a fine allegory upon the implied power of society that the poet Marvell used when he said he "would not drink wine with any one to whom he could not trust his life."

Titian painted his women with all their best points visible. There was a careful shadow or drapery which hid the defects which none of us are without; but defects to the eye of the optimist make beauty more attractive by contrast; in a portrait they may better be hid perhaps.

To poetize the truth in the science of charity and forgiveness can never be a great sin. If it is one, the recording angel will probably drop a tear. This tendency to optimism is, we think, more like that magic wand which the great idealist waved over a troubled sea, or like those sudden sunsets after a storm, which not only control the wave, but gild the leaden mass with crimson and unexpected gold, whose brightness may reach some storm-driven sail, giving it the light of hope, bringing the ship to a well-defined and hospitable shore, and regulating, with a new attraction, the lately distracted compass. Therefore, we do not hesitate to say that the philosophy, and the creed, and the manners of the optimist are good for society. However, his excellence may well be criticised; it may even sometimes take its place amid those excesses which are catalogued as amid the "deformities of exaggerated virtues." We may be too good, some of us, in one single direction.

But the rounded and harmonious Greek calm is hard to find. "For repose and serenity of mind," says a modern author, "we must go back to the Greek temple and statue, the Greek epic and drama, the Greek oration and moral treatise; and modern education will never become truly effectual till it brings more minds into happy contact with the ideal of a balanced, harmonious development of all the powers of mind, body, conscience, and heart."

And who was a greater optimist than your Athenian? He had a passionate love of nature, a rapt and infinite adoration of beauty, and he diffused the splendid radiance of his genius in making life more attractive and the grave less gloomy. Perhaps we of a brighter faith and a more certain revelation may borrow something from this "heathen" Greek.

CHAPTER LIV

THE MANNERS OF THE SYMPATHETIC.

Sympathy is the most delicate tendril of the mind, and the most fascinating gift which nature can give to us. The most precious associations of the human heart cluster around the word, and we love to remember those who have sorrowed with us in sorrow, and rejoiced with us when we were glad. But for the awkward and the shy, the sympathetic are the very worst company. They do not wish to be sympathized with--they wish to be with people who are cold and indifferent; they like shy people like themselves. Put two shy people in a room together, and they begin to talk with unaccustomed glibness. A shy woman always attracts a shy man. But women who are gifted with that rapid, gay impressionability which puts them en rapport with their surroundings, who have fancy and an excitable disposition, a quick susceptibility to the influences around them, are very charming in general society, but they are terrible to the awkward and the shy. They sympathize too much, they are too aware of that burning shame which the sufferer desires to conceal.

The moment that a shy person sees before him a perfectly unsympathetic person, one who is neither thinking nor caring for him, his shyness begins to flee; the moment that he recognizes a fellow-sufferer he begins to feel a reinforcement of energy. If he be a lover, especially, the almost certain embarrassment of the lady inspires him with hope and with renewed courage. A woman who has a bashful lover, even if she is afflicted with shyness, has been known to find a way to help the poor fellow out of his dilemma more than once. Hawthorne, who has left us the most complete and most tragic history of shyness which belongs to "that long rosary on which the blushes of a life are strung," found a woman (the most perfect character, apparently, who ever married and made happy a great genius) who, fortunately for him, was shy naturally, although without that morbid shyness which accompanied him through life. Those who knew Mrs. Hawthorne later found her possessed of great fascination of manner, even in general society, where Hawthorne was quite impenetrable. The story of his running down to the Concord River and taking boat to escape his visitors has been long familiar to us all. Mrs. Hawthorne, no doubt, with a woman's tact and a woman's generosity, overcame her own shyness in order to receive those guests whom Hawthorne ran away from, and through life remained his better angel. It was through this absence of expressed sympathy that English people became very agreeable to Hawthorne. He describes, in his "Note Book," a speech made by him at a dinner in England: "When I was called upon," he says, "I rapped my head, and it returned a hollow sound."

He had, however, been sitting next to a shy English lawyer, a man who won upon him by his quiet, unobtrusive simplicity, and who, in some well-chosen words, rather made light of dinner-speaking and its terrors. When Hawthorne finally got up and made his speech, his "voice, meantime, having a far-off and remote echo," and when, as we learn from others, a burst of applause greeted the few well-chosen words drawn up from that full well of thought, that pellucid rill of "English undefiled," the unobtrusive gentleman by his side applauded, and said to him, "It was handsomely done." The compliment pleased the shy man. It is the only compliment to himself which Hawthorne ever recorded.

Now, had Hawthorne been congratulated by a sympathetic, effusive

American who had clapped him on the back, and who had said, "Oh, never fear--you will speak well!" he would have said nothing. The shy sprite in his own eyes would have read in his neighbor's eyes the dreadful truth that his sympathetic neighbor would have indubitably betrayed--a fear that he would not do well. The phlegmatic and stony Englishman neither felt nor cared whether Hawthorne spoke well or ill; and, although pleased that he did speak well, invested no particular sympathy in the matter, either for or against, and so spared Hawthorne's shyness the last bitter drop in the cup, which would have been a recognition of his own moral dread. Hawthorne bitterly records his own sufferings. He says, in one of his books, "At this time I acquired this accursed habit of solitude." It has been said that the Hawthorne family were, in the earlier generation, afflicted with shyness almost as a disease-- certainly a curious freak of nature in a family descended from robust sea-captains. It only goes to prove how far away are the influences which control our natures and our actions.

Whether, if Hawthorne had not been a shy man, afflicted with a sort of horror of his species at times, always averse to letting himself go, miserable and morbid, we should have been the inheritors of the great fortune which he has left us, is not for us to decide. Whether we should have owned "The Gentle Boy," the immortal "Scarlet Letter," "The House with Seven Gables," the "Marble Faun," and all the other wonderful things which grew out of that secluded and gifted nature, had he been born a cheerful, popular, and sympathetic boy, with a dancing-school manner, instead of an awkward and shy youth (although an exceedingly handsome one), we cannot tell. That is the great secret behind the veil. The answer is not yet made, the oracle has not spoken, and we must not invade the penumbra of genius.

It has always been a comfort to the awkward and the shy that Washington could not make an after-dinner speech; and the well-known anecdote--"Sit down, Mr. Washington, your modesty is even greater than your valor "--must have consoled many a voiceless hero. Washington Irving tried to welcome Dickens, but failed in the attempt, while Dickens was as voluble as he was gifted. Probably the very surroundings of sympathetic admirers unnerved both Washington and Irving, although there are some men who can never "speak on their legs," as the saying goes, in any society.

Other shy men--men who fear general society, and show embarrassment in the every-day surroundings--are eloquent when they get on their feet. Many a shy boy at college has astonished his friends by his ability in an after-dinner speech. Many a voluble, glib boy, who has been appointed the orator of the occasion, fails utterly, disappoints public expectation, and sits down with an uncomfortable mantle of failure upon his shoulders. Therefore, the ways of shyness are inscrutable. Many a woman who has never known what it was to be bashful or shy has, when called upon to read a copy of verses, even to a circle of intimate friends, lost her voice, and has utterly broken down, to her own and her friends' great astonishment.

The voice is a treacherous servant; it deserts us, trembles, makes a failure of it, is "not present or accounted for" often when we need its help. It is not alone in the shriek of the hysterical that we learn of its lawlessness, it is in its complete retirement. A bride, often, even when she felt no other embarrassment, has found that she had no voice with which to make her responses. It simply was not there!

A lady who was presented at court, and who felt--as she described herself-- wonderfully at her ease, began talking, and, without wishing to speak loud, discovered that she was shouting like a trumpeter. The somewhat unusual strain which she had put upon herself, during the ordeal of being presented at the English court, revenged itself by an outpouring of voice which she could not control.

Many shy people have recognized in themselves this curious and unconscious elevation of the voice. It is not so common as a loss of voice, but it is quite as uncontrollable.

The bronchial tubes play us another trick when we are frightened: the voice is the voice of somebody else, it has no resemblance to our own. Ventriloquism might well study the phenomena of shyness, for the voice becomes bass that was treble, and soprano that which was contralto.

"I dislike to have Wilthorpe come to see me," said a very shy woman --"I know my voice will squeak so." With her Wilthorpe, who for some reason drove her into an agony of shyness, had the effect of making her talk in a high, unnatural strain, excessively fatiguing.

The presence of one's own family, who are naturally painfully sympathetic, has always had upon the bashful and the shy a most evil effect.

"I can never plead a cause before my father?" "Nor I before my son," said two distinguished lawyers. "If mamma is in the room, I shall never be able to get through my part," said a young amateur actor.

But here we must pause to note another exception in the laws of shyness.

In the false perspective of the stage shyness often disappears. The shy man, speaking the words, and assuming the character of another, often loses his shyness. It is himself of whom he is afraid, not of Tony Lumpkin or of Charles Surface, of Hamlet or of Claude Melnotte. Behind their masks he can speak well; but if he at his own dinner- table essays to speak, and mamma watches him with sympathetic eyes, and his brothers and sisters are all listening, he fails.

"Lord Percy sees me fall."

Yet it is with our own people that we must stand or fall, live or die; it is in our own circle that we must conquer our shyness.

Now, these reflections are not intended as an argument against sympathy properly expressed. A reasonable and judiciously expressed sympathy with our fellow-beings is the very highest attribute of our nature. "It unravels secrets more surely than the highest critical faculty. Analysis of motives that sway men and women is like the knife of the anatomist: it works on the dead. Unite sympathy to observation, and the dead Spring to life." It is thus to the shy, in their moments of tremor, that we should endeavor to be calmly unsympathetic; not cruel, but indifferent, unobservant.

Now, women of genius who obtain a reflected comprehension of certain aspects of life through sympathy often arrive at the admirable result of apprehending the sufferings of the shy without seeming to observe them. Such a woman, in talking to a shy man, will not seem to see him; she will prattle on about herself, or tell some funny anecdote of how she was tumbled out into the snow, or how she spilled her glass of claret at dinner, or how she got just too late to the lecture; and while she is thus absorbed in her little improvised autobiography, the shy man gets hold of himself and ceases to be afraid of her. This is the secret of tact.

Madame R‚camier, the famous beauty, was always somewhat shy. She was not a wit, but she possessed the gift of drawing out what was best in others. Her biographers have blamed her that she had not a more impressionable temper, that she was not more sympathetic. Perhaps (in spite of her courage when she took up contributions in the churches dressed as a Neo-Greek) she was always hampered by shyness. She certainly attracted all the best and most gifted of her time, and had a noble fearlessness in friendship, and a constancy which she showed by following Madame de Sta‰l into exile, and in her devotion to Ballenche and Chateaubriand. She had the genius of friendship, a native sincerity, a certain reality of nature--those fine qualities which so often accompany the shy that we almost, as we read biography and history, begin to think that shyness is but a veil for all the virtues.

Perhaps to this shyness, or to this hidden sympathy, did Madame R‚camier owe that power over all men which survived her wonderful beauty. The blind and poor old woman of the Abbaye had not lost her charm; the most eminent men and women of her day followed her there, and enjoyed her quiet (not very eloquent) conversation. She had a wholesome heart; it kept her from folly when she was young, from a too over-facile sensitiveness to which an impressionable, sympathetic temperament would have betrayed her. Her firm, sweet nature was not flurried by excitement; she had a steadfastness in her social relations which has left behind an everlasting renown to her name.

And what are, after all, these social relations which call for so much courage, and which can create so much suffering to most of us as we conquer for them our awkwardness and our shyness? Let us pause for a moment, and try to be just. Let us contemplate these social ethics, which call for so much that is, perhaps, artificial and troublesome and contradictory. Society, so long as it is the congregation of the good, the witty, the bright, the intelligent, and the gifted, is the thing most necessary to us all. We are apt to like it and its excitements almost too well, or to hate it, with its excesses and its mistakes, too bitterly. We are rarely just to society.

The rounded and harmonious and temperate understanding and use of society is, however, the very end and aim of education. We are born to live with each other and not for ourselves; if we are cheerful, our cheerfulness was given to us to make bright the lives of those about us; if we have genius, that is a sacred trust; if we have beauty, wit, joyousness, it was given us for the delectation of others, not for ourselves; if we are awkward and shy, we are bound to break the crust and to show that within us is beauty, cheerfulness, and wit. "It is but the fool who loves excess." The best human being should moderately like society.

CHAPTER LV

CERTAIN QUESTIONS ANSWERED.

We are asked by a correspondent as to when a gentleman should wear his hat and when take it off. A gentleman wears his hat in the street, on a steamboat deck, raising it to a lady acquaintance; also in a promenade concert-room and picture-gallery. He never wears it in a theatre or opera-house, and seldom in the parlors of a hotel. The etiquette of raising the hat on the staircases and in the halls of a hotel as gentlemen pass ladies is much commended. In Europe each man raises his hat as he passes a bier, or if a hearse carrying a dead body passes him. In this country men simply raise their hats as a funeral _cort‚ge_ passes into a church, or at the grave. If a gentleman, particularly an elderly one, takes off his hat and stands uncovered in a draughty place, as the foyer of an opera-house, while talking to ladies, it is proper for one of them to say, "Pray resume your hat "--a delicate attention deeply prized by a respectful man, who, perhaps, would not otherwise cover his head.

Again, our young lady friends ask us many questions on the subject of _propriety_, showing how anxious they are to do right, but also proving how far they are from apprehending what in Old-World customs has been always considered propriety. In our new country the relations of men and women are necessarily simple. The whole business of etiquette is, of course, reduced to each one's sense of propriety, and the standard must be changed as the circumstances demand. As, for instance, a lady writes to know if she should thank a gentleman for paying for her on an excursion. Now this involves a long answer. In Europe no young lady could accept an invitation to go as the guest of a young gentleman on "an excursion," and allow him to pay for her, without losing much reputation. She would not in either England or France be received in society again. She should be invited by the gentleman through her father or mother, and one or both should accompany an her. Even then it is not customary for gentlemen to invite ladies to go on an excursion. He could invite the lady's mother to chaperon a theatre party which he had paid for.

Another young lady asks if she could with propriety buy the tickets and take a young gentleman to the theatre. Of course she could, if her mother or chaperon would go with her; but even then the mother or chaperon should write the note of invitation.

But in our free country it is, we hear, particularly in the West, allowable for a young lady and gentleman to go off on, "an excursion" together, the gentleman paying all the expenses. If that is allowed, then, of course--to answer our correspondent's question she should thank him. But if we were to answer the young lady's later question, "Would this be considered etiquette?" we should say, decidedly, No.

Another question which we are perpetually asked is this: How to allow a gentleman a proper degree of friendly intimacy without allowing him to think himself too much of a favorite. Here we cannot bring in either etiquette or custom to decide. One very general law would be not to accept too many attentions, to show a certain reserve in dancing with him or driving with him. It is always proper for a gentleman to take a young lady out to drive in his dog-cart with his servant behind, if her parents approve; but if it is done very often, of course it looks conspicuous, and the lady runs the risk of being considered engaged. And she knows, of course, whether her looks and words give him reason to think that he is a favorite. She must decide all that herself.

Another writes to ask us if she should take a gentleman's hat and coat when he calls. Never. Let him take care of those. Christianity and chivalry, modern and ancient custom, make a man the servant of women. The old form of salutation used by Sir Walter Raleigh and other courtiers was always, "Your servant, madam," and it is the prettiest and most admirable way for a man to address a woman in any language.

Another asks if she should introduce a gentleman who calls to her mother.

This, we should say, would answer itself did not the question re-appear. Of course she should; and her mother should always sit with her when she is receiving a call from a gentleman.

But if in our lesser fashionable circles the restrictions of etiquette are relaxed, let a young lady always remember these general principles, that men will like and respect her far better if she is extremely particular about allowing them to pay for her, if she refuses two invitations out of three, if she is dignified and reserved rather than if she is the reverse.

At Newport it is now the fashion for young ladies to drive young men out in their pony-phaetons with a groom behind, or even without a groom; but a gentleman never takes out a lady in his own carriage without a servant.

Gentlemen and ladies walk together in the daytime unattended, but if they ride on horseback a groom is always in attendance on the lady. In rural neighborhoods where there are no grooms, and where a young lady and gentleman go off for a drive unattended, they have thrown Old-World etiquette out of the window, and must make a new etiquette of their own. Propriety, mutual respect, and American chivalry have done for women what all the surveillance of Spanish duennas and of French etiquette has done for the young girl of Europe. If a woman is a worker, an artist, a student, or an author, she can walk the Quartier Latin of Paris unharmed.

But she has in work an armor of proof. This is not etiquette when she comes into the world of fashion. She must observe etiquette, as she would do the laws of Prussia or of England, if she stands on foreign shores.

Perhaps we can illustrate this. Given a pretty young girl who shall arrive on the steamer Germania after being several years at school in Paris, another who comes in by rail from Kansas, another from some quiet, remote part of Georgia, and leave them all at the New York Hotel for a winter. Let us imagine them all introduced at a New York ball to three gentlemen, who shall call on them the next day. If the girl educated in Paris, sitting by her mamma, hears the others talk to the young men she will be shocked. The girls who have been brought up far from the centres of etiquette seem to her to have no modesty, no propriety. They accept invitations from the young men to go to the theatre alone, to take drives, and perhaps, as we have said, to "go on an excursion."

To the French girl this seems to be a violation of propriety; but later on she accepts an invitation to go out on a coach, with perhaps ten or twelve others, and with a very young chaperon. The party does not return until twelve at night, and as they walk through the corridors to a late supper the young Western girl meets them, and sees that the young men are already the worse for wine: she is apt to say, "What a rowdy crowd!" and to think that, after all, etiquette permits its own sins, in which she is right.

In a general statement it may be as well to say that a severe etiquette would prevent a young lady from receiving gifts from a young man, except bonbonnieres and bouquets. It is not considered proper for him to offer her clothing of any sort--as gowns, bonnets, shawls, or shoes--even if he is engaged to her. She may use her discretion about accepting a camel's-hair shawl from a man old enough to be her father, but she should never receive jewellery from any one but a relative or her _fianc‚_ just before marriage. The reason for this is obvious. It has been abused--the privilege which all men desire, that of decking women with finery.

A young lady should not write letters to young men, or send them presents, or take the initiative in any way. A friendly correspondence is very proper if the mother approves, but even this has its dangers. Let a young lady always remember that she is to the young man an angel to reverence until she lessens the distance between them and extinguishes respect.

Young women often write to us as to whether it is proper for them to write letters of condolence or congratulation to ladies older than themselves. We should say, Yes. The respect of young girls is always felt gratefully by older ladies. The manners of the present are vastly to be objected to on account of a lack of respect. The rather bitter Mr. Carlyle wrote satirically of the manners of young ladies. He even had his fling at their laugh: "Few are able to laugh what can be called laughing, but only sniff and titter from the throat outward, or at best produce some whiffling husky cachinnations as if they were laughing through wool. Of none such comes good." A young lady must not speak too loud or be too boisterous; she must even tone down her wit, lest she be misunderstood. But she need not be dull, or grumpy, or ill-tempered, or careless of her manners, particularly to her mother's old friends. She must not talk slang, or be in any way masculine; if she is, she loses the battle. A young lady is sometimes called upon to be a hostess if her mother is dead. Here her liberty becomes greater, but she should always have an aunt or some elderly friend by her side to play chaperon.

A young lady may do any manual labor without losing caste. She may be a good cook, a fine laundress, a carver of wood, a painter, a sculptor, an embroideress, a writer, a physician, and she will be eligible, if her manners are good, to the best society anywhere. But if she outrage the laws of good-breeding in the place where she is, she cannot expect to take her place in society. Should she be seen at Newport driving two gentlemen in her pony-phaeton, or should she and another young woman take a gentleman between them and drive down Bellevue Avenue, she would be tabooed. It would not be a wicked act, but it would not look well; it would not be convenable. If she dresses "loudly," with peculiar hats and a suspicious complexion, she must take the consequences. She must be careful (if she is unknown) not to attempt to copy the follies of well-known fashionable women. What will be forgiven to Mrs. Well Known Uptown will never be forgiven to Miss Kansas. Society in this respect is very unjust--the world is always unjust--but that is a part of the truth of etiquette which is to be remembered; it is founded on the accidental conditions of society, having for its background, however, the eternal principles of kindness, politeness, and the greatest good of society.

A young lady who is very prominent in society should not make herself too common; she should not appear in too many charades, private theatricals, tableaux, etc. She should think of the "violet by the mossy stone." She must, also, at a watering-place remember that every act of hers is being criticised by a set of lookers-on who are not all friendly, and she must, ere she allow herself to be too much of a belle, remember to silence envious tongues.

CHAPTER LVI

ENGLISH TABLE MANNERS AND SOCIAL USAGES.

In no respect can American and English etiquette be contrasted more fully than in the matter of the every-day dinner, which in America finds a lady in a plain silk dress, high-necked and long-sleeved, but at which the English lady always appears in a semi-grand toilette, with open Pompadour corsage and elbow sleeves, if not in low-necked, full-dress attire; while her daughters are uniformly sleeveless, and generally in white dresses, often low-necked in depth of winter. At dinner all the men are in evening dress, even if there is no one present at the time but the family.

The dinner is not so good as the ordinary American dinner, except in the matter of fish, which is universally very fine. The vegetables are few and poor, and the "sweets," as they call dessert, are very bad. A gooseberry tart is all that is offered to one at an ordinary dinner, although fine strawberries and a pine are often brought in afterwards. The dinner is always served with much state, and afterwards the ladies all combine to amuse the guests by their talents. There is no false shame in England about singing and playing the piano. Even poor performers do their best, and contribute very much to the pleasure of the company. At the table people do not talk much, nor do they gesticulate as Americans do. They eat very quietly, and speak in low tones. No matters of family history or religion or political differences are discussed before the servants. Talking with the mouth full is considered an unpardonable vulgarity. All small preferences for any particular dish are kept in the background. No hostess ever apologizes, or appears to hear or see anything disagreeable. If the omelette souffle is a failure, she does not observe it; the servant offers and withdraws it, nor is any one disturbed thereby. As soon as one is helped he must begin to eat, not waiting for any one else. If the viand is too hot or too cold, or is not what the visitor likes, he pretends to eat it, playing with knife and fork.

No guest ever passes a plate or helps to anything; the servant does all that. Soup is taken from the side of the spoon noiselessly. Soup and fish are not partaken of a second time. If there is a joint, and the master carves, it is proper, however, to ask for a second cut. Bread is passed by the servants, and must be broken, not cut, afterwards. It is considered gauche to be undecided as to whether you will take clear soup or thick soup; decide quickly. In refusing wine, simply say, "Thanks;" the servant knows then that you do not take any.

The servants retire after handing the dessert, and a few minutes' free conversation is allowed. Then the lady of the house gives the signal for rising. Toasts and taking wine with people are entirely out of fashion; nor do the gentlemen remain long in the dining-room.

At the English dinner-table, from the plainest to the highest, there is etiquette, manner, fine service, and everything that Englishmen enjoy. The wit, the courtier, the beauty, and the poet aim at appearing well at dinner. The pleasures of the table, says Savarin, bring neither enchantment, ecstasy, nor transports, but they gain in duration what they lose in intensity; they incline us favorably towards all other pleasures--at least help to console us for the loss of them.

At very few houses, even that of a duke, does one see so elegant a table and such a profusion of flowers as at every millionaire's table in New York; but one does see superb old family silver and the most beautiful table-linen even at a very plain abode. The table is almost uniformly lighted with wax candles. Hot coffee is served immediately after dinner in the drawing-room. Plum-pudding, a sweet omelet, or a very rich plum-tart is often served in the middle of dinner, before the game. The salad always comes last, with the cheese. This is utterly unlike our American etiquette.

Tea is served in English country-houses four or five times a day. It is always brought to your bedside before rising; it is poured at breakfast and at lunch; it is a necessary of life at five o'clock; it is drunk just before going to bed. Probably the cold, damp climate has much to do with this; and the tea is never very strong, but is excellent, being always freshly drawn, not steeped, and is most refreshing.

Servants make the round of the table in pairs, offering the condiments, the sauces, the vegetables, and the wines. The common- sense of the English nation breaks out in their dinners. Nothing is offered out of season. To make too great a display of wealth is considered bourgeois and vulgar to a degree. A choice but not oversumptuous dinner meets you in the best houses. But to sit down to the plainest dinners, as we do, _in plain clothes_, would never be permitted. Even ladies in deep mourning are expected to make some slight change at dinner.

Iced drinks are never offered in England, nor in truth are they needed.

In England no one speaks of "sherry wine," "port wine;" "champagne wine," he always says "sherry," "port," "claret," etc. But in France one always says "vin de Champagne," "vin de Bordeaux," etc. It goes to show that what is proper in one country is vulgar in another.

It is still considered proper for the man of the house to know how to carve, and at breakfast and lunch the gentlemen present always cut the cold beef, the fowl, the pressed veal and the tongue. At a country-house dinner the lady often helps the soup herself. Even at very quiet dinners a menu is written out by the hostess and placed at each plate. The ceremony of the "first lady" being taken in first and allowed to go out first is always observed at even a family dinner. No one apologizes for any accident, such as overturning a glass of claret, or dropping a spoon, or even breaking a glass. It is passed over in silence.

No English lady ever reproves her servants at table, nor even before her husband and children. Her duty at table is to appear serene and unruffled. She puts her guests at their ease by appearing at ease herself. In this respect English hostesses are far ahead of American ones.

In the matter of public holidays and of their amusements the English people behave very unlike American people. If there is a week of holidays, as at Whitsuntide, all the laboring classes go out of town and spend the day in the parks, the woods, or the country. By this we mean shop-girls, clerks in banks, lawyer's clerks, young artists, and physicians, all, in fact, who make their bread by the sweat of their brows. As for the privileged classes, they go from London to their estates, put on plain clothes, and fish or bunt, or the ladies go into the woods to pick wild-flowers. The real love of nature, which is so honorable a part of the English character, breaks out in great and small. In America a holiday is a day when people dress in their best, and either walk the streets of a great city, or else take drives, or go to museums or theatres, or do something which smacks of civilization. How few put on their plain clothes and stout shoes and go into the woods! How much better it would be for them if they did!

At Whitsuntide the shop-girls of London--a hard worked class--go down to Epping Forest, or to Hampton Court, or to Windsor, with their basket of lunch, and everywhere one sees the sign "Hot Water for Tea," which means that they go into the humble inn and pay a penny for the use of the teapot and cup and the hot water, bringing their own tea and sugar. The economy which is a part of every Englishman's religion could well be copied in America. Even a duchess tries to save money, saying wisely that it is better to give it away in charity than to waste it.

An unpleasant feature of English life is, however, the open palm, every one being willing to take a fee, from a penny up to a shilling, for the smallest service. The etiquette of giving has to be learned. A shilling is, however, as good as a guinea for ordinary use; no one but an American gives more.

The carriage etiquette differs from ours, as the gentleman of the family rides beside his wife, allowing his daughters to ride backwards. He also smokes in the Park in the company of ladies, which looks boorish. However, no gentleman sits beside a lady in driving unless he is her husband, father, son, or brother. Not even an affianced lover is permitted this seat.

It must be confessed that the groups in Hyde Park and in Rotten Row and about the Serpentine have a solemn look, the people in the carriages rarely chatting, but sitting up in state to be looked at, the people in chairs gravely staring at the others. None but the people on horseback seem at their ease; they chat as they ride, and, all faultlessly caparisoned as they are, with well-groomed horses, and servants behind, they seem gay and jolly. In America it is the equestrian who always looks preoccupied and solemn, and as if the horse were quite enough to manage. The footmen are generally powdered and very neatly dressed in livery, in the swell carriages, but the coachmen are not so highly gotten up as formerly. Occasionally one sees a very grand fat old coachman in wig and knee- breeches, but Jeames Yellowplush is growing a thing of the past even in London.

A lady does not walk alone in the Park. She may walk alone to church, or to do her shopping, but even this is not common. She had better take a hansom, it now being proper for ladies to go out to dinner alone in full dress in one of these singularly open and exposed-looking carriages. It is not an uncommon sight to see a lady in a diamond tiara in a London hansom by the blazing light of a summer sun. Thus what we should shun as a very public thing the reserved English woman does in crowded London, and regards it as proper, while she smiles if she sees an American lady alone in a victoria in Hyde Park, and would consider her a very improper person if she asked a gentleman to drive out with her--as we do in our Park every day of our lives--in an open carriage. Truly etiquette is a curious and arbitrary thing, and differs in every country.

In France, where they consider English people frightfully _gauche_, all this etiquette is reversed, and is very much more like ours in America. A Frenchman always takes off his hat on entering or leaving a railway carriage if ladies are in it. An Englishman never takes his hat off unless the Princess of Wales is passing, or he meets an acquaintance. He sits with it on in the House of Commons, in the reading-room of a hotel, at his club, where it is his privilege to sulk; but in his own house he is the most charming of hosts. The rudest and almost the most unkind persons in the world, if you meet them without a letter or an introduction in a public place, the English become in their own houses the most gentle, lovely, and polite of all people. If the ladies meet in a friend's parlor, there is none of that snobbish rudeness which is the fashion in America, where one lady treats another as if she were afraid of contamination, and will not speak to her. The lady-in-waiting to Queen Victoria, the duchess, is not afraid of her nobility; her friend's roof is an introduction; she speaks.

There is a great sense of the value of a note. If a lady writes a pretty note expressing thanks for civilities offered to her, all the family call on her and thank her for her politeness. It is to be feared that in this latter piece of good-breeding we are behind our English cousins. The English call immediately after a party, an invitation, or a letter of introduction. An elegant and easy epistolary style is of great use in England; and indeed a lady is expected even to write to an artist asking permission to call and see his pictures--a thing rarely thought of in America.

CHAPTER LVII

AMERICAN AND ENGLISH ETIQUETTE CONTRASTED.

No sooner does the American traveller land in England than are forced upon his consideration the striking differences in the etiquette of the two countries, the language for common things, the different system of intercourse between the employee and the employer, the intense respectfulness of the guard on the railway, the waiter at the hotel, and the porter who shoulders a trunk, and the Stately "manageress" of the hotel, who greets a traveller as "my lady," and holds out her hand for a shilling. This respect strikes him forcibly. The American in a similar position would not show the politeness, but she would disdain the shilling. No American woman likes to take a "fee," least of all an American landlady. In England there is no such sensitiveness. Everybody can be feed who does even the most elevated service. The stately gentlemen who show Windsor Castle expect a shilling. Now as to the language for common things. No American must ask for an apothecary's shop; he would not be understood. He must inquire for the "chemist's" if he wants a dose of medicine. Apothecaries existed in Shakespeare's time, as we learn from "Romeo and Juliet," but they are "gone out" since. The chemist has been born, and very good chemicals he keeps. As soon as an American can divest himself of his habit of saying "baggage," and remark that he desires his "luggage sent up by the four train," the better for him. And it is the better for him if he learns the language of the country quickly. Language in England, in all classes, is a much more elaborate and finished science than with us. Every one, from the cad to the cabinet minister, speaks his sentences with what seems to us at first a stilted effort. There is none of the easy drawl, the oblivion of consonants, which mark our daily talk, It is very beautiful in the speech of women in England, this clear enunciation and the proper use of words. Even the maid who lights your fire asks your permission to do so in a studied manner, giving each letter its place. The slang of England is the affectation of the few. The "general public," as we should say, speak our common language most correctly. At first it sounds affected and strained, but soon the American ear grows to appreciate it, and finds the pure well of English undefiled.

The American lady will be sure to be charmed with the manners of the very respectable person who lets lodgings, and she will be equally sure to be shocked at the extortions of even the most honest and best-meaning of them. Ice, lights, an extra egg for breakfast, all these common luxuries, which are given away in America, and considered as necessaries of existence, are charged for in England, and if a bath is required in the morning in the tub which always stands near the wash-stand, an extra sixpence is required for that commonplace adjunct of the toilette. If ladies carry their own wine from the steamer to a lodging-house, and drink it there, or offer it to their friends, they are charged "corkage." On asking the meaning of this now almost obsolete relic of barbarism, they are informed that the lodging-house keeper pays a tax of twenty pounds a year for the privilege of using wine or spirits on the premises, and seven shillings--equal to nearly two dollars of our money--

was charged an invalid lady who opened one bottle of port and two little bottles of champagne of her own in a lodging-house in Half-moon Street. As it was left on the sideboard and nearly all drunk up by the waiter, the lady demurred, but she had no redress. A friend told her afterwards that she should have uncorked her bottles in her bedroom, and called it medicine.

These abuses, practised principally on Americans, are leading to the far wiser and more generous plan of hotel living, where, as with us, a man may know how much he is paying a day, and may lose this disagreeable sense of being perpetually plucked. No doubt to English people, who know how to cope with the landlady, who are accustomed to dole out their stores very carefully, who know how to save a sixpence, and will go without a lump of sugar in their tea rather than pay for it, the lodging-house living has its conveniences. It certainly is quieter and in some respects more comfortable than a hotel, but it goes against the grain for any one accustomed to the good breakfasts, the hearty lunch, and the excellent dinners of an American hotel of the better class, to have to pay for a drink of ice-water, and to be told that the landlady cannot give him soup and fish on the same day unless her pay is raised. Indeed, it is difficult to make any positive terms; the "extras" will come in. This has led to the building of gigantic hotels in London on the American plan, which arise rapidly on all sides. The Grand Hotel, the Bristol, the First Avenue Hotel, the Midland, the Northwestern, the Langham, and the Royal are all better places for an American than the lodging-house, and they are very little if any more expensive. In a lodging-house a lady must have a parlor, but in a hotel she can sit in the reading-room, or write her letters at one of the half-dozen little tables which she will find in each of the many waiting-rooms.

London is a very convenient city for the writing and posting of letters. Foreigners send out their letters of introduction and cards, expecting a reply in a few days, when, lo! the visitor is announced as being outside. Here, again, London has the advantage of New York. The immediate attention paid to a letter of introduction might shame our more tardy hospitality. Never in the course of the history of England has self-respecting Londoner neglected a letter of introduction. If he is well-to-do, he asks the person who brings the letter to dinner; if he is poor, he does what he can. He is not ashamed to offer merely the hospitality of a cup of tea if he can do no more. But he calls, and he sends you tickets for the "Zoo," or he does something to show his appreciation of the friend who has given the letter. Now in America we are very tardy about all this, and often, to our shame, take no notice of letters of introduction.

In the matter of dress the American lady finds a complete bouleversement of her own ideas. Who would not stare, on alighting at the Fifth Avenue Hotel in the hot sunshine of a June evening, to find ladies trooping in at the public entrance dressed in red and blue and gold, with short sleeves or no sleeves, and very low corsage, no cloak, no head-covering? And yet at the Grand Hotel in London this is the nightly custom. These ladies are dressed for theatre or opera, and they go to dine at a hotel first. No bonnet is allowed at any theatre, so the full dress (which we should deem very improper at Wallack's) is demanded at every theatre in London. Of course elderly and quiet ladies can go in high dresses, but they must not wear bonnets. The laws of the Medes and Persians were not more strictly enforced than is this law by the custodians of the theatre, who are neatly dressed women ushers with becoming caps. Here, again, is a difference of custom, as we have no women ushers in America, and in this respect the English fashion is the prettier. It would be well, if we could introduce the habit of going to the theatre bonnetless, for our high hats are universally denounced by those who sit behind us.

The appearance of English women now to the stranger in London partakes of a character of loudness, excepting when on the top of a coach. There they are most modestly and plainly dressed. While our American women wear coaching dresses of bright orange silks and white satins, pink trimmed with lace, and so on, the English woman wears a plain colored dress, with a black mantilla or wrap, and carries a dark parasol. No brighter dress than a fawn-colored foulard appears on a coach in the great London parade of the Four-in-Hands.

Here the London woman is more sensible than her American cousin. The Americans who now visit London are apt to be so plain and undemonstrative in dress that they are called shabby. Perhaps alarmed at the comments once made on their loudness of dress, the American woman has toned down, and finds herself less gay than she sees is fashionable at the theatre and opera. But she may be sure of one thing--she should be plainly dressed rather than overdressed.

As for dinner parties, one is asked at eight or half-past eight; no one is introduced, but every one talks. The conversation is apt to be low-voiced, but very bright and cordial--all English people unbending at dinner. It is etiquette to leave a card next day after a ball, and to call on a lady's reception day. For the out-of-door _fˆtes_ at Hurlington and Sandhurst and the race days very brilliant toilettes of short dresses, gay bonnets, and so on, are proper, and as no one can go to the first two without a special invitation, the people present are apt to be "swells," and well worth seeing. The coaches which come out to these festivities have well-dressed women on top, but they usually conceal their gay dresses with a wrap of some sombre color while driving through London. No one makes the slightest advance towards an acquaintance or an intimacy in London. All is begun very formally by the presentation of letters, and after that the invitation must be immediately accepted or declined, and no person can, without offending his host, withdraw from a lunch or dinner without making a most reasonable excuse. An American gentleman long resident in London complains of his country-people in this respect.

He says they accept his invitations to dinner, he gets together a most distinguished company to meet them, and at the last moment they send him word: "So sorry, but have come in tired from Richmond. Think we won't come. Thank you."

Now where is his dinner party? Three or four angry Londoners, who might have gone to a dozen different dinners, are sulkily sitting about waiting for these Americans who take a dinner invitation so lightly.

The London luncheon, which is a very plain meal compared with ours--indeed, only a family dinner--is a favorite hospitality as extended to Americans by busy men. Thus Sir John Millais, whose hours are worth twenty pounds apiece, receives his friends at a plain lunch in his magnificent house, at a table at which his handsome wife and rosy daughters assist. So with Alma Tadema, and the literary people whose time is money. Many of the noble people, whose time is not worth so much, also invite one to lunch, and always the meal is an informal one.

English ladies are very accomplished as a rule, and sometimes come into the drawing-room with their painting aprons over their gowns. They never look so well as on horseback, where they have a perfection of outfit and such horses and grooms as our American ladies as yet cannot approach. The scene at the corner of Rotten Row of a bright afternoon in the Derby week is unapproachable in any country in the world.

Many American ladies, not knowing the customs of the country, have, with their gentlemen friends, mounted a coach at the Langham Hotel, and have driven to the Derby, coming home very much shocked because they were rudely accosted.

Now ladies should never go to the Derby. It is not a "lady" race. It is five hundred thousand people out on a spree, and no lady is safe there. Ascot, on the contrary, is a lady's race. But then she should have a box, or else sit on the top of a coach. Such is the etiquette.

It would be better for all Americans, before entering London society, to learn the etiquette of these things from some resident.

In driving about, the most aristocratic lady can use the most plebeian conveyance. The "four-wheeler" is the favorite carriage. A servant calls them from the door-step with a whistle. They are very cheap--one-and-sixpence for two miles, including a call not to exceed fifteen minutes (the call). The hansom cab with one horse is equally cheap, but not so easy to get in and out of. Both these vehicles, with trunks on top of them, and a lady within, drive through the Park side by side with the stately carriages. In this respect London is more democratic than New York.

CHAPTER LVIII

HOW TO TREAT ENGLISH PEOPLE.

The highest lady in the realm, Queen Victoria, is always addressed by the ladies and gentlemen of her household, and by all members of the aristocracy and gentry, as "Ma'am," not "Madam," or "Your Majesty," but simply, "Yes, ma'am," "No, ma'am." All classes not coming within the category of gentry, such as the lower professional classes, the middle classes, the lower middle classes, the lower classes (servants), would address her as "Your Majesty," and not as "Ma'am." The Prince of Wales is addressed as "Sir" by the aristocracy and gentry, and never as "Your Royal Highness" by either of these classes, but by all other people he is addressed as "Your Royal Highness."

The other sons of Queen Victoria are addressed as "Sir" by the upper classes, but as "Your Royal Highness" by the middle and lower classes, and by all persons not coming within the category of gentry; and by gentry, English people mean not only the landed gentry, but all persons belonging to the army and navy, the clergy, the bar, the medical and other professions, the aristocracy of art (Sir Frederick Leighton, the President of the Royal Academy, can always claim a private audience with the sovereign), the aristocracy of wealth, merchant princes, and the leading City merchants and bankers. The Princess of Wales and all the princesses of the blood royal are addressed as "Ma'am" by the aristocracy and gentry, but as "Your Royal Highness" by all other classes.

A foreign prince is addressed as "Prince" and "Sir" by the aristocracy and gentry, and as "Your Serene Highness" by all other classes; and a foreign princess would be addressed as "Princess" by the aristocracy, or "Your Serene Highness" by the lower grades, but never as "Ma'am."

An English duke is addressed as "Duke" by the aristocracy and gentry, and never as "Your Grace" by the members of either of these classes; but all other classes address him as "Your Grace." A marquis is sometimes conversationally addressed by the upper classes as "Markis," but generally as "Lord A--," and a marchioness as "Lady B--;" all other classes would address them as "Marquis" or "Marchioness." The same remark holds good as to earls, countesses, barons, baronnesses--all are "Lord B--" or "Lady B--."

But Americans, who are always, if presented at court, entitled to be considered as aristocracy and gentry, and as such are always received, must observe that English people do not use titles often even in speaking to a duke. It is only an ignorant person who garnishes his conversation with these titles. Let the conversation with Lord B flow on without saying "My lord" or "Lord B--" more frequently than is absolutely necessary. One very ignorant American in London was laughed at for saying, "That isn't so, lord," to a nobleman. He should have said, "That isn't so, I think," or, "That isn't so, Lord B--," or "my lord."

The daughters of dukes, marquises, and earls are addressed as "Lady Mary," "Lady Gwendoline," etc. This must never be forgotten, and the younger sons of dukes and marquises are called "Lord John B--," "Lord Randolph Churchill," etc. The wife of the younger son should always be addressed by both the Christian and surname of her husband by those slightly acquainted with her, and by her husband's Christian name only by her intimate friends. Thus those who know Lady Randolph Churchill well address her as "Lady Randolph." The younger sons of earls, viscounts, and barons bear the courtesy title of "Honorable," as do the female members of the family; but this is never used colloquially under any circumstances, although always in addressing a letter to them.

Baronets are addressed by their full title and surname, as "Sir Stafford Northcote," etc., by persons of the upper classes, and by their titles and Christian names by all lower classes. Baronets' wives are addressed as "Lady B--"or "Lady C--." They should not be addressed as "Lady Thomas B--'" that would be to give them the rank of the wife of a younger son of a duke or marquis, instead of that of a baronet's wife only.

In addressing foreigners of rank colloquially the received rule is to address them by their individual titles without the addition of the surname to their titles. In case of a prince being a younger son he is addressed as "Prince Henry," as in the case of Prince Henry of Battenberg. The sons of the reigning monarchs are addressed as "Your Imperial Highness." A foreign nobleman is addressed as "Monsieur le Duc," "Monsieur le Comte," "Monsieur le Baron," etc.; but if there is no prefix of "de," the individual is addressed as "Baron Rothschild," "Count Hohenthal," etc.

While it is proper on the Continent to address an unmarried woman as mademoiselle, without the surname, in England it would be considered very vulgar. "Miss" must be followed by the surname. The wives of archbishops, bishops, and deans are simply Mrs. A--, Mrs. B--, etc., while the archbishop and bishop are always addressed as "Your Grace" and as "My lord," their wives deriving no precedency and no title from their husbands' ecclesiastical rank. It is the same with military personages.

Peeresses invariably address their husbands by their title; thus the Duchess of Sutherland calls her husband "Sutherland," etc. Baronets' wives call their husbands "Sir John" or "Sir George," etc.

The order of precedency in England is strictly adhered to, and English matrons declare that it is the greatest convenience, as it saves them all the trouble of choosing who shall go in first, etc. For this reason, among others, the "Book of the Peerage" has been called the Englishman's Bible, it is so often consulted.

But the question of how to treat English people has many another phase than that of mere title, as we look at it from an American point of view.

When we visit England we take rank with the highest, and can well afford to address the queen as "Ma'am." In fact, we are expected to do so. A well-bred, well-educated, well-introduced American has the highest position in the social scale. He may not go in to dinner with a duchess, but he is generally very well placed. As for a well- bred, handsome woman, there is no end to the privileges of her position in England, if she observes two or three rules. She should not effuse too much, nor be too generous of titles, nor should she fail of the necessary courtesy due always from guest to hostess. She should have herself presented at court by her Minister or by some distinguished friend, if She wishes to enter fashionable society. Then she has the privilege of attending any subsequent Drawing-room, and is eligible to invitations to the court bails and royal concerts, etc.

American women have succeeded wonderfully of late years in all foreign society from their beauty, their wit, and their originality. From the somewhat perilous admiration of the Prince of Wales and other Royal Highnesses for American beauties, there has grown up, however, a rather presumptuous boldness in some women, which has rather speedily brought them into trouble, and therefore it may be advisable that even a witty and very pretty woman should hold herself in check in England.

English people are very kind in illness, grief, or in anything which is inevitable, but they are speedily chilled by any step towards a too sudden intimacy. They resent anything like "pushing" more than any other people in the world. In no country has intellect, reading, cultivation, and knowledge such "success" as in England. If a lady, especially, can talk well, she is invited everywhere. If she can do anything to amuse the company--as to sing well, tell fortunes by the hand, recite, or play in charades or private theatricals-- she is almost sure of the highest social recognition. She is expected to dress well, and Americans are sure to do this. The excess of dressing too much is to be discouraged. It is far better to be too plain than too fine in England, as, indeed, it is everywhere; an overdressed woman is undeniably vulgar in any country.

If we could learn to treat English people as they treat us in the matter of _introductions_, it would be a great advance. The English regard a letter of introduction as a sacred institution and an obligation which cannot be disregarded. If a lady takes a letter to Sir John Bowring, and he has illness in his family and cannot ask her to dinner, he comes to call on her, he sends her tickets for every sort of flower show, the museums, the Botanical Garden, and all the fine things; he sends her his carriage--he evidently has her on his mind. Sir Frederick Leighton, the most courted, the busiest man in London, is really so kind, so attentive, so assiduous in his response to letters of introduction that one hesitates to present a letter for fear of intruding on his industrious and valuable life.

Of course there are disagreeable English people, and there is an animal known as the English snob, than which there is no Tasmanian devil more disagreeable. Travellers everywhere have met this variety, and one would think that formerly it must have been more common than it is now. There are also English families who have a Continental, one might say a cosmopolitan, reputation for disagreeability, as we have some American families, well known to history, who have an almost patrician and hereditary claim to the worst manners in the universe. Well-born bears are known all over the world, but they are in the minority. It is almost a sure sign of base and ignoble blood to be badly mannered. And if the American visitor treats his English host half as well as the host treats him, he may feel assured that the entente cordiale will soon be perfect.

One need not treat the average Englishman either with a too effusive cordiality or with that half-contemptuous fear of being snubbed which is of all things the most disagreeable. A sort of "chip on the shoulder" spread-eagleism formerly made a class of Americans unpopular; now Americans are in favor in England, and are treated most cordially.

CHAPTER LIX

A FOREIGN TABLE D'HOTE, AND CASINO LIFE ABROAD.

Life at a French watering-place differs so essentially from that at our own Saratoga, Sharon, Richfield, Newport, and Long Branch, that a few items of observation may be indulged in to show us what an immense improvement we could introduce into our study of amusement by following the foreign fashions of simplicity in eating and drinking.

The Continental people never eat that heavy early meal which we call breakfast. They take in their rooms at eight o'clock a cup of coffee and a roll, what they call _caf‚ complet_, or they may prefer tea and oatmeal, the whole thing very simple. Then at Aix-les Rains or Vichy the people under treatment go to the bath, taking a rest afterwards. All this occupies an hour. They then rise and dress for the eleven o'clock _d‚jeuner … la fourchette_, which is a formal meal served in courses, with red wine instead of coffee or tea. This is all that one has to do in the eating line until dinner. Imagine what a fine clear day that gives one. How much uninterrupted time! How much better for the housekeeper in a small boarding-house! And at a hotel where the long, heavy breakfast, from seven to eleven, keeps the dining-room greasy and badly ventilated until the tables must be cleared for a one or two o'clock dinner, it is to contrast order with disorder, and neatness with its reverse.

The foreign breakfast at eleven is a delicious meal, as will be seen by the following bills of fare: _oeufs au beurre noir_; _saut‚ printanier_ (a sort of stew of meat and fresh vegetables); _viande froide panach‚e_; _salade de saison_; _compote de fruit et pƒtisserie_; _fromage_, _fruit_, _caf‚_.

Another breakfast is: _oeufs au plat_; _poulet … la Godard_; _c'telettes de mouton grillees_; _reviere pommes de terre_; _flans d'apricot_; and so on, with every variety of stewed pigeon, trout from the lake, delicious preparations of spinach, and always a variety of the cheeses which are so fresh and so healthful, just brought from the Alpine valleys. The highly flavored Alpine strawberries are added to this meal. Then all eating is done for the day until the six or seven o'clock dinner. This gives the visitor a long and desirable day for excursions, which in the neighborhood of Aix are especially charming, particularly the drive to Chambery, one of the most quaintly interesting of towns, through the magnificent break in the Alps at whose southern portal stands La Grande Chartreuse. All this truly healthy disposition of time and of eating is one reason why a person comes home from a foreign watering-place in so much better trim, morally, mentally, and physically, than from the unhealthy gorging of our American summer resorts.

At twelve or one begins the music at the Casino, usually a pretty building in a garden. In this shady park the mammas with their children sit and listen to the strains of the best bands in Europe. Paris sends her artists from the Chƒtelet, and the morning finds itself gone and well into the afternoon before the outside pleasures of the Casino are exhausted. Here, of course, trip up and down on the light fantastic toe, and in the prettiest costumes of the day, all the daughters of the earth, with their attendant cavaliers. There are certain aspects of a foreign watering-place with which we have nothing to do here, such as the gambling and the overdressing of a certain class, but all is externally most respectable. At four or earlier every one goes to drive in the voiture de place or the _voiture de remise_, the latter being a handsome hired carriage of a superior class. But the _voiture de place_, with a Savoyard driver, is good enough. He knows the road; his sturdy horse is accustomed to the hills; he takes one for three francs an hour--about half what is charged at Saratoga or Sharon or Richfield; he expects a few cents as pourboire, that is all. The vehicle is a humble sort of victoria, very easy and safe, and the drive is generally through scenery of the most magnificent description.

Ladies at a foreign watering-place have generally much to amuse them at the shops. Antiquities of all sorts, especially old china (particularly old Saxe), also old carved furniture from the well- known chateaux of Savoy, are found at Aix. The prices are so small compared with what such curiosities would bring in New York that the buyer is tempted to buy what she does not want, forgetting how much it will cost to get it home. Old lace and bits of embroidery and stuffs are brought to the door. There is nothing too rococo for the peripatetic vender in these foreign watering-places.

The dinner is a very good one. Cooked by Italian or French cooks, it may be something of this sort: _potage de riz_; _lavarets St. Houlade_; filets de boeuf

Beaumaire_ (a delicious sauce with basil mixed in it, a slight taste of aniseed); _bouchers … la reine_; _chapon roti au cresson_; _asperge au branches_; _glace au chocolat_; _caf‚_; or: _potage au Cr‚cy_; _turbot aux cƒpres_; _langue de boeuf_; _petits pois, lies au beurre_; _bombe vanille_; with fruits, cheese, and cakes, and always the wine of the country, for which no extra charge is made. These delicious meals cost--the breakfast four francs (wine included), the dinner ten francs. It would be difficult in our country to find such cooking anywhere, and for that price simply impossible.

Music in the Casino grounds follows the dinner. The pretty women, by this time in the short, gay foulards and in the dressy hats in which they will appear later at the Casino ball, are tripping up and down in the gas-lighted grounds. The scene is often illuminated by fireworks. At eight and a half the whole motley crew has entered the Casino, and there the most amusing dancing--valse, galop, and polka --is in vogue. The Pole is known by his violent dancing; "he strikes and flutters like a cock, he capers in the air, he kicks his heels up to the stars." There is heartiness in the dancing of the Swedes and Danes, there is mettle in their heels, but no people caper like the Poles. The Russians and the Americans dance the best. They are the elegant dancers of the world. French women dance beautifully:

"A fine, sweet earthquake, gently moved By the soft wind of their dispersing silks."

No lady appears at the Casino bareheaded; it is always with hat or bonnet, and she lives in her bonnet more or less even at the balls.

If a concert or a play is going on in the little theatre, the same people take their places in boxes or seats, until every face becomes familiar, as one knows one's shipmates. Sometimes pleasant acquaintances are thus formed. A very free-and-easy system of etiquette permits dancing between parties who have not been introduced, and the same privilege extends to the asking of a party of ladies to take an ice. All acquaintance ceases on leaving the Casino, however, unless the lady chooses to bow to her cavalier.

Sometimes the steward of the Casino gets up a fancy-dress ball under the patronage of some lady, and then the motley crew appear as historical characters. It is a unique and gay spectacle. Here in the land of the old masters some very fine representations of the best pictures are hastily improvised, and almost without any apparent effort the whole ball is gotten up with spirit and ingenuity. This, too, among people who never met the day before yesterday. There is a wide range of costume allowed for those who take part in these revelries.

The parquet floor of a foreign Casino is the most perfect thing for good dancing. They understand laying these floors there better than we do, and the climate does not alter them, as with us. They are the pleasantest and easiest of all floors to dance upon.

Not the least striking episode to an American eye is the sight of many priests and men in ecclesiastical garments at these Casinos. The number of priestly robes everywhere strikes the visitor to a French watering-place most emphatically. The schoolmasters are young priests, and walk about with their boys, and the old priests are everywhere. A solemn procession crosses the gay scene occasionally. Three or four acolytes bearing censers, a group of mourners, a tall and stately nun in gray robes and veil walking magnificently, and moving her lips in prayer; then a group of people; then a priest with book in hand saying aloud the prayers for the dead; then the black box, the coffin, carried on a bier by men, the motley crowd uncovering as the majesty passes; and the boys follow, chanting,

"The glories of our birth and state Are shadows, not substantial things; There is no armor against fate; Death lays his icy hand on kings."

Yes, and on the gay visitor at the Casino. These simple and unostentatious funerals are very impressive. The priests always walk bareheaded through the streets on these occasions, and on many others. Indeed, the priestly head seems impatient of a hat.

The fˆtes of the peasants are things to go and see, and the unalterable differences of rank are deeply impressed on the American mind. An old peasant woman has brought cheese and milk into Aix for forty years, and now, in her sixties, she still brings them, and walks eight miles a day. There is no hope that her daughter will ever join in the gayeties of the Casino, as in America she might certainly aspire to do. The daughter will be a peasant, as her mother was, and far happier and more respectable for it, and certainly more picturesque. How many of the peasant dresses have given an idea to the modiste! And one sees in the fields of Savoy the high hat with conical crown, with brim either wide or flat, which has now become so fashionable; also the flat mushroom hat of straw with the natural bunch of corn and red poppy, which has gone from Fanchon up to the duchess. They both come from the fields.

Of course horse-races, formed after the plan of Longchamps, are inseparable from the amusements of a French watering-place; and in proportion to the number of guests to be amused; the horses come down from the various stables. Pigeon-shooting goes on all the time.

It is said that the French have a greater hatred of ennui than any other people in the world. They do not know what it means. They amuse themselves all the time, and are never at a loss. The well- bred French women have as much energy and industry as any New England woman, but they take their amusement more resolutely, never losing music, gayety, and "distraction." Perhaps what amuses them might not amuse the more sober Saxon, but the delicate embroidery of their lives, with all that comes thus cheaply to them, certainly makes them a very delightful set. Their manners are most fascinating, never selfish, never ponderous, never self-conscious, but always most agreeable. The French woman is sui generis. She may no longer be very young; she never was very handsome. Every sensation that the human mind can experience she has experienced; every caprice, whim, and fancy that human imagination can conceive she has gratified. She is very intelligent; she was born with a perfect taste in dress; and she is--all the novelists to the contrary notwithstanding--a very good wife, an excellent mother, a charming companion, a most useful and sensible helpmeet, with a perfect idea of doing her half of the business of life, and of getting out of her hours of leisure all the amusement she can. At a French watering-place the French women of the better class are most entirely at home and intensely agreeable.

###

Made in the USA
Middletown, DE
12 February 2016